Praise for Paul Loeb's Revolutionary Training Techniques and

SMARTER THAN YOU THINK

"[Loeb's] emphasis on achieving absolute clarity in master-to-dog communication sets him apart. . . . His humor, passion and experience—forty years of animal training—come across as if the book were a seminar."
—*Press-Telegram* (Long Beach, CA)

"A witty, sensitive and practical approach to matters involving living with pups and dogs. . . . Loeb gives quick, practical, easily understood and responsible dog-ownership and training methods to prevent objectionable behavior. There are some interesting diet proposals and practical housebreaking tips as well."
—*The Pilot* (Southern Pines, NC)

"*SMARTER THAN YOU THINK* is intriguing . . . worth a try."
—*Grand Rapids Press* (MI)

"Presents excellent training techniques."
—*Library Journal*

As featured on *Leeza*

Previous Works by Paul Loeb

Paul Loeb's Complete Book of Dog Training
You Can Train your Cat
Supertraining Your Dog
Cathletics
Nutrition and Your Dog

Smarter
than you **THINK**

A Revolutionary Approach to
Teaching and Understanding
Your Dog in Just a Few Hours

Paul Loeb
& Suzanne Hlavacek

POCKET BOOKS
New York   London   Toronto   Sydney   Tokyo   Singapore

Originally published in hardcover in 1997 by Pocket Books

POCKET BOOKS, a division of Simon & Schuster Inc.
1230 Avenue of the Americas, New York, NY 10020

ISBN: 0-671-02328-4

First Pocket Books trade paperback printing August 1998

10 9 8 7 6 5 4 3 2 1

Cover design by Joseph Perez
Front cover photos: top, Ann Shamel/Graphistock/PNI; bottom left,
Henry Ausloos/Animals Animals; bottom right, Barbara Reed/Animals
Animals; back cover photo by William Silliker, Jr./Animals Animals

Printed in the U.S.A.

Here's to all the dogs in the world. And a special thanks to our dogs, Willy and Tibby, who are here now, and to the memory of Plum, Inches, Sleepy Joe, and Snapper Dan—for letting us get to know them and love them.

For ease of writing we have referred to all the dogs in this book using the impersonal pronoun *he*. This in no way implies favoritism. We love all dogs equally.

CONTENTS

Contents

INTRODUCTION

One day you've got your life well in order, and things are running smoothly. The next day, chaos. Your house has been destroyed, your patience exhausted, and you feel like your well-ordered life is in shambles. What natural disaster struck, spinning you out of control? You've got a *new* dog!

Is your house all chewed up? And as time goes by do you believe this is because your dog is still teething? After all these years? What about housebreaking? Is that ever going to be over with? Perhaps you suspect your dog has a learning disability or that he suffers from an acute separation anxiety complex. Maybe you think he is handicapped with all of the above.

No matter what your findings and conclusions are, you still must find the answers to survive, to combat this home wrecker and put your house and mind back together.

You buy fifty different dog books, determined to solve all your problems. You go to a dog training school; your dog learns to "sit." You're told if you don't practice "sit" diligently for five, six, or even eight hours a day, your dog will forget to "sit." So you try. But you can't. You do need some time for yourself. You have to go to work, that's eight hours. You have to sleep, that's eight hours. You have to eat, that's three hours. You might want to shower and dress. When you get home from work you might want to change your clothes, which takes time. Read a newspaper, more time. Be with your family and friends and maybe get a night out to go to the movies. More time. There just isn't enough time in a day for you to practice your doggy lessons. So ultimately you're doomed to fail. Unless, of course, you quit your job, don't eat, don't sleep, don't read, don't shower or relax, and don't go to the movies. Just practice, practice, practice, sit, stay, heel, and no, all day . . .

In spite of your best efforts, the books you read, and the classes you took your dog to, you both failed. It didn't work. So now you bring an expert into your home. He looks at your dog, shakes his head, and blames all your dog's problems on you. You now have guilt. He shows you how he makes your dog sit. At this point, you don't care if your dog ever sits again. You now feel inadequate and defeated. Then the expert puts your dog in a cage and leaves. Oh, yes, he charges you lots of $$$$$$.

I'm sure you have heard all kinds of excuses and solutions from professionals and professionals and professionals, including psychics, soothsayers, and your neighbors. It seems everyone is an expert. So how come with all this intelligence, both solicited and unsolicited, nothing works? Oh, yes, your dog does sit for you, when he feels like it.

You can have a well-behaved, responsible dog *in no time at all, and without endless and overbearing practice sessions.* It's not magic and it's not mysterious. Quite simply, you are going to be learning a new and better way to communicate with your dog. In fact, we will take the confusion and myths out of understanding and educating your dog altogether and redefine those terms.

When I work with a new dog or puppy and his owner, it takes no more than three hours to fully teach both of them everything necessary for a successful relationship. I'm not saying that *you* could or couldn't learn in three hours; what I am saying is that if you read this book from cover to cover, you will have all the information you need to accomplish this. This book is a successful three-hour seminar, with real solutions to real problems.

When I started out over forty years ago, there wasn't much information available on dog training. In the area of animal behavior there was information, but there was no way to practically apply this information to our dogs. For dogs, what information there was consisted of simple one-word commands, (sit, stay, no, heel, come) with a lot of practice. I was led to believe that dogs were not capable of understanding anything more sophisticated or complex. Not enough emphasis was placed on their intelligence. And if one starts with the premise that dogs are "stupid" and are very limited in their understanding, then one is stuck with old, limited dog-training methods and techniques.

I laugh now when I see how in my first book (written in 1975), I cautioned owners about first mastering "no" before going on to other commands like "sit" and "stay," and that "repetition" was very important. As for diet and nutrition, I relied on experts, like dog-food companies. It was rather like me relying on a giant commercial food company for all the information I would ever need for all my nutritional needs. I didn't question their nutritional claims, nor did I fully understand to what degree diet was important in training and behavior.

In my first books and even today, the human element is still what fascinates me. The human-animal interaction. No dog responds in quite the same way as another. And differences and idiosyncrasies can be found in the behavior patterns of their owners. So both the owner and the dog are my students. But still it's the dog's owner who must learn to train his own dog in his own way. That's what I taught then and that's what I teach now. This I call "transference"—making sure that the dog recognizes his owner as the authority figure, or pack leader. What good is it for me to teach the dog my way, and to listen to me, when the dog isn't mine and doesn't live with me?

Early on I realized that most training methods were very rigid and followed inflexible rules, as if each dog and owner were the same. Owners would emulate their trainers, using a deep loud voice and transforming themselves into drill sergeants every time they asked their dogs to respond. If a dog failed his six- to eight-week course, the two standard excuses would be, "Your dog is untrainable, for whatever reason" or "It's your fault." The dynamics of dog behavior and the owner-dog relationship were never dealt with, and this created more problems. I never, not back then and not now, taught with rigid, inflexible rules and excuses, as if every dog on earth came in a standard size, shape, and color, like a sofa. They don't. And neither do their owners. You must consider and be sensitive to both in order to teach successfully.

Even when I wrote my first books, although I was still teaching one-word commands and asking owners to practice, I had already included a humanistic and holistic approach in my work, which was different then and is still different today. That was why I could successfully teach a dog more quickly and more easily than other trainers.

Today I know that it doesn't take six to eight weeks, or forever, to teach a dog his main behaviors, that you don't need one-word commands or a lot of practice, and that he is far more intelligent then you might realize. That is why I now can give you a blueprint for successfully teaching your dog immediately, with no practice and without a separate language. It works, it's fun, and it's easy.

This book continues where my previous ones left off, and

brings my study of human-animal interaction to a much higher plane, to a new level benefiting both species coexisting in the same environment. Yes, we can teach both you and your dog in just a few hours.

This book is different from others in its philosophy. Most experts say a dog, especially a puppy, has a very short attention span, that certain breeds are smarter than others, and that puppies shouldn't be trained until they are six months old. That just isn't true, and if you believe it is true, then you're limiting your ability to train your dog and to understand him from the very beginning. Dogs or puppies can be taught complex behaviors very quickly. Attention span is related to boredom; they get bored if they don't understand you, or if they just don't want to listen to you. Remember, a student is only as good as his teacher and the curriculum.

When I was in school, about a hundred years ago, if my classes were boring or if I had problems understanding a subject, my attention span became very short and limited. My father called it selective memory. It isn't any different with your dog. The more you exercise the muscle in his head (the brain), the more you increase his ability to learn.

We don't need to use such training aids as crates or cages for housebreaking or controlling destructive habits, or choke collars, pinch collars, or leashes for control when walking. We don't use one-word commands or a loud voice when teaching or as a reprimand. There is no more endless practicing and no more excuses as to why your dog doesn't listen. He will listen. That means he will come to you, follow you, and count on you for all of his security, education, and guidance, in the same way a dog would depend on his real mother to teach him everything about the world. He learns from her immediately; his life depends on it. And in a sense his life is now in your hands. If you can't teach him anything and you give him away, what are his options for the future going to be?

You'll be taught about diet and nutrition and how it plays a major role in his education. You should know what, when, and how much your dog should eat. We're not going to leave this important information to the food companies or veterinarians alone. We'll teach you to know your dog better than all the experts, including us. This book will give you all the tools you'll ever need.

I'm not just coming out of the woodwork like some latter-day prophet, although I realize I may be one of the lone voices in the wilderness right now. I'm not throwing out ideas and concepts with no foundation in experience. Granted, many so-called dog experts will want to say this is impossible, and many people consider themselves "experts." This tells me that long-held and cherished ideas, even if wrong or outdated, are hard to let go of.

Today, many trainers and writers continue to write about and teach old methods, although claiming to find new ways of teaching them. It's like the emperor with his new clothes. You can dress him up and say he looks great, but he's still got nothing on.

Shaking a can of pennies, blowing up balloons all over your house, or squirting a water pistol at your dog are just temporary gimmicks. They only work until the dog figures out that they are silly and no threat to him. That will happen overnight, or at the most a couple of days.

I know all about these "cures." I wrote about them twenty years ago. They were ridiculous then and they are ridiculous now. If you want to stop a bad habit you stop a bad habit. You don't shake pennies or burst balloons or squirt water pistols.

This isn't a gimmick book, and we're not recycling old ideas. We're teaching you another way, a much better way. Our new teaching style is organic, allowing you and your dog to interact naturally without adopting artificial aids and mannerisms.

Introduction

This book is a complete package of behavior, training, nutrition, and psychology. This is paramount. By combining these fields we can give you *Smarter Than You Think*.

Just as there are major breakthroughs in other areas of animal behavior, such as the new findings on intelligence, communication and social structures of chimps, gorillas, and dolphins, and just as my first book was a breakthrough in 1975, this new book will be a complete breakthrough in the world of dogs, dramatically different from anything in the marketplace today.

The success rate of my teaching philosophy and the understanding of these techniques is virtually 100 percent. It's taken me forty years to work out this formula, and it's taken Suzanne six years of studying with me and learning my work. She was very determined to learn it all, and she did.

This book will make teaching and understanding your dog plain and simple, so you will be able to succeed very quickly, with none of those long, drawn-out, tedious hours of practicing. If the puppy's mother can succeed immediately, why can't you?

Remember, if you can't understand your dog, then you can't teach him, and if you can't teach him, then he could be put on the bottom of an intelligence list even though he might be a genius.

We know that explorers defied tradition and discovered a new and round world when every expert declared it was flat. Take this journey with us; you might find out that the world of dog training, nutrition, and behavior is perfectly round.

Author Background

There are animal trainers and then there's Paul Loeb. His unique knowledge of animals and his abilities to understand them have always put him in a class by himself. He is truly different; his thinking and his work have always been ahead of their time.

The Wall Street Journal said . . .

He considers himself an animal behaviorist. What does this mean exactly?

Well, *The Wall Street Journal* compared Paul Loeb's work with animals to the work of B. F. Skinner. Loeb takes

practical approaches to physical needs as a means to psychological (read "behavioral") cures . . . He is to the canine world what B. F. Skinner, the noted Harvard psychologist who devoted himself to the techniques of shaping behavior, was to the study of man. (January 17, 1985)

The *Chicago Tribune* said . . .

Loeb has been identified as an animal psychiatrist, animal psychic, or animal trainer. Whatever the appellation, he's a success in a wide range of activities involving animals.

His credits include more than 600 television commercials, ranging from pet foods to men's underwear. He also cured 8,000 family pets of such bad habits as biting, drooling, wetting, chewing, wandering, and intimidation.

The *Chicago Tribune* published this article in June 4, 1975. Today the number of "cured" pets would be tripled.

When Loeb was twelve years old, a new neighbor moved onto his block in Brooklyn. Her name was Sarah Reinman. She had lived in eastern Europe and was an animal trainer who had spent years with the circus. Sharing her apartment with her were her birds, monkeys, and cats. Loeb was fascinated by her pets and by her uncanny ability to communicate with them. She hardly spoke to them, and yet it seemed her animals understood her every thought.

Needless to say, she left a lasting impression on a twelve-year-old street kid. In fact, nonverbal communication would become one of the hallmarks of Loeb's later work, earning him the title of animal psychic among many of his clients.

Born in 1935 and raised in New York City, Paul Loeb has been a leader in the field of animal behavior, specializing in dogs and cats for more than four decades. His great passion and understanding for animals and his rare ability to communicate that understanding are what sets him apart from the rest of the pack.

Paul Loeb has extensive experience with the print and electronic media, and promotional experience with *Fortune* 100 marketers. His innovative ideas have always attracted a large audience in all of these media, including television. In a "seeing is believing" format, right in front of the camera's eye, he would immediately transform dogs with "problems" into well-behaved citizens, creating a lively experience for the audience and home viewers. He amazed audiences with an innate ability to "read" animals so quickly.

He appeared on many television shows, including Johnny Carson's *Tonight Show*. But Loeb's first and most memorable experience was on the Mike Douglas show in 1969 with his wonder dog Plum, a beautiful taupe-colored weimaraner. Plum could and did add and subtract, differentiate magazines—*Newsweek* from *Time*—and even tell the difference between a hundred-dollar bill and a one. When Loeb jokingly would complain to Plum that he hadn't any money, Plum would bound off into the audience, steal a pocketbook, and return with it to the stage.

With five successful books, he has set a standard in his field. Part of his tremendous appeal has been his humorous way of delivering the goods. This flair for comedy is an added bonus for all of his written and visual work. Getting people to relax and enjoy themselves when working with their animals enhances their ability to succeed.

He has achieved worldwide recognition, being featured alongside Jane Goodall and Konrad Lorenz in *National Geographic*'s Behavioral Education series, which was shown to schools and universities throughout this country.

He directed education in animal behavior and training for the ASPCA in New York City. Working at this large shelter with groups of dog owners and their dogs, Loeb developed many revolutionary ideas and techniques in the area of human-animal interaction.

He knew these pound dogs had to be trained fast and successfully or else; this was sometimes a matter of life and death. Not a joke. He knew that if he couldn't help these adopted animals and if their new owners couldn't understand how to deal with their problems, these dogs could be dumped back into the maelstrom of the pound before an emotional bond could be fused.

For the Animal Medical Center in New York City, the largest small-animal hospital in the world, Loeb consulted on animal behavioral problems. He also maintained close working relationships with veterinarians throughout the country. One is Dr. William J. Kay, the former director and chief of staff of the AMC. He endorsed one of Paul's books (*Supertraining*, 1979), referring to it as the "champion of training books" and Loeb as an "internationally acclaimed expert" in the field.

With over thirty years of experience and more than one hundred thousand surgeries, Dr. Martin De Angelis, DVM, board certified ACVS (American College of Veterinary Surgeons), is many times the surgeon of last resort, when no one else can help. Martin is also acknowledged as a leading specialist in orthopedic surgery, and is considered to have the best pair of hands in the business. Dr. De Angelis acknowledged Loeb's work, calling him a pioneer in the field and one of the "premier animal trainers in the world today."

Loeb was asked to help with the federal government's Open Cities program. He did. He taught children in the New York City public school system an awareness and understanding of the sensitivities of animals, underlining their intelligence, and abilities, to respond and communicate. This was also accomplished in "The Pet Set," his monthly column in *Parents* magazine (1979–1982).

In 1974, at Bellevue Hospital in New York City and New York University Hospital, Paul Loeb introduced the idea of using animals to help comfort the sick and the elderly.

Among his many accomplishments he is also recognized by the city and state of New York as a trainer of companion-aide dogs. In this specialized area, his ability to transform the household pet into a super and very valuable helper for the physically challenged is unique. Being able to use their own pet allows challenged persons many more options, of time and choice, than are currently available. This technique, developed over many years, is vintage Paul Loeb.

His work has been written up in many magazines and newspapers, including *Esquire, Glamour, Newsweek, Cosmopolitan, Family Circle, The Christian Science Monitor,* the *New York Times, New York Post, New York Daily News, Chicago Sun-Times,* the *Philadelphia Inquirer,* and many more.

Although the seeds of his new techniques are evident in his large body of work on animals, Loeb has honed and refined them to a new level. What has taken him over forty years to develop is now available to you. He can teach your dog all the basics in approximately three hours, while other trainers take weeks, months, or even years. His philosophy is quite simple. Animals have the ability to learn more and faster in a shorter time if information is delivered properly.

In this age of instant communication, computers, fax machines, E-Mail, and video, and of time-saving devices like microwaves and instant foods, no one seems to have time to waste. Technological advances have appeared in every field and facet of life. Except for one. Your dog. Now his time has finally come.

Six years ago, Suzanne Hlavacek got two Westy terriers, Tibby and Willy. Not knowing anything about dogs, and seeing her house being systematically dismantled, bite by bite, she figured she better find out what to do and fast before it was totaled.

Everyone wanted to help and everyone seemed to be an "expert." One "expert" told her to put her dogs in a crate. Another "expert" said "fill a can with pennies, and shake it, or squirt a water pistol at them." Those gimmicks didn't work and putting her dogs in a crate was an unthinkable, inhumane, prison sentence.

Then there were the trainers and schools. Driving with her two puppies jumping around out of control for two hours round trip twice a week for eight weeks to group classes was impossible. One school, after an evaluation, concluded the dogs would have to be kept for at least six weeks. Having just gotten the puppies, she wasn't giving them away.

A friend recommended Paul Loeb, saying that this guy gets the job done in just a few hours. He did. It was fun and it worked for both Suzanne and the dogs.

Suzanne now knows to trust her instincts, and to use common sense to understand and communicate with her dogs. She developed an even greater admiration for their intelligence, super senses, and their ability to learn so quickly. There was a lot more to them than just being lovable but simple creatures. Like any mother she concluded that her little dogs had to be the two smartest in the world. She could be right, because Willy and Tibby were the ones responsible for Suzanne's last six years of working with and writing about animals.

Suzanne Hlavacek, an accomplished screenwriter, born in Bombay, India, graduated from Barnard College in New York City, where she currently lives.

CHAPTER 1

Breaking Away from Tradition

Charley was exhausted. His one-sided relationship with Ginger, his cocker spaniel, had been going on for months, and he was pretty damn tired of getting nowhere fast. "She thinks she owns me, the damn house, and everything in it!" Charley cried. "But I own this house, I pay the rent, I pay for her food, and for her health insurance and medical bills. Now I'm paying for those damn classes every week, and she's failing! Damn! Damn!" Stamping his foot, Charley continued, "She had better listen to me or else I'll just get rid of her."

Ginger, the cocker, thought to herself, "I'm so tired of this, nothing ever seems to work for me. Every time I go to class all they ever tell me is 'Sit' 'Stay!' 'Heel!' or they keep yelling 'No!' at me. And then I have to hear the teacher telling Charley I'm flunking in school. I get so mad, I just want to run away."

Or what about this?

"Where did I go wrong?" Peggy asks herself aloud. "I give

this puppy everything, I should have named him 'NO,' because all I ever say to him is NO don't do this, and NO don't
do that, NO, NO, NO. . . . Why won't he listen to me? How
can I stop him from chewing up my shoes?" The defeated dog
owner continues: "I saw his real mom succeed with a litter of
her pups, carrying one in her mouth while the others just followed along behind. I'm as smart as she is, aren't I?"

The Japanese call it *kansei*, which means completion or perfection, creating a harmony where there was none, a whole-
ness and a oneness where before there was separation and
misunderstanding.

The bottom line is communication in all of its forms. How
you communicate, what you communicate, when you communicate, and why you communicate. Human beings are very
complex animals and have many ways to communicate with
each other—television, radio, newspapers. One could say
there is an overload of communication and a limited amount
of time to absorb it all. The world moves very fast; the most
valuable commodity we have is time. Time is money and there
is none to waste.

Even with so much information out there, there is a lot of
miscommunication and wrong signals. Human beings are animals famous for saying one thing and doing another. Relationships, both personal and business, go off the rails because
human animals are adept at deception, wearing masks, and living by formulas. Relationships can be difficult and confusing.

Now you bring a member of a different species home to live
with you, a dog. How is he supposed to fit in with this complicated and time-deficient human animal? At least with the dog,
what you see is what you get. He's honest, loyal, and true. He
won't be spiteful, because that isn't in his vocabulary, and he
won't punish you by running away from home, joining the
drug culture, or marrying wrong. It's easier in some ways to
have a friendship with your dog because you can depend on

2

his character and nature to be true. Many people prefer the company of their dog to the company of humans, and it's easy to see why.

But inherent complications can also exist in this relationship between you and your dog because you are two different species coexisting in the same environment. Your dog needs to reach an understanding with you and you with him. Every dog is unique and complex, whether he is six to eight weeks old or between one year and twenty years. And each owner is different. Coexistence, harmony, and getting to a successful level of understanding between the two of you is an art. This advanced art form, this direct communication, is something you will have to achieve if you want your dog to fit comfortably into your lifestyle naturally and very quickly. Traditional dog training will not even come close to the mark. There is no way to reach this harmonious design unless you break from the old ways. So leave tradition in the past with the horse and buggy and let's take an incredible journey into your dog's mind and understand just how smart he is and how easy it is to teach him your world.

A successful athlete achieves the optimum level in his sport by first learning the basics. He then creates his own way to deliver the goods. You can also achieve this kind of success and perfection in the teaching of your dog. Once you learn the elementary principles of this form of teaching, you then can develop your own style. Just as the successful athlete, or for that matter the artist, the doctor, even the candlestick maker, has developed his own technique, you will be able to develop yours.

A piano player has to learn technique to play the piano; you have to learn technique to be able to teach your dog. Some of the things you're going to learn will seem so obvious that you'll wonder why you never thought of them yourself. Rather like not seeing the forest for the trees. The only difficulty at first will be forgetting the methods that you've read about or were told about or the traditional training you were taught.

This advanced form of teaching breaks away from traditional dog-training methods and the philosophies on which they are based. Put aside all of that stuff for now and take a fresh look at the whole picture. You'll see. We think it's time to redefine many of the accepted standards of dog behavior and training, because the old stuff, the ideas and methods on which it's based, can't get you to a new level of understanding and communication with your dog. The foundation isn't there, and therefore you can't build on it.

We use this type of communication when we work on television commercials or in film. It's perfect because it's fast. We only have a limited amount of time to make a connection with the animals' thought process and get them to learn and to perform their important starring roles.

We taught Denise and Bob how to bring up their thirteen-week-old Saint Bernard puppy, Max. Big Max not only grew fast but also learned fast and easy how to fit in perfectly with them. Four months later we were approached by a commercial production company, an advertising agency, and their product people, Brawny paper towels, to do a national commercial. This group had had four months to put their commercial together. But they had a major problem. All the dog experts and all the animal talent agencies, from coast to coast, had said that a Saint Bernard puppy could never and would never perform the complex behaviors that the script called for. In other words, everyone said, "It couldn't be done, it was impossible." We were called as the last resort a week and a half before shooting. It took us three days of preparing Max and getting him to understand what he had to do, and two days to shoot the commercial.

Max did everything that was asked of him and he did it successfully. He carried a half-gallon milk container in his mouth as he ran from room to room in someone's home. Up the stairs and down the stairs, spilling milk everywhere he went, all the while a three-year-old child chasing him with paper towels, trying to clean up after him. These stairs were steep, narrow, and high, not very secure for a puppy this young and this size. In another scene, Max had to knock over his water dish while the little boy stood next to it. In the opening scene, Max had to come in out of the rain and just inside the door he had to shake himself off. Some might think this is easy to do, but Max had to be taught to hold this milk container with milk coming out of it, and then perform all of the other behaviors asked of him, and he had to do them time after time, and always the same way. As for the running up and down the stairs, giant-size puppies generally can't and won't do this because a lack of coordination on their part makes them insecure and frightened. There was much more to this commercial, but you get the idea. Max smiled while he easily accomplished the impossible. We took on this job only because we had Big Max. He had been brought up our way, and therefore we knew that we would be able to teach him these complex behaviors very quickly and make this job look like a piece of cake. And by the way, it did not take hours and hours and hours of practice, just a few reminders from time to time that he was a paid actor when he seemed to forget why he was there. Just think, Max learned and performed these behaviors in only a few days.

To achieve this type of communication with your dog, what's important is for you to understand not only our technique but also our philosophy, for it is the key to our world of academe.

Dogs are very smart animals, and they will understand and accept you with all your shortcomings. Up to now people have felt that dogs were very limited in what and how they could learn. It's time to meet the dog halfway. We are going to use your dog's intelligence and all of his incredible senses to help us teach him to understand what you want of him, and very quickly at that. We are going to use your instincts, your intelligence, and your senses, especially your common sense, to teach him to understand you.

You will also realize that what we are telling you to do is to be comfortable, have fun, relax, trust, and be yourself. Don't worry. Being yourself is not as difficult as learning to play the piano. As a matter of fact it's as easy as looking into a mirror.

Your dog is a very intelligent animal. With the right training he can become a companion-aide dog for the physically disabled or a seeing eye specialist. He can save people that have been buried in earthquakes, sniff out bombs and drugs better than mechanical devices, and he can protect. He is even used in hospitals to help the sick and elderly. So teaching him just to be your pal should be no problem at all.

Our techniques are geared to respect your dog and his ability to learn complex behaviors from the very beginning. Most experts will teach only simple one-word commands. They figure your dog has a limited attention span and he's not that bright. This is not true. If you can keep your dog's interest, then common sense will dictate that his attention span becomes greater. If you can't, then he will get bored quickly and you will mistake his boredom for a limited attention span. Or as a lack of intelligence. That's wrong. You, the boring teacher, are responsible.

We're not going to tempt him with food rewards. Those are bribes, and he will expect them and learn very quickly how to get a bigger bribe or a better one. If you train your dog with treats, then you better use the greatest treat in the world. Because the minute someone comes along with a better treat, your dog will listen to them, and not to you. That's not to say we won't give him treats when he does exactly what we want perfectly. Then, you can give him whatever you want. And I hope it's something really good. Not a silly dog treat.

Of the many phone calls we get from prospective clients, a large percentage tell us that their dog is 99 percent trained, they just need that extra 1 percent to make him perfect. "I know you charge $650 for three hours; how much would you charge me?" Our question to them is plain and simple. "What is the 1 percent that your dog doesn't do?" Their answer is: "He won't come back when he's off the leash, he only has accidents when I leave him alone or when he's angry at me, and he chews things when I'm gone." "Generally," one client said, "generally he only chews up my right shoes." When we ask them about the 99 percent, we're told that when he's in the crate he's perfect, when he's on a leash and no dogs or people are around he walks wonderfully, and he sits but he won't stay. Our answer to them is always, "We charge only twenty-five cents to teach sit and stay." We've even had clients deduct twenty-five cents off the bill after we helped them with their dogs.

Our approach to dog training is a holistic one. You have to understand your dog in all dimensions in order to teach him effectively and bond with him. This humanistic connection between you and your dog will set the groundwork for a more sophisticated and contemporary form of education, getting you to see things and do things beyond the traditional scope of dog training and behavior. Your reward will be the dog you've always wanted, the perfect pet, a real best friend. You might even forget he's a dog.

You must understand that it's not just behavior that's important here. It's also understanding that food experts, health experts, and training experts, and even expert experts, have brainwashed, tainted, and clouded an entire culture when it comes to understanding, caring for, and teaching your dog. We are going to unravel what we call the three Ms: mysteries, myths, and misconceptions. We're going to use as our magic weapon common sense. No excuses, no blame, no nonsense.

Just answers. And you don't even have to agree with us on everything. You'll still have a good friend and a healthy one.

Fitting Your Dog into Your Lifestyle

Whether you live on a boat or a plane, in a house, a large apartment, a tiny apartment, or even a cardboard box; if you take your dog to work, if you work at home, or if you're out of work, both you and your dog; this is what we mean by lifestyle. Your dog has to be customized to fit this lifestyle. In order for this to happen you have to learn how to bring him into your lifestyle.

Remember, you brought this dog or puppy home not just because he matches your paintings. This is an emotional purchase. You brought him home to fill a void. You thought you'd live longer, or maybe he was a frustration outlet, or a child substitute, or possibly that fantasy of freedom. You know, sometimes you can't find a good man or a good woman, but you can always find a good dog.

Whatever the reason, you don't want him to be your interior decorator, customize your car, or walk off with your best shoes. Or eat them for that matter. You want him to behave. If not, then you might start to rationalize and compromise, and eventually he is not there for the reasons you originally wanted. Which means you must adjust to him, and I don't know of many human-dog relationships that have worked where the dog was in charge.

Misty and Magic are a pair of giant schnauzers who live in Westhampton in the summer and Florida in the winter. They are considered snowbird dogs. That's not a breed, that's a lifestyle. These two beauties, the size of small horses, are not kept in cages or in the garage or even on an outdoor exercise chain. They have the run of the house and property. They swim laps in their swimming pools, go for boat rides, and lay out on the deck to get some sun. When they go to town they don't even have to be on a leash, unless it's the law. They can sit near the table when everybody is eating breakfast, lunch, or dinner. They've been taught the house rules laid down by their owners, Dan and Susan, and that is not to annoy anybody unless they are told to. That's their lifestyle.

Billie June and her German shepherd, Dorrie, live in a small studio apartment on New York's Upper West Side. She adopted Dorrie from a shelter. Dorrie was a large, adult dog weighing as much as Billie. "Help me with Dorrie, she's a handful," Billie said. I did. Dorrie became a great friend to Billie and vice versa. A couple of years later, Billie's rheumatoid arthritis became crippling and she needed help. Her doctor suggested a companion-aide dog.

Billie called several schools and asked them to train Dorrie for her as a companion-aide dog. She was told she would have to come to their school, live there for four to six weeks, and train with and apply for one of their dogs. Billie physically couldn't do this. She asked them if they could train Dorrie. She was told that no one would train her dog. The schools told her that she would just have to have two dogs, her pet Dorrie and the one they would give her as a companion-aide dog. This was an impossibility for Billie because she could hardly walk now. What was she going to do with two dogs? The school didn't have an answer for her.

The facts were Billie would have had to give Dorrie away and she couldn't and wouldn't do this. Billie said, "My emotional attachment to Dorrie is too strong. How can I give away a dog that's been so loyal to me for all these years?"

Billie called me and asked me if I could teach Dorrie to be a companion-aide dog for her. I said I could. Dorrie was already a super pet so I was able to transform her into a super companion-aide dog. I taught her how to help Billie in and out of bed, in and out of a tub, up and down steps, to wait at the curb, push revolving doors, pick up her cane if she dropped it, and protect her on the street.

This extension training was accomplished by using the basic techniques and the abilities of her dog to learn more complex behaviors and increase her basic reasoning. Even though Billie's lifestyle changed drastically, Dorrie was able to change along with her, from being a pet to taking on a more professional role. This is what we mean by fitting your dog into your lifestyle, no matter what it is. This is Billie and Dorrie's lifestyle.

Billie found me through Sparkle's owner, Harvey. Sparkle is a small poodle who does a lot of traveling, is an avid theater and movie buff, and loves to go to restaurants. She does all of this by riding in her owner's shoulder bag. That's Sparkle's way of fitting into her owner's lifestyle. Oh, by the way, Sparkle's owner also loves traveling, movies, the theater, and restaurants. But he doesn't ride in a bag, poor guy; he has to walk and pay all the bills. What a life Sparkle has.

There is a reasonable explanation for everything. A most important tool to use is your common sense, something we generally forget about when it comes to understanding our dog.

How God or Mother Nature Intervened

It was August, a very hot sunny day, over one hundred degrees. A five-year-old boy was fishing in a lake near the Weather Castle in Central Park. The boy's mother was sunbathing and totally submerged in her boom box.

The sunbather's poor little hot Yorkie couldn't find any shade. This little hot dog kept trying to hide underneath the boom-boxed mother's dress, but she kept pushing her dog away screaming, "Stop it, stop it, go away, leave me alone, don't be a pest, what's wrong with you!" As if this little dog didn't exist, wasn't real, was nothing more than a bothersome insect.

I was about to go over to this dog owner and explain that her little dog was a good candidate for heat stroke. But just then, Mother Nature intervened and told her in no uncertain terms to smarten up. The message came by way of a tremendous torrential thunderstorm with lots of strong corrective dialogue in the form of thunder and lightning.

I stood there laughing till my belly hurt. The little dog was jumping around, wagging his tail and barking, having a great time in the cool rain. Mom had to gather up all of her belongings: the wet blanket, the wet son, and all of the wet things, including the soaked boom box. She ran screaming for shelter, cursing all the way. It was wonderful.

Another example of someone who probably cares about their dog but is just not thinking when it comes to their dog's health and well-being is the person who takes their dog exercising with them believing that the exercise will be good for the dog. But in many cases, it isn't. And this truly is a major problem.

Running the Dog Down

We saw a guy jogging in Central Park one hot summer's day during a July heat wave. Running alongside him and almost tripping over his tongue was his exhausted sheepdog.

My God! Did he ever look hot in his thick, long coat. The poor dog's tongue was hanging out so far it looked like he was wearing an extra large red necktie. We wanted to take him and put him into an ice cold tub.

The jogger stumbled, dropping his radio. He stopped to pick it up and cursed his bad luck, hoping the radio wasn't broken. All the while he ignored his dog, as if the dog were nothing but an old sneaker.

We were pissed off and it showed as we walked over to this runner and asked him, "Why the hell are you running this poor dog in this unbearably hot weather? He could collapse and die right here, right now, from heat stroke." At first, while looking at the radio he thought might have been broken, and not even paying attention to what we said, he told us to mind our own business. And then, staring angrily at us, he gave us this incredibly nonsensical explanation.

He said, "*Its* heavy coat and long hair actually insulated *it* from the heat, and kept *it* cool." He said he knew this for a "*fact*." He then told us to, "f— off!" His radio, not broken after all, came back on as he blasted away.

We hope the dog was okay, but who knows? What we do know from the little conversation that we had with him was that his dog was only an "it" to him.

If you stop and think, a heavy coat worn in hot weather does not keep you cool or keep you insulated from the heat—not you, and not your dog. Furthermore, dogs should not be made to accompany you on your running exercises on days when the weather is extreme. In hot weather all you have to do is put on a winter coat and go out running, and you'll get a good idea of how a dog feels.

When jogging, rollerblading, biking, or running, don't take your dog with you because he has to run to your rhythms and pace and he's generally not comfortable loping along to your moves. It rubs the bottom of his feet raw. If it's very warm outside, he could be a candidate for heat stroke. If you must take him with you on your exercising journeys, then teach him to stay with you off a lead. Then he will be able to adjust better to your pace. And if you must take your dog with you when you are sunbathing, make sure he has plenty of shade and water available.

You might think that because your dog is a totally different animal, his needs are totally different from yours. That he needs a totally different language, a totally different food, a totally different shampoo and soap. In fact, he might as well live in a totally different world. But that ain't so. He's in your world, he should have what you have, except for your bank account and your clothes. All products that you personally use—soaps, shampoos, colognes—sad to say, are tested on animals before you are allowed to use them. Products that are made for dogs are not tested on dogs. The test is real life. Again, sad to say.

On many dog products you'll see warning signs, "Keep out of the reach of children." Children and dogs have been synonymous since time immemorial, so if it's bad for the child it's bad for the dog. Why not get your dog products that have been tested safe? Like your shampoo, your soap, your mouthwash, and your toothpaste.

You bring a dog home and then you buy and read fifty dog-training books and they all say the same thing—teach him to SIT. What is this preoccupation with sit? Why do you have to practice "sit" for hours and hours on end? We guarantee you that when your dog is tired, he'll sit down.

And as for the universal word "NO" for everything that goes wrong, why do you have to read books or pay a trainer a lot of money just to teach you to say "No!" To just say "no" doesn't work. To teach and use "no" and "sit" as main communication tools is an insult to the intelligence of both you and your dog.

You go to your veterinarian and you would like to ask questions about your dog. Some will give you answers, but some practice a theocratic policy where they rule by divine authority and won't tell you anything, won't let you ask questions, and won't even allow you in the examining room with your dog. You are supposed to listen to them, no questions asked. You must be able to ask questions because, just like you with your doctor, you might want to get a second opinion. Or you might want to question his diagnosis. Don't be embarrassed. Ask questions. Lots of them. Remember, you do know your dog, or you should know your dog, better than anyone.

You should also know about proper diet and nutrition, how

it was before there were dog-food companies. How it changed as the dog-food companies grew and became more important in your dog's life, or so they say. These multibillion-dollar dog-food companies care about profit first, you second, because you pay the bills, and your dog a distant third.

You are told certain dog foods give your dog a firm stool. Who cares about the pursuit of the perfect stool? It isn't important. You are told certain dog foods clean teeth. Think about that. How can they? They don't, they can't. You are told if your dog doesn't eat dog food he won't get a proper balanced diet. That's not true either.

When to eat, what to eat, how much to eat—you should know all of these things. Don't rely solely on dog-food companies and their commercial profit-making claims, or the veterinarians, who are not really experts on diet and nutrition but who rely on the food companies for their knowledge, to supply you with all of this vital information. Let's break from this tradition of only one source of information and get on to the information highway. It's much wider, and there are more and better alternatives.

Other misconceptions are that your dog needs a choke collar or a spike collar. If you think about it you'll see that these are not necessary and could even injure your dog. How can you believe that a choke collar doesn't choke a dog? It does! How can you believe that a choke collar, by any other name, is not a choke collar? It is. Or that a spike collar doesn't hurt your dog. It does! Just put these contraptions on your own neck. And by the way, experts get around this choke collar business by calling it a "release collar" or just by giving it another name. I'm sure when a hanged man is cut down, the rope "releases." If you insist that your dog must wear a choke collar, make sure he doesn't wear it in the house. It can get caught on the bottom hinges of doors and he could hang himself.

For decades crates and cages have been the accepted way to

stop destructive habits, housebreak, and control your dog. The wisdom is that dogs are cave animals and they need their privacy. Another way experts get around this small prison is by saying that the cage or crate is like the dog's own personal apartment. Not true. If it were true, then people would be looking for their comfort and security in very small places for themselves to live in instead of nice, big, open, spacious, wonderful places to live in and around. We're sure if your dog were given a choice he would choose more room rather than less room, which equates to more freedom, not less freedom.

If you put your dog in a crate or a cage, you could pay an even bigger price. Instead of growing up bonding with you and depending on you for his security, he becomes dependent on a crate or a cage. This imprint becomes permanent and can have an insidious effect on his well-being and behavior. In case of an emergency such as a fire, an earthquake, or any disaster, instead of coming to you when he's frightened or hurt, he will run into that so-called "cave security," that wonderful small prison. That means hiding in his cage or crate, or under a bed, or in a closet, or even running away. You could lose him, forever.

Common sense will tell you that a dog is a social creature and wants to be with his family. Not in solitary confinement. We don't use a crate or a cage. We have a better way.

Appropriate actions should be taken. Be clear in your thinking so that you can be clear when communicating with your dog.

If you want your dog to stop barking, tell him to stop barking. Don't tell him to "sit." Don't tell him "no." And don't tell him "bad dog." Plain and simply tell him to stop barking, and make him stop. Praise him after he stops. That's the true meaning of positive reinforcement. We call it common sense. And that goes for all other communications problems. If your dog runs out the door, jumps on people, begs, bites, stop these problems using appropriate action and appropriate terms. You cannot use no and sit for everything that happens in your dog's world.

Thinking things through and asking lots of questions is the way to go to understand good information and filter out what doesn't make any sense. Because there are a lot of so-called experts out there and the wrong information given to you becomes the wrong information that you will give to your dog. And your dog will do the wrong thing in a very "expert" way.

Lots of Expert Advice and Opinions

Everybody seems to be an expert dog trainer. There's the actor-trainer expert, the doorman-trainer expert, the lawyer-trainer expert, the doctor-trainer expert, the person-on-the-street-trainer expert. You name them and they are all trainers and experts, ready with advice and opinions.

This reminds me of a Bob Hope movie, *The Paleface*, where Bob is about to get into a gunfight with a fast gun and everybody is giving him advice: "He draws from the left, so lean to the right. The sun's in the west, so walk to the east. He crouches when he draws, so stand on your toes." Jane Russell had to step in and kill the gunfighter because Bob was too busy trying to digest and remember all the information he was given. It was a funny movie, but too much advice can often be confusing and the wrong advice can get you shot.

It makes sense to be relaxed, and to be yourself with your dog.

An old friend of ours, Peggy, came to visit. She brought along her tiny Yorkie, Rippah. Since it was such a beautiful day, we decided to sit outside in the sun and have lunch.

Peggy was nervous. She had never taken her dog to a restaurant before, and didn't know if the Rippah would behave. We sat down at a table and sure enough the dog went bonkers, and so did Peggy.

I took Rippah from Peggy and put her in my lap. She quieted down and relaxed immediately. I had worked with Rippah and she remembered me. Peggy was amazed to see how fast her dog calmed down. I explained to Peggy that if you want your dog to behave and relax you must set an example. If you're nervous, your dog will pick it up and react in the same way. You will make her feel insecure. The more confidence you have with your dog, the more he will believe in you.

A movie was made out of Jack London's book *Call of the Wild*. It starred Clark Gable and a giant Saint Bernard who played Buck. Buck was loyal and would have given his life for Clark. If you want to have a Buck, then you will have to get a Jack London to write you one. If you want to be Clark Gable, then you will have to study his life, become an actor, and live in the north country. Or, you can be yourself. You can still have a dog that will be your best friend and loyal to you. Not to a trainer, not to your neighbor, not to your friends, but to you. And you don't even have to change who you truly are.

People have described their training experiences. How their dogs wouldn't listen to them but loved their trainers and they were so perfect with them. To us that's not *your* trained dog, that's the *trainer's* trained dog. We want your dog to hate the trainer and to love you. Can you imagine going to a marriage counselor because you're having problems with your marriage and your partner falls in love with the marriage counselor? It's the same thing.

I remember during a *Tonight Show* appearance I was working with two dogs whose owners said were untrainable. I made them stop jumping and sit down and stay put, immediately. Because all of this was so easy, I asked them to do these things in three different languages. It wasn't magic. In fact it was quite easy. I just got their attention and made them do it for me. They did. It looked great and everybody was pleased. About a week later the dog's owners called and asked me what they were doing wrong because the dogs weren't listening to them the way they had listened to me. "Nothing," I said. "What I did was teach the dogs to listen to me, but only temporarily. You will still have to teach your dogs about you and to listen to you if you want to fit them into your lifestyle. These dogs will have to know who you are and your way of being."

A dog will respond more quickly to a dog trainer than to you because the trainer seems to know what he's doing and trains the dog in a way that has been successful for him. If you try to emulate the trainer, it won't work, because eventually you will have to relax and be yourself. And when you are you, you look different to your dog than when you are trying to imitate a trainer's voice or body language.

Remember, you are the surrogate parent; you must get your dog to respond to you. If your dog were living with his real mother, he would follow her and listen to her totally and she would never utter even a single word. You must be yourself. Don't copy the moves of a trainer or animal expert unless you want to be just like that person. Chances are you don't. Your dog or puppy—age makes little difference—will pick up habits and respond to voice and body language very quickly. It would be a good idea if the language that your dog sees, hears, and learns is yours.

It has taken you many years to develop your own habit patterns, so if you're most comfortable telling your dog what you want him to do with a certain hand gesture, then that's the way you teach him. If you have a habit of stuttering, talking fast, or using your hands to express yourself, then teach him in that way. Don't force yourself to use hand gestures or verbal communications that are uncomfortable or totally foreign to you. You want the dog to understand that this is the real you. You may be a soft-spoken person and suddenly you're told to use a deep loud voice for a command. Don't. It isn't you and you might frighten yourself and your dog. It won't work because it simply isn't you talking. You won't feel comfortable or natural saying it that way.

By being yourself, you will be at your optimum level, relaxed, confident, and at your best. This will increase your dog's trust in you and enhance his ability to learn quickly. Just think, no matter what problems you have, no matter what your personality is, no matter what you look like, no matter how much money you have, no matter what your shortcomings, your dog will accept and love you anyway, 100 percent. Now you can have your own version of Buck, and in his eyes you will always be his Clark Gable.

A Member of the Family

If you consider your dog a member of your family, like another person living in your home, you would then be more aware of potential problems that you might not have realized existed. This is in the same way that a parent takes care of his or her children, developing a sixth sense about their safety, well-being, needs, moods, and wants. As a dog owner or as a parent, this sensitivity is essential. You will think twice about what you're subjecting your dog to before doing it. And if you do consider your dog a member of the family, he's protected in another way. Nobody, but nobody, gives away a family member, no matter what the situation. You'll always find a way to take care of and keep your dog. This awareness and relationship is your dog's health and life insurance policy.

Adult dogs and puppies are often brought home because they are cute and cuddly, or you saw one by chance and fell in love with him at first sight (a *coup de foudre*). They're brought home as presents for our loved ones, our children, our friends, or for ourselves.

Everything is great until the "present" goes out of control;

then things begin to change. Depersonalizing thoughts start to fill your mind. You begin to think of your dog as nothing more than a bothersome possession. Something that you have to get rid of in order to go on with your life. This type of thinking is very selfish and callous. However, some people do think this way.

First, these inconsiderate and selfish dog owners ask themselves, "Why is my dog so destructive? Why won't he listen to me?" Then, they start telling themselves, "I give this dog everything, he just doesn't understand me," or "My dog is stupid," or "My dog doesn't like me," and finally, "My dog is untrainable." This sets the stage for rationalizing and making up all the great excuses as to why they are now going to give up their dogs. Because now the dog has become an inconvenience.

They justify their reasoning and put it into action. This way they are blameless and have no responsibility, because now the dog has been totally depersonalized and has become an all-too-common *it*. "I'm moving to a new apartment, and *it* isn't allowed; I'm allergic to *it* and I didn't know it when I got *it*; I think *it* has brain damage; I'm leaving the country and they don't allow *it* where I'm going; I think *it* should have a home in the country where *it* has room to roam, and be free; I can't stop *it* from barking and I'll be evicted if I don't get rid of *it*; I'll give *it* to a shelter and they'll get *it* a home. I'll take *it* somewhere, tie *it* up, someone will surely find *it*." And many more creative reasons and solutions. But the dog is gone, however they got rid of him and for whatever reason. A cruel end for a loyal and helpless creature. And none of this was necessary.

The truth is, the owner never knew how to communicate with his dog, never understood his dog, and never knew how to bring up his dog, and therefore he could never teach his dog to fit into his life. The dog never became a family member. The owner's limit of time and patience ran out, so it was good-bye dog.

Once you decide to get rid of your dog and you give him away, his next owner will have the dog that you brought up wrong because you inadvertently followed wrong information or just didn't know how to teach him the right things, and now this dog carries all the bad habits as baggage to his new home. If he's lucky. If your dog is not lucky and doesn't get a new home because of all his wrong imprinting and bad habits, then he's a dead dog. In some cases dogs are even drowned or shot. Sad to say.

Some of these "giveaway" dogs now have legitimate problems that new owners will have to contend with. They really are biters, incessant barkers, destructive chewers, or they can't be housebroken, making it difficult to find new homes. All of these problems were solvable and are solvable, and very quickly at that. When I worked with the ASPCA (a very large shelter) in New York City, the dogs I helped, and helped very successfully and very quickly, were these same types of dogs. All that was needed was the right kind of direction and understanding.

Dogs Are Responsibilities, Not Just Possessions

If you are going to get a dog or a puppy for your child, remember he will be your responsibility overall. As children grow up and start their own lives, going to school, staying with friends, playing with friends, you will find that the dog you got for your child is now your dog. This happening is a fact of life. If your child moves into his own apartment, or goes away to school, the dog stays home and is your dog. We're stating the obvious here, because every parent who has ever brought a dog home for their child knows that they ended up taking care of the dog, feeding him, walking him, taking care of his health and well-being, including baby-sitting. These dogs are also given away if the child loses interest, moves away, and the parent can't be bothered.

Then there are people who get dogs because they fit in with the new country house, or they go well with a new lifestyle or self-image, or they are the most popular flavor-of-the-month dog. These dogs are given away for the most part if they don't measure up to the original reasons they were bought and the aesthetic expectations of their owners.

Let's not forget, if you are thinking of getting a dog, this is usually a fifteen-year investment. Dogs are not possessions like a car or a washing machine or an extra pair of shoes to be given away when they don't fit in with your current schedule, a vacation, or a move. Dogs are responsibilities. They are living, breathing, intelligent creatures; they are smart and they do have feelings. So if you can't take care of your responsibility, don't get a dog.

When traditional training fails, when it breaks down, and you give your dog away, you might have paid a price monetarily, but your dog pays the ultimate price, which could mean the end of his life. And that is one of the prime failures of traditional dog training. If you never achieved a bond, a connection, or an understanding with your dog, and you can't control your dog; if all the books you've read and the trainers you've hired to train and the experts you've listened to failed you, then the bottom line is that you are going to give your dog away. That is not in his best interest.

If you want to enjoy your dog for the next fifteen or so years, then the two of you have to reach an understanding so that rules and parameters can be set up. This way your dog will immediately start to learn your ways, and that will make teaching more enjoyable and a lot easier.

Understand that dogs will form permanent imprints by about thirteen weeks and that they can successfully learn between eighty and a hundred behaviors within the first year of their life. Understand that an adult dog or even an older adult dog can be taught your way of life, can be taught new habit patterns, and can be taught very quickly. Remember you can even teach an old person new tricks. Understand that by learning your dog and communicating with him in the right way, you'll be able to bring him up with proper behavior and proper nutrition, and prevent many possible health problems. And you will not have to count on the dog-food industry to be the last word on his diet and nutrition, or your veterinarian for the last word on your dog's behavior, or put up with an "expert" blaming you for not practicing enough. And last but not least, relying on that sage wisdom from your local pet shop, where they probably know less than you do.

Your dog is very smart and can learn complex behaviors in a very short time. You will be able to fit him into your lifestyle and in a very reasonable and holistic way. Remember, a little common sense should help you wade through the overload of information and misconceptions surrounding you and your dog. It will give you the dog you've always wanted, purely and simply done. Break with tradition and enjoy a new lease on life. With your dog, that is.

A good rule and philosophy for the life of your dog is that if you are always doing the right things for him, he can and will do the right things for you. He will be the yin to your yang.

By truly understanding your dog, you will be able to experience unconditional love and loyalty, a rare occurrence in our own species. This will happen only if you break from the tradition of thinking that your dog is a one-dimensional, one-word creature with limited intelligence.

CHAPTER 2
The Magic Touch

Coming to You Once and for All

Claudette Did

In the movie *The Egg and I* Claudette Colbert watches from a terrace while her husband, played by Fred MacMurray, flirts with another woman in the garden below. Annoyed, Claudette takes off her shoe and throws it at Fred. The shoe sails through the air and hits him in the head. Fred picks up the shoe, looks at it, and takes a moment to think about what just happened. He then immediately comes to her, rubbing his head with one hand and holding the shoe in the other. Claudette used a very powerful technique.

Eddie Got It

A friend of ours tells a story about why he always listened to his mother. He explained that it was because he never saw the

24

shoe that hit him, or from where it came, or when it was coming.

The Bribe

He used to come to me whenever I offered him a dog biscuit. Then the range and variety of necessary treats became exhaustive. Not long after that he'd only listen to me in his own sweet time, waiting for the best deal, until he found better pickings elsewhere. He now hangs out at the better restaurants in town. I guess he's a very enterprising young dog, being able to figure out how to successfully extract a bribe.

The Gift

A client of mine would let his dog out of his house every morning to go to the bathroom. He would leave the door open so his dog could get back in. But many times she would bring back a dead mouse and drop it near the breakfast table. She had learned this from her owner, who used to call her and give her a treat as a reward for listening. So now, she is returning the favor.

He must learn to come to you before anything else is taught.

Getting your dog to come to you is the most important behavior and should be the first one you teach your dog. If you can't get your dog to come to you, then you really can't control him. Which means he can never be let off his leash. You will always have to be careful never to leave a door open, including a car door, an apartment door, or for that matter any exit. You can never truly relax around him because to err is human and to err could mean losing your dog. When walking your dog, you might drop your leash, the leash could break, the leash could get stuck in an elevator door. There's no end to the problems that you could have if you can't get your dog to come to you.

It could add up to this. If you can't get your dog back when he's loose, he could be badly injured, stolen, or even killed. If he is an aggressive dog, he could hurt or kill someone else's dog or even attack a person. None of these would be pleasant experiences for either of you.

You're also missing out on lots of fun, the fun you would be having with your dog if you could get him to come back to you when you want him. Then when you take him to the beach or to the country or to a park, or just to visit some friends, he'd be free and so would you.

Many people will still take their dogs along with them wherever they go even if the dogs are not well behaved, but the dogs that are under control are the ones that are most welcome.

The Obnoxious Visitor

Have you ever had a friend bring their dog or new puppy over to your house for a visit and then the dog either attacked your cat, if you had one, or lifted his leg and copiously peed on the corner of your expensive couch, then it dripped down to include that very nice oriental rug? Or maybe the puppy left you a deposit that was not bankable but was transferred all over your house by one or more shoe bottoms. How about sitting down to a nice dinner only to find your guest's drooling canine companion climbing all over the dinner table or up onto your lap?

One Sunday afternoon we were invited over to a friend's house to watch a Super Bowl game. As we sat down on a couch to eat, another couple arrived bringing with them their beagle dog.

The minute they took his leash off, the dog ran wildly around the apartment using two to three feet of the wall to make his incredible hairpin turns, then catapulted up onto the couch where we were sitting. He raced across our bodies, vacuuming the food off our plates, and stopped just long enough to check and see if we were hiding anything in our mouths.

Noticing where we went to refill our plates, he very quickly discovered the smorgasbord table and proceeded to dive into it, spreading everything evenly to all parts of the room, including the ceiling.

When you take the leash off your dog and he becomes a pest, stop him immediately. Don't make good-sounding irrational excuses such as my dog didn't get enough exercise today, my dog has been depressed and needs an outlet, my dog gets excited at parties. There are many, many more. But the truth is you couldn't control your dog. Don't subject everyone to your dog's obnoxious behavior. You might think it's cute, but nobody else does. If you teach your dog to come to you and stay with you, this problem becomes moot and you can take your dog anywhere.

Sparky's Bitten Ear

Sparky is a young German short-haired pointer. Central Park is her home turf. Whenever Sparky would see a squirrel in her park, she would run off and try to catch it.

She quickly learned to fake a run straight at the squirrel and then head the squirrel off at his tree. This worked, and she caught a squirrel. Surprised by the success, the Sparker dropped her catch. The squirrel, not hurt, but a little dazed by what had just happened, shook his head to clear it, got his bearings, then quickly scampered up his tree to home. This squirrel was lucky to be alive, because killing is a learned behavior and Sparky hadn't learned it yet.

Squirrels don't hurt anyone, and their zany acrobatics are a joy to watch. They will even let you feed them if and when they get to trust you. So, for the life of the squirrels, this game of Sparky's had to be stopped before she did learn how to kill.

Sparky wouldn't come back to her owners, Nina and Teddy, until she was good and ready. Sometimes that meant a couple of hours. If they had a one o'clock appointment, they had to take Sparky out at ten or eleven just in case Sparky decided to hang out in the park for a while.

She also had a bad habit of running up to strange dogs. On one of these occasions a stranger she didn't know almost removed her ear when she excitedly ran up to say hello. The bill for Sparky's ear job was rather expensive, as is all medical attention for anyone without health insurance.

These stories all have happy endings. The dogs, along with their owners, have all been put through our training program and are doing just fine. They all listen to their owners 100 percent of the time, and it doesn't matter if they are on or off a lead. The only time they need to wear a lead now is when the law requires it.

Running Away

During the North Ridge, California, earthquake in 1994, I was with my two dogs, Tibby and Willy, when the 6.8 earthquake hit at around five o'clock in the morning. My dogs were barking and very upset but stayed with me as I ran to a secure place.

I recalled how a few years earlier, before I learned this technique from Paul, Tibby liked to get out the door and run away. She didn't listen to me at all then.

I was living in a large apartment complex in Los Angeles with her. She was less than a year old at that time. One day Tibby got out the front door and went running down the hall with me chasing after her. I chased her down the hall, up a flight of stairs, and out into the parking lot, where there was always lots of traffic. I couldn't get her back; she thought this was some kind of a game. Smiling and wagging her tail at me, she ran under cars and all over the place playing hide-and-seek while I kept chasing her and trying to get her to come back to me. I was terrified at the thought of losing my dog. I didn't know what to do. She could have been run over.

Finally, with the help of a neighbor and lots of luck, we caught her. If I had known how to teach Tibby to come back to me or not to run out the door in the first place, then I would have saved myself all of this unnecessary anxiety. Tibby used to come to me only when she felt like it.

In the months after the earthquake there were many news reports about lost, injured, or dead pets. People were being told to check all the animal shelters, the police, neighbors, fire departments, and so on for their missing dogs and cats. I'm not saying all, but many of these casualties could have been avoided had these dogs and cats been taught to go to their owners in times of danger.

You need to teach your dog to come to you, first and foremost, and that's through fire, water, earthquakes, hurricanes, tornadoes, and any and all calamities. He can sit down later, when he's tired.

What's "Sit" Got to Do with It?
Absolutely Nothing

To control your dog and avoid the problems illustrated in the above stories, you must teach your dog to come to you. Teaching your dog to sit will be absolutely useless in times of crisis.

The first lesson most dog trainers, most dog books, and the rest of the world's experts will tell you is to teach your dog to sit. If the first permanent behavior you teach your dog is to sit down and your dog runs away from you and you yell "Sit!", he might sit but he may be dragging his butt for a mile, causing a lot of smoke while burning up the roads. Or he might sit, but he could be a mile away, sitting. Then what? You can't call him back to you because you haven't taught him to come to you. If you run after him he might run away thinking that either you're angry or you're playing a game with him. Just think, if you had taught your dog to come to you in the first place, then you wouldn't have this "What do I do now?" mystery on your hands.

Many dog owners use sit as one of the three "control all" commands. The other two are "stay" and "no." For example, to control their dogs they'll yell these three so-called magic words, "sit, stay, no," or "no, sit, stay," or, "stay, no, sit." And on and on. The dog isn't listening because this is very confusing to him. It would be very confusing to anybody; just reading this paragraph is confusing. If your dog runs away you should be able to say to him "Come back here," and he should come back to you.

Eleanor Roosevelt would simply say to her pet Scottie, "Fala, come over here this instant." And he would. And because Fala listened, I don't think he was ever excluded from important meetings.

I took my dogs Plum, Snapper Dan, Sleepy Joe, and Inches to Hyde Park to see where Fala, the Roosevelts' beloved Scottish terrier, lived. They especially wanted to see the little ottoman that Fala rested on when he would keep his president and Mrs. Roosevelt company. My dogs seemed very impressed. We don't know what influence Fala might have had on the shaping of world policy, but because they loved him so much, he must've had some influence on their private lives.

Now you should realize the importance of teaching your dog to come to you as the first and most important behavior you'll ever need in your relationship with him. Everything else is nice but doesn't mean a damn thing unless your dog listens to you and comes back to you. How will you ever be able to teach him any or all of the other social graces if he's not around to learn them?

This reckoning goes for any and all of the other behaviors: lie down, walk with you, stay here, and any other ones. These should be learned after you teach your dog to come to you. And then, as if by magic, real magic, all of these other behaviors will be learned in a matter of minutes, with no boring, tedious, time-consuming practice sessions.

Everything else you want your dog to learn to make your lives together easier is great but will never be as important as teaching him to come back to you. We can't *overstate* the importance of this behavior.

What's wrong with teaching your dog to come to you with a long line?

Traditional training requires a six-foot training lead and then a long, long line to teach the dog to come to his owner from a distance.

The six-footer will give your dog a vague clue as to what you want and nothing more. As far as the long line is concerned, it isn't necessary and it can work against you. Those fifty-footers tangle everybody and everything within their reach. If you pull your dog on a long line or a six-footer, he will come to you, but only when he is attached to that line.

Remember, dogs are smarter than you think, and when your dog knows there is no line holding him, he will take off. Your dog is very sensitive to any physical changes on his body no matter how slight they might be. He will know that the line isn't there by the absence of its weight. Why should he come to you? He was never taught to come to you without a leash. Even if you have a four- or six-foot lead attached to him and you drop it, he'll know you dropped it, and again you will not be certain he will come back to you.

Some dog owners always keep a leash on their dog even when they let them run free. They hope to maintain some control over their dog this way, to grab the lead if they have to. But this presents a greater problem. Dog owners who allow their dogs to run with the lead dragging behind them are putting their dogs in harm's way. For example, a dog runs into an elevator, the elevator door closes, the lead is outside, the elevator goes up. No more dog. Your dog's leash can get caught in the door of a taxicab, or any car. When the driver takes off, good-bye dog. Or your dog is running and the lead gets caught on something; the dog can choke himself and get hurt. These are not rare instances; these are common problems.

Training your dog with a line limits your control. He will learn very quickly that you can't reach him past your fingertips once he is free. Did you ever notice how your dog will come within inches of you when you call him but stay just out of your reach? When you call him to you and you say, "Good boy," he says, "Good-bye." That's because he has not really learned that he must come to you off his lead. He's learned to come near you when he's free, and near you can mean five feet, ten feet, fifty feet, or even a thousand feet. Near you becomes only relative to him. Eventually, he will think that when you call him all he has to do is look at you and that's enough. This is another problem of training your dog to come to you with leashes or lines.

Although your dog might come back to you at times if you train him with the short or long line, when you really want him, when it's a question of his safety, you will never be 100 percent sure that he will come back to you. The only way that you can truly be certain that you can get your dog back to you is if he is taught to come back to you, without a lead, freestyle.

An umbilical cord is removed at birth because it's unnecessary after that. It won't teach a child or a dog to come back to or to stay with his mother. A dog's mother teaches this imprint immediately and freestyle. It's most important that no binding contraptions hinder the direct communication of this lesson.

Contrary to the accepted wisdom, teaching your dog to listen to you and to come to you without a leash isn't difficult. In fact, you both can learn this in less than an hour. It's fast, it's sure, and it works.

The Old Way

For many years, I followed the long line principle. I put a six-foot cotton training lead on the dog and pulled him and called him and pulled him and called him, until I felt he understood what I wanted. Then I would take the lead off the dog and using an enclosed area somewhere, I would chase the dog to his owner. This eventually worked but it took a long time, usually four or five weeks, and even then I was never truly certain that it would work 100 percent of the time. But I was certain of keeping my weight down because I burned a lot of calories chasing dogs.

Even though chasing the dog to his owner without a leash was a new twist on an old technique, and worked, it was still limited, it still took too long, and in my mind, I wasn't 100 percent certain of having the control that I wanted over the dog with this behavior.

All this racing around, chasing, pulling, and complicated, involved, primitive form of teaching used to drive me up a wall, because I knew dogs were smarter than all this archaic teaching implied. The lack was in these traditional teachings, not in the dog. There had to be a simpler, faster, and more direct way to communicate this all-important command. After all, the mother dog teaches this quickly and permanently to her puppies without all this sweat and effort.

The Accidental Discovery

One day I was walking my dog Plum in Central Park. He was a puppy then and not yet the famous dog he was to become later. I let him free so he could run around and get some exercise. When I wanted to leave the park I called him to me. He looked at me, wagged his tail, and smiled as if to say, "No way." Turning around he bounced and bounded in any direction he pleased, doing whatever he felt like doing, as long as he didn't have to come to me. I chased him, I called after him, "Plum, come here! No! Sit, stay!!!" And of course he couldn't have cared less. He did whatever he wanted to do. He was free, he was faster than me, and he was in charge.

Out of frustration and now fearful of losing my dog, I threw my leash at him, and to my surprise, it hit him. It also surprised him, and he stopped in his tracks. He then smelled the leash, and looked at me. Again to my surprise, he came back to me. I was so relieved to get him back that I didn't think too much about the mechanics of what had just happened. I put his lead back on and we went home.

While walking home, I went over the episode in my mind. He was running, I threw the lead, he stopped, he smelled the lead and came back to me. The lead had become an extension of me, and he had immediately listened to that extension. It was as if I had reached out across a long distance to tap him on the shoulder and say, "Hey, Plum, remember me? Come over here." I was amazed at how simply and how quickly it had worked, this magic long-distance touch.

It's hard to believe that this simple, accidental toss of Plum's leash became the key that would unlock a door that allowed me in a flash to move from the past into a future that had unlimited possibilities in all dimensions of training and behavior. The change was total. It was revolutionary. This toss was the catalyst for how all of my training would evolve to this very day.

I had been looking for this answer, and Plum, with the help of Mother Nature, had given it to me.

Reached at a Distance Anytime and from Anywhere

Imagine this. You open the window to let in some air. Along with the air, a strange-looking two-foot being with large eyes and one large forefinger floats into your living room. Staring at you, he comes to rest about three feet off the floor, nose to nose with you. Are you nervous? Are you frightened? Are you angry? Are you annoyed? Or are you just plain curious? This creature then floats backwards a few feet, points a long finger at you, and you start to levitate. You're now suspended in space, a little frightened and nervous. You could possibly even be pants-wetting nervous. He moves you around a bit and then places you back on the floor. He asks you in a very nice way to come over to him. Do you listen to him? Or do you stamp your foot on the floor and obstinately tell him, "No, I won't." We think you will do as he asked. We know we would. We think you will listen to him not only because he's doing things that you can't understand, but he is asserting a power that you can't even believe exists. It's mind-boggling to you.

When you learn how to use our throwing technique to show your dog how powerful you are, that you can reach him and touch him from anywhere and at anytime, it will have the same affect on him as the strange-looking two-foot being had on you. Your dog will listen. He might even be pants-wetting nervous at first, but he will listen. And listen perfectly, as if you truly were a respected parent. We don't know if you would love and trust the alien; we do know your dog will still love and trust you.

When the throwing technique teaches your dog to come to you, you are not simply teaching a solitary command. That's

35

old thinking and old doings. The magic touch changes everything forever in the way you and your dog look and act toward one another. In this one swift move you will dramatically change forever your standing in the eyes of your dog. Why?

Two different species of animal are coexisting in your environment. Your dog and a strange-looking being, you. One of you is going to have to adapt to the other's lifestyle. One of you must become the dominant species. Right now your dog feels that he is, and this is with good reason. His sense of smell is better than yours, his sight and hearing are better than yours, he can run faster and jump higher than you. So why should he listen to you? Why should he be the one to adapt? You can show him your bank account or your new car, but he won't be impressed. What can you do to so impress your dog that he will hand the reins of dominance back to you?

Because your dog is not a primate, he has no idea how to throw or what a throw is and how you were able to accomplish this incredible feat. He is not physically able to throw an object; he's not built that way. If he were a primate, he would imitate you and throw the object back at you, probably with a better aim and much harder.

The throwing technique is a very powerful tool when used properly. In your dog's eyes you will become his total security blanket. You will be able to get his attention and teach him anything. Your dog will look to you for direction at all times and without a question. He won't play the come-and-catch-me-if-you-can game anymore. Because now your reach extends beyond your fingertips. And far beyond the length of any leash. It's like tapping him on the shoulder from twenty feet away and reminding him to pay attention to you and to come to you if that's what you want. He will never understand your magic, he will just listen to it.

You will notice that when you toss an object at him, first he will look at it, then he will smell it. He will try to identify the object and how it got there. Since he knows your smell he knows you were the source of the thrown object. He will come to you. This will give you total control over your dog.

Here are a few helpful pointers to keep in mind; they are essential elements.

1. *Use positive reinforcement.* Means first your dog does what you want him to do, then you reward him by praising him. He should want to learn from you because he knows he is secure with you, he can trust you, and that by doing the right things for you, he makes you happy, and therefore you will make him happy. Then you can give him the whole wide world. Remember, any animal will mistake kindness for weakness and will look to take advantage of it. So only be a pushover and a softy when your dog listens to you.

2. *Never use the word "no" as a punishment.* If you claim to train your dog with positive reinforcement, why do you say "no" every time you talk to your dog? "No" happens to be a negative term.

Many dog trainers and dog owners claim to train their dogs with positive reinforcement. But they use the word "no" as frequently as they breathe. It seems to be another one of those all-encompassing, for every situation words that's supposed to solve any and all problems. It doesn't. You might as well name your dog "No," since it's said more frequently than his name.

"No" is so frequently misused in training that it actually will confuse a dog. But no matter how you say it, it's a negative term, and it's negative reinforcement, so don't use it.

Never use the word "no" when you are physically reprimanding your dog. For example, if you have to slap or shake your dog as a disciplinary measure when he does something wrong, don't also use the word "no." If you do, it then becomes a double negative and will be very confusing to him. It could work against what you are trying to teach him. Guaranteed your dog won't get the message you're trying to send to him. You're much better off using a sentence. "Don't do that again!" or "Stop it this instant!" or whatever you feel comfortable saying after you discipline your dog.

Showing your displeasure this way gives you a more natural body language and emphasizes that you are not happy much more effectively than the word "no."

3. *Never call your dog to punish him.* If your dog has done something wrong—soiled your rug, chewed up your favorite shoes, or only destroyed the left leg of that beautiful old chair you found at a flea market—wait until all those pictures in your mind of what you would like to do to him fade away. Calm down. Then go and get your dog; without saying a word to him, quietly bring him over to the scene of the crime, then show him you're not pleased. Never, never call him over to his dirty deed and then punish him, because you'll find that it will be the last time your dog will probably ever come to you. He will think that to call him means he will be punished.

4. *When first teaching your dog to come to you by throwing, don't wave objects around in the air as if they were toys and don't try to teach your dog to retrieve at the same time.* Keep whatever the object is, whether it's a slipper, a magazine, or a pair of socks, either under your arm or somewhere nearby. To brandish something in your hand when calling your dog, especially when first teaching your dog to come to you with this throwing method, would be like holding up an ax to me and then asking me to come over to you. I wouldn't. But once your dog does learn to come to you, and that shouldn't take more than an hour at the most, then anything you have in your hand after that won't bother him at all.

Don't try to teach your dog, especially a puppy, to retrieve or to fetch until you teach him to come to you. If you do it will certainly confuse your dog and our training method could be compromised.

5. *To bribe or not to bribe.* Don't offer your dog a bribe in the form of a food treat when asking him to come to you. Bad habits are learned much faster then good ones, even with humans. Dogs are very smart and learn very quickly to hold out for bigger and better bribes. You must make sure your dog listens to you first and then show him how grateful you are. Hey, you can spoil him rotten when he listens. We do.

6. *Call your dog once; don't repeat yourself.* When you call your dog to you, you should call him just once, not two times, not three times. Don't repeat yourself. If you repeat his name or what you want him to do, for example, "Max, Max, come here, come here, come here," the imprint might read in the dog's mind that he should come to you only if you say everything three times in succession and that his name is Max Max. The correct way to call him is just once and then make him do what you want.

7. *Wait about ten seconds.* You must hesitate for ten seconds after asking your dog to come to you. It will take your dog between six and ten seconds to get your message, think about it, and then to do what you asked him. For example: "Max, come over here." Give him about ten seconds to respond. This will be true for anything you teach your dog.

If you look at the second hand on your watch after you ask your dog to do something for you, you'll see that he will respond within six to ten seconds. Assuming that he has been taught the behavior that you are asking him to do.

8. *Call your dog in your own way; don't use one-word commands. You don't have to create a separate, single-word, simple, incomplete-sentence language for him.* Most dog books, dog trainers and dog experts will tell you to use one-word commands when training your dog. Their reasoning is that the dog

will not be able to understand more than that. But then, why repeat the one word over and over again? "Sit, Sit, Sit, Sit, Sit." Sounds like a one-word sentence to us.

You went to school, you learned how to speak in sentences; you learned how to use grammar properly, so use it. Teach your dog from the very beginning to understand you the way you are. He can learn more and much faster if you teach him English the way you learned it.

When you're talking on the telephone, or to your friends, or with your family, anytime you are in a social situation, your dog will be listening and he will be part of the gang because he's part of your life and language now. Unless you communicate in your world with a language consisting of one-word, simple, incomplete sentences, well, in that case you should teach your dog that other language.

To clarify what we mean, Edgar Rice Burroughs's character, Tarzan, spoke this way when he was with Jane. "Me, Tarzan, you, Jane. Jane, see, Simba?" So, if you feel you're a Tarzan, then you can express yourself to your dog in Tarzan's language. "Me, Tarzan, you, dog, come, sit, stay, no."

We like to say, "Come over here" if we want our dogs *to* come to us, or "Let's go," or even "Come on," if we want our dogs to come *with* us. Whatever we want our dogs to do, we will ask them in a language that we were taught, English, and use it as correctly as we can.

You might also want to gesture with your hand for him to come to you or with you. All of this is okay because you must teach your dog to listen to you in the way you feel most comfortable and natural. Then your dog can learn from the real you.

9. *You must be stationary when calling your dog to you.* It's very important to be clear and direct when communicating with your dog. When you want your dog to come to you, you

must be stationary and let him come to you. If you are moving when you call him to you, then he can't come to you, he can only come with you. Make sure that when you are first teaching your dog to come to you, you don't move around. It might sound silly to you, but it can be very confusing to your dog.

10. *Always take him by his collar first.* If your dog comes almost to you, then he really doesn't come to you at all. Your dog is the expert on body language and knows very well the length of your arm. He is always able to stay just out of your reach when you want him to come to you. To prevent this from happening, you must always hold him by his collar first before you tell him how good he is. This teaches your dog to come all-l-l-l the way to you. All the time.

Plum was trained not to go to people and not to let people touch him unless I said it was okay. So, he always stayed just out of everyone's reach. If anybody came over to touch him, Plum would move away from them, ever so slightly, just far enough away so that the person trying to pet him couldn't touch him, and didn't realize that Plum was moving, just out of reach. The person would literally lose his balance and fall down. I guess you could say that people always fell for Plum.

Teaching Your Dog to Come to You

Bring your dog to an enclosed area. We like to use a room where the dog can't run out. Sit down and relax. It's important to be relaxed. Your dog is the real expert on body language and will know whether you are relaxed, nervous, angry, or just not sure of yourself. Since your dog looks to you for guidance, he will key off of your behavior. Call your dog to you. Give him the ten-second time frame. If he comes to you, hold him by the collar and tell him how good he is. If you don't take hold of his collar, he might think it's enough just to come near you, then when you praise him, he will leave. This distance will increase until your dog doesn't come to you at all.

Throwing Not to Hurt but to Teach

If he does not come to you, take some keys, a small soft-covered book, a magazine, a soft slipper, or anything that you can think of that won't hurt your dog but is substantial enough to reach your dog when thrown. Don't use a feather (just kidding), but don't throw something that won't reach your dog. For a puppy we like to use a rolled-up pair of socks and toss that in his direction. It should make contact with him, but not hurt him. Use your common sense. For a small dog or a puppy use a small object and throw it gently. For a larger dog use a more substantial object and throw it more substantially. We don't want the dog to think that this is a game; on the other hand, we don't want to hurt him either.

Don't use objects such as hard-covered books or heavy shoes. We want to emphasize that you shouldn't use objects that can hurt your dog. This is most important. But you must make contact with him when you throw. It's all right if you miss once in a while, but if you never make contact with your dog, then all you are doing is teaching him that you're a person who throws things around and that you have a terrible aim. He will never come to you and might even decide to leave home and look for a less stressful, easier-to-understand place to live.

Once you have thrown the object of your choice at your dog, he will immediately react to this in two ways. First, you will have his undivided attention, and second, he will smell the object you have thrown and discover that it's an extension of you since it has your smell on it. You have now become a super person with incredibly long arms.

Your dog might come to you, and if he does, praise him. Again, always take hold of his collar first. If he does not come to you and decides to run away, sit down, or do something else, your next move is to remember where you were when you called him, and *quietly, without saying a word,* go and get your dog. Take him by the collar, and pull him all the way back to the spot where you were when you first called him. *Don't talk and don't let go of his collar.* When you get back to your original spot, give him a lot of praise. Let him know that he was really, really a good dog for coming to you, even if you had to pull him the length of a New York City block.

You have learned to make sure that when you ask your dog to come to you, he comes to you, and if not, then you can make him do it. He has learned, he hasn't any choice. Spoil him rotten after he listens.

Once you feel confident that your dog knows what you want, you're ready for the next step. If you have been working in your living room and you've been calling him to you from your couch, now walk to another part of the room, say to a chair or to the door. At this point, we want your dog to follow you and stay by you without your having to call him at all. If he does not follow you, throw something at him *without saying anything.* He should smell the object again and go right to you, or even walk with you.

Your Dog Should Not Go to Anyone Without Your Okay

If somebody calls your dog, your dog is not to go to them unless you say it is okay. You're not to say, "No," you're to physically stop him. How? A well-placed slap on the behind, or if you can't reach him, throw something. He should stop and come back to you. Then you can praise him or give him a steak dinner; if he's a vegetarian, a carrot will do. *He is not to go to anybody.* He has to bond with you first, and only later, after he listens to you 100 percent of the time, can he then be allowed to go to other people or play with other dogs. He can have the freedom to do anything you approve of when you tell him he can.

You don't have to wait for this situation to happen; you should set it up as part of your teaching program. Ask a friend to call your dog; make sure not to let the friend call him by name. If he starts to go to your friend, stop him physically. If you have to throw something at him, do it; don't say anything to him and don't hold him back. He must come back to you on his own. If he comes back to you, praise him. If he does not, then go and get him by the collar, don't say a word, show him you're not happy with him, and pull him back to you. Repeat the process until your dog does not go to that person even if that person has the most incredible food treat in the world. Then you give your dog the world for listening only to you and to no one else.

This is very important because it means that your dog is bonding to you. He becomes part of your family. Then he will accept and be friendly only to those you accept and are friendly with. You teach your children not to talk to strangers for their protection. It's no different with your dog. Socializing your dog with the whole world makes your dog the whole world's dog and not yours.

Within a half hour to an hour your dog will learn to come to you. You are then ready to open up his range to the whole house or apartment. You want him to come to you from any-where—upstairs, downstairs, from the attic or the basement. From anywhere and at anytime. Even if he is out of sight when you call him, he must come to you. But don't bother your dog when he's having his dinner. It's not necessary to call him away from his meal or when he's sleeping. We're sure you wouldn't want to be annoyed during meals or when you are sleeping.

When your dog comes to you 100 percent of the time in a controlled area, when your dog stays and listens to you no matter what distractions there are in his path (people or dogs), he will come to you and stay with you when you are outside. Especially when he knows you're armed with your magic touch.

Some People Are Blessed, Being Perfect from the Very Beginning

Some people have to work very hard to achieve perfection. The same goes for owning a dog. Some dog owners feel they are blessed with the perfect dog, and some have to work hard to achieve the same result. Even with the "perfect" dog, though, we often hear, "He's always perfect except when he . . ." However, some dogs do seem to learn more quickly than others. This does not have to do with a dog's intelligence, it has to do with how you teach him, or what your dog might have learned before you got him, and of course what habits he has picked up along the way.

Their names are Chagall, Matisse, and Zoie, and although they're not painters or writers, they are creative personalities as well as being three small white Westies. When we first went to work with them and Paula, their owner, the three "kids" were sitting on their couch, very excited because they knew that whatever was going to happen, it was about them. Everybody loves attention and they loved every minute of it, even if it included a higher education—the dynamics of flight to be more exact.

Paula did what we told her. She took off a slipper and casually threw it in their direction. It landed on Zoie, who didn't need to be asked more than once. Not only did she go to Paula immediately, she bounded across the room, jumped in her lap, and kissed her. We all laughed because Zoie was having such a good time. And then the next ones were waiting for their turn to play this new game. Everyone fully enjoyed themselves: Paula, because she couldn't believe how quickly this technique had worked, and the dogs, because they were having fun being so important. Remember, Paula kept telling each of them how good they were for flying across the room to her. It was so fast. It's nice when they listen. Teaching these three little guys was very simple, and the way they responded was a pleasure.

. . . A Little More Work

Spot and Topper are two cocker spaniels who are good friends and who have always played together. Spot was a puppy and Topper about a year or so old. The owners of the puppy had heard about our program and had hired us. They had insisted that their daughter and son-in-law be there because they could no longer tolerate the visits of Topper, who belonged to the children. Topper would race wildly through their house, jumping and peeing. He was totally obnoxious. And the little puppy was learning all of these habits from his older cousin, how to be wild and out of control and how to get away with it. In this case we worked with Topper and his owner Karen first. The puppy watched with great interest, as puppies generally do, while his friend was being taught the rules of the road.

Only one person at a time should work with their dog. This means that if you are a couple, either you or your partner works with the dog first, and the other one stays out of it until the lesson is completed. And vice versa. You will notice how a dog will try to go to any person other than the one working with him. He is not doing this out of love or for security; he's doing it because he doesn't want to listen. He would rather go to somebody who cannot control him or who won't ask anything of him. If given the choice he would rather do nothing your way and everything his way. When one of you works with your dog, and your dog immediately tries to distract both of you by playing one against the other, don't allow it. Don't touch your dog and don't talk to your dog when your partner is working with him.

With Topper and Spot and six adults there, this is exactly what happened. Topper wanted to go to Spot, his grandfather, his father, to everyone else in the room, but not necessarily to Karen, who had called him. We all maintained a hands-off policy. Topper was working with Karen. She had to pull him out from under the table, and out from behind the plants and away from everybody. He was reluctant at first; maybe he hated giving up his old wild ways. That was too bad for him. All of a sudden he got the idea that he hadn't any choice, and he knew what was expected of him.

You could actually see the pieces fitting together when Topper suddenly understood what Karen wanted from him. It was amazing and gratifying to see how Topper was able to reason this whole episode out. At the end of the session, Topper was treated to a nice piece of roasted chicken breast (without the bones, of course) when he was perfect. You can treat your dog to anything after he does what you want. He loved being perfect after that.

When it was time to work with the puppy, Spot, he had basically learned from watching his pal go through his paces. Wagging his tail he seemed to say, "See I'm perfect now myself, so let's have some of that roasted stuff you gave that bigger-than-me guy." We didn't fall for this con job Spot was trying to lay on us. We made him go through his paces and only after he was perfect did he get his piece of crispy roast chicken. Now, these two can play together in total freedom without destroying the house or patience of their families.

That sense of security your dog feels he has by being in a cage or a crate must be transferred over to you where it truly belongs. You then become your dog's real security, which is the way it should be. You can help your dog if he is in trouble. A cage or a crate cannot. In times of emergency, a cage or a crate can become the ultimate trap.

Carlyle, a very hairy Lhasa apso, and Shari, a sparsely spotted Dalmatian, were both crate-trained before we met them. When we first applied our throwing technique, these two dogs, uncertain of what was taking place, ran right into their respective crates for security instead of going to their owners as they should have. When we closed the entrances to these "caves of security," the two dogs then tried to climb into book-shelves, into the stereo unit, into a closet, or under a bed. But still they did not go to their owners. Think of this. In the event of an emergency, such as the earthquake we mentioned ear-lier, or a fire, or any emergency, if these dogs are ever fright-ened or in any danger and are running for their lives, where they are going is right into their "caves of security," the crate or cage (the ultimate trap), instead of going to their owners for their safety.

If you have been using a cage or a crate to control your dog before using our techniques, it might take you a little longer, and a little more effort, to get your dog to come to you. Re-member, you are breaking and restructuring a very strong se-curity habit. But you can still teach your dog to come to you in a very short time using this technique. Usually in an hour or less. So, if your dog is a Shari or a Carlyle or any dog trained in a crate or cage, now you know exactly what to expect. Do not lose your temper, don't scream or yell at your dog, don't get frustrated. Be patient, stay calm. He will come to you. And by using this throwing technique you have actually taught him even more than to come to you. You have taught him that you are his security blanket, and not his cage or crate. And that's the way it should be.

Don't practice. There's no need for it and it will bore your dog to tears. He will feel that he only has to listen to you during a practice session. When your dog has learned some-thing, he's learned something. If you think he "forgot" something, just remind him when necessary. Because chances are he didn't forget, but he might have felt he didn't have to listen to you.

Don't endlessly practice "coming to you" with your dog. Once he's got it, he's got it. When you learned something in class, your teacher didn't make you repeat what you learned hundreds of times; your teacher went on to the next lesson.

Do it for real. Whenever you want your dog, call him. If he doesn't come to you, go find him and throw something. Walk away. He should follow you or come to you. If not, get him by the collar and pull him along all the way back to where you first called him from. Then tell him how good he is. This we call a reminder; some call it reinforcing a learned behavior. Remember, your dog is not a robot; he has a mind, he does think, and he might not think that at this particular time he should or has to listen to you. Then, remind him that he does.

Don't get angry with him. If you feel you are losing your patience, stop, do something else, read a book, learn to control yourself. Don't work with your dog.

Throwing and teaching your dog to come to you has nothing to do with being angry or impatient with him, nor is it punishment. Sometimes a dog owner will become impatient, his voice changes, his body language changes, and he starts to get defensive and angry. You better believe that your dog can read all these changes. Why would he want to listen to someone like that? He'd have to be crazy. Stay calm and cool, then your dog will listen and will come to you. If he doesn't, you know how to make him listen.

Getting the Puppy to Come to You

Experts say you can't teach your puppy complex behaviors until he is six months old.

The reasoning behind this is that the puppy has a very limited attention span and that he is too young to understand anything. *Poppycock*. Erase this limited-attention-span theory from your mind. Puppies can pay attention and will pay attention as long as they need or want to. However, if your dog or puppy gets bored, he may not want to listen. And if you do not give him a clear message and direction about what you want, he also might decide to ignore you altogether and just pee on the floor and look confused. But this is an entirely different situation than having the *ability* to listen and understand. The more you exercise the muscles in your puppy's head (his brain), the more you will increase his ability to learn.

In the wild, a wild dog mother or a wolf mother bonds with her babies immediately. She doesn't wait until the puppy is six months old and has had all of his inoculations. She teaches him all of his survival behaviors at once: to come to her, to follow her, to stay with her, or to stay behind when she leaves to find food.

The wild puppy listens for two reasons: because his life depends on it, which he doesn't realize, and because he hasn't any choice, which he does understand.

If the wild dog mother and the wolf mother are able to imprint all of these behaviors successfully from the very beginning on their pups, then your puppy can learn many behaviors from you, even some very complex ones, from the first moment he steps into your life.

Using Your Lead or Leash with a Puppy

If the throwing technique seems to be confusing to you and to your new puppy, put a lead on him and pull him toward you. Call him to you in your own way. When he starts in your direction, release the pressure on the lead and call him. You want him to come to you on his own, not because you are pulling him on a lead. If he stops, pull the lead toward you to get him moving again.

Don't praise him until you have hold of his collar. Even when using a lead as a temporary tool, you must still throw something and it has to touch him. Take his lead off when he starts listening to you and then use the throwing technique alone.

Now He Can Play with Other Dogs

People insist that their puppies or dogs must play with other dogs for the purposes of socializing. When you can get your dog to listen to you and come back to you 100 percent of the time when you want him, then you can let him play and socialize with other dogs. Because you know when it's time to stop playing he'll come back to you when you ask him. If he doesn't, throw the leash or something else at him, and he'll come back. That's called control.

The downside of your dog playing with other dogs is that he will only pick up bad habits and parasites, and he could get into fights with other dogs. If you must let him play with dogs, it's a good idea to know the dogs that you are going to let him play with. It's the same with children; you wouldn't let your child play with strangers.

Swimming—An Extension of Getting Your Dog to Come to You

It's a sunny afternoon in the Hamptons. Behind a beautiful contemporary Westhampton beach house is an Olympic-size swimming pool. In this pool two giant schnauzers, Misty and Magic, are swimming laps. Near the pool's edge are their owners, Susan and Dan, watching proudly. A bell rings, and as lunch is brought out the schnauzers climb out of their pool, shake themselves off, and proceed to leisurely walk over and lie down under the shade of an aging mulberry tree.

How'd these guys learn to swim? They took lessons, and this afternoon they're going to get diving instructions. They learn very fast.

Have you ever been in a swimming pool and someone's dog, or maybe even your own dog, was racing and running around the pool barking and yelling frantically at you? No, the dog wasn't crazy; in fact, he was concerned for your safety. Since he doesn't know how to swim and is not secure in the water over his head, he was frightened for the both of you.

If your dog knew how to swim he would be in the water with you. Swimming is a learned behavior, one that a dog should learn for fun as well as for his safety. On a hot day all of those people and their dogs who are not afraid of going into the water are in the water to the last warm-blooded body. All of them.

Other benefits of teaching your dog to swim, especially in a pool, is that the chlorine will kill fleas and ticks. Also, swimming is great exercise.

Getting your dog to swim and to come to you in the water is a very good way to make sure your dog will come back to you in any situation. And basically you can teach your dog to swim using the same techniques that you learned when you taught your dog to come to you on dry land.

If you teach a puppy to swim at an early age, he will take to it like a duck takes to water. The puppy will be fearless and become a champion swimmer. We like to start teaching our dogs to swim as early as six weeks of age. Older dogs take a little more time to teach and a little more encouragement, but it still will happen quickly. Some dogs do just naturally take to the water. Generally, those dogs are the ones that have strong owners and they have been taught to listen to their owners early on. Don't throw your dog or puppy into the water. You could frighten him and he might never want to go near the water or near you for that matter. It's like calling your dog to you and punishing him.

Since you have taught your dog to come to you, he now feels 100 percent secure with you and should follow you anywhere on the globe. However, he will probably not follow you into the water. Many dogs have to be pulled or carried in for the first few times. Pick him up and take him in if he is a puppy or a small dog. Even if your dog or puppy swims with you because you carried him into the pool, you still have to teach him to follow you into the water on his own for his safety.

Keep in mind if your dog swims in a pool, as many dogs do, your dog should be taught where the steps are for his safety to ensure that if he jumps or falls into the pool he knows how to get out. Even if he is a very good swimmer he can still drown if he can't find his way out of the pool.

Put a six-foot lead on your dog or puppy, bring him to the edge of the pool, and sit him down on the steps. If you are near the ocean or a lake, bring him to the water's edge. Walk out to the end of your lead. Then call your dog to you. If he comes to you, praise him and continue to walk backwards out and deeper into the water until he starts swimming and there is no pressure on the lead.

He should follow you, on his own, without pressure on the lead. If he does, praise him. If he doesn't, pull on his lead slowly; a steady pressure should be applied. Don't jerk or snap the lead. If and when he starts to swim to you, then let the pressure off the lead.

Remember, we want him coming to you on his own. If he starts to come to you and then he decides to turn and leave, just put pressure back on his lead until he changes his mind and comes back to you. He might try to swim to you but can't stay afloat, so help him by putting your hands under his belly and chest, keeping him afloat until he gets the idea of how to stay afloat on his own. This will happen very quickly.

Your dog is to come to you in the water, and he is not to come out until you leave or until you tell him it's okay to go out. Once your dog goes into the water and starts swimming with you and there is no pressure on his lead, then and only then can you take his lead off. He now knows how to swim.

It's real easy. Once your dog feels secure in the water, from then on it's all fun and games for him. You will have a hard time keeping this expert swimmer on dry land.

"Shane, Come Back"

George called us one Saturday from his house at the beach, complaining that his dog, Shane, wouldn't swim. What really ticked George off, and he screamed his disappointment out to the world, was that, "My Shane is a yellow Labrador retriever, he has webbed feet and is supposed to be a born swimmer and he can't swim!" In fact, George said, "Shane hates the water! Even after I bought him a house with a pool, he still refuses to get his feet wet."

We went out to help George and Shane. First, George had to get ready to go swimming, putting on his wetsuit, his flippers, his mask, and snorkel. It looked like a scene from the movie *The Graduate*. Anyway, while George was dressing for his date in the chilly waters of Long Island (his heated pool), we put a lead on Shane, walked over to the steps of the pool, walked into the pool, which wasn't so cold, and pulled Shane into it with us. He swam, and he swam, and he swam.

But still we had to make sure he came into the pool on his own. We took him out of the pool and then all of us went back in. Shane didn't; he hesitated. George threw the lead at him and in he happily came. Of course, he was also given a nice piece of apple pie for his good work after we finally were able to drag him out of the pool.

When it was all over, George explained to us he didn't know he had to pull Shane into the pool and teach him how to swim. He thought Shane would just naturally want to swim because this breed was supposed to be a water breed. I guess nobody told the dog of his ancestry.

George now tells us that his pal Shane has been seen diving into swimming pools all over Long Island. He goes on to tell us that whenever they visit friends, if a swimming pool is on the premises, Shane will jump into it. That could be a new definition of a split second.

The reason Shane learned how to swim in such a quick fashion was that the first behavior taught to him was to come when called, and the incredible results of this Magic Touch. The reason we first had to pull Shane into the pool was that he had to learn how to swim so that he could go to George in the water when George called him.

Once your dog learns to come to you 100 percent of the time, then everything else you want to teach him after that will be a piece of cake, easily learned in a matter of minutes with either little or no practice involved.

Remember:

1. Stay calm and relaxed.
2. Give your dog time to think; he will.
3. Don't use one-word commands.
4. Don't repeat yourself.
5. Don't practice. It gets to be boring for both of you. If you want your dog to do something for you, make him do it. Your dog didn't forget and he did hear you. He might just feel that he doesn't have to listen to you. A simple reminder will tell him he could be wrong.
6. Make sure that your dog comes all the way to you before praising him.
7. Never call your dog to punish him.

8. Do not bribe your dog to come to you. Spoil him rotten after he listens to you.
9. You don't need the crate or the cage.
10. Only socialize your dog with other dogs or people after he listens to you 100 percent of the time.

CHAPTER 3

You Are What You Eat

Now that we've left tradition in the dust, along with your dog's one-dimensional lifestyle, let's take a break and relax. Oh, yes, please call that new kid on the block over to you. If he doesn't come over, pick up a good, soft-cover gourmet cookbook and magically touch him with it. We want him to hear this too. We are going to discuss a most important facet of his life, his diet. Whether it's going to be dry and boring, and hazardous to his health, or an exciting culinary experience for his supersensitive taste buds and his even more incredible nose. One of the greatest pleasures in life is enjoying good food. If you give your dog lots of that pleasure, you'll keep him healthy and happy and you'll keep him a long, long time.

Say It Ain't So, You Little So-and-So

Donna stepped on her scale and watched the needle climb. She screamed when she saw where it stopped. "Oh, my God!

One hundred and fifty pounds!" She turned and pointed at Moose, her five-pound poodle, and with teeth clenched, she said in a very angry whisper, "It's all your fault, you little so-and-so, you forced me out into that pouring rain last night, just so you could have your Chinese food and two chocolate eclairs."

Is It Genetic or Behavioral?

Harry gave Waffle, his adorable two-year-old Maltese, a three-hour lecture about not taking food from the table and then he went to bed. When Waffle was certain Harry was fast asleep, she proceeded to empty his pockets of the peanuts he was saving for a family of squirrels in Central Park. Waffle ate them and left the empty shells strewn all over the living-room floor. I guess Harry forgot to lecture Waffle about not going into his pants pockets, but even if he did, it probably wouldn't have helped, because Harry's three former wives had had the same successful habit. But not for peanuts.

By Invitation Only

One client told me how she hated when her dogs would beg at the table. She explained, "I shouldn't have given them my food in the first place. That way they wouldn't know about people food, and they wouldn't beg to get it." My answer was plain and simple: "Why don't you teach them not to beg?"

Sixty years ago dog-food companies were a rarity. The few that existed used to collect the animal parts that people wouldn't or couldn't eat. These were collected from slaughter-houses and butcher shops, then chopped up and put in cans. You could very well open up a can and find a heart part or a kidney part in there—cut-up identifiable parts. They were parts of the animal that were soon classified by the government as four-d meats: dying, dead, disabled, and diseased, better known as by-products. They were not to be used for human consumption. Many people were put off by this. The people I knew that had cats and dogs didn't bother with these dog foods, preferring to feed their pets whatever the family was having for dinner. At that time, people didn't take the dog-food industry very seriously.

When I was a kid, it wasn't unheard of for a dog to live to a ripe old age of eighteen, nineteen, or even twenty years. Guess what they ate? They ate what we ate, from table scraps to even joining us at the table.

Our Dog, Rebel

Rebel was a mixed breed (I don't know what the mixtures were but they came out just right). He was a beautiful two-shaded brown hound who lived for nineteen years eating eastern European Jewish cooking, including blintzes, bagels, kasha varnishkes, flanken and cabbage, and gefilte fish, with a nice sour pickle or tomato on the side.

That's Show Business

When I was in the business of training animals for movies and commercials, a certain dog-food company, which shall remain nameless, asked me to get them a dog for a commercial, an old dog, the very oldest dog I could find. I did. That's how I gave my Rebel his show-biz debut. Rebel was eighteen at the time, but that's show biz; some people get a break at an early age and some have to wait until they're a little long in the tooth. Anyway, records from his veterinarian and a receipt from the ASPCA where we had adopted him, plus some of his old dog licenses, authenticated his age. His age was also visible by the way he walked and his wise old gray-bearded face. His sight wasn't what it used to be, and he was hard of hearing. Hey! I think I'm describing me.

The commercial was completed and well liked by this dog-food company. They asked me would I give them an affidavit testifying to the fact that Rebel had reached this ripe old age by eating and loving their primo dog food. This I couldn't do because it wasn't true. Rebel ate what we ate. I also told them that their food company wasn't even in business at the time Rebel was growing up. Needless to say, two things did happen: They didn't use the commercial and I was never hired by them again.

Out of the Tree of Life I Picked Me a Plum

Rebel was our family pet; he belonged to all of us. Plum, a handsome taupe-colored weimaraner with pale green eyes that started out as baby blue, belonged to me. This guy was smart as a whip. He was my best friend. Anyone who could put up with all my bad habits without complaining had to be a good and loyal friend. He became my star student. Actually I became his student for a new way of teaching. He taught me everything I know that's worth knowing. I had ideas and experience, but Plum brought them to life. I tried out all my ideas on him and I went with him everywhere: to see all my private clients, on television interviews and book tours, and whenever I worked on commercials and movies. Plum loved all this attention and fame. But never became affected by it. He remained cool. He had soul.

The Subtle Mind Control of Marketing

In the early sixties, dog-food companies became very popular, rich, and powerful. They had produced an image, benevolent and caring, and became the last word on a dog's balanced diet. They said their food was best for dogs, and they even created a fear in dog owners that your dog could die if he didn't eat a diet of dog food every day. Many veterinarians agreed and some became paid consultants. Their control of the minds of dog owners went unchallenged for years, and eventually became the accepted way.

I also bought into these marketing claims and fed Plum dog food. Not only that, I fed him dry dog food because they said it was the highest in nutrition. I depended on the experts (food companies and veterinarians) to deliver a proper diet for him. I shouldn't have. Although diet had always been included in my training philosophies, I had simply relied on the information I read on dog-food labels, without questioning it. The true importance of the quality and the proper amount of food, I learned later. And almost at the cost of my Plum's life.

The Twist, a Danger to a Large Dog

Certain events can happen that will change your life forever. For me, one of these events happened on a spring evening in the middle of May 1972 when Plum was six years old.

I fed him his usual dry dog food, in the usual way, as I always had for the past six years. He ate as he always did. Plum was never sick, and he never missed a meal. Then he had his usual drink of water, after dinner, as he always did for the past six years. Then, as usual, he went to lie down as he normally did for the past six years. Nothing unusual, nothing eventful. Or so I thought. But then I noticed something strange happening, something he hadn't ever done before. He started to nervously pace back and forth, and then run in circles. He was trying desperately to throw up, but he couldn't. I noticed that his stomach was much larger than normal. I touched it, and it was hard as a rock. He was frantically pacing and running and his stomach continued to swell. I didn't know what to do. I'd never seen this before and I was getting nervous and more than a little frightened. I called Martin, my veterinarian, who also happens to be a good friend. Reaching him at home, I explained as best as I could what was happening to Plum and asked him what to do. Martin told me to bring him over the Animal Medical Center immediately, and that he would meet me there. Martin was being very professional—too professional, I thought. Now I knew this was urgent.

I put Plum in the back of my station wagon and started driving across town. At first I tried to stay calm. No way. Sensing Plum was in a lot of pain, I started to race through traffic, fast and crazy, zigzagging all the way. I was crossing Second Avenue on Sixty-fourth Street heading east. Not seeing a large pothole in front of me, I hit it at top speed and we really took a hard bounce. Plum was thrown into the air and off his feet. As he got up, he started throwing everything up, all over the car. I was surprised to see this. It was as if the food he had eaten had tripled in size. I knew that I hadn't fed him that much dry dog food. No more than usual, and there was no way he could have gotten any more food anywhere else, because he was with me all day. But I didn't spend too much time thinking about this because my immediate concern was to get Plum to Dr. Martin De Angelis.

We arrived at the Animal Medical Center about twenty minutes later; Plum seemed to be feeling a lot better. Martin was waiting there for me. He checked the "Plummer" over while I told him of the scene in the car. Martin figured that the car hitting the pothole probably saved Plum's life. He explained further: When Plum was thrown into the air the jolt released the trapped food in his stomach, allowing him to throw up. It had put his stomach into a position so he could get the food out, and he did. I guess I can say thanks to one of New York's grand potholes for saving my dog's life. If it wasn't for that pothole, they would have had to try and get a tube down into his stomach to release the food or cut him open to clean out his stomach and straighten it, then tack it down to try and prevent this from happening again. Martin explained Plum had suffered from bloat. If not caught soon enough, bloat could evolve into a condition called gastric torsion, and this is usually fatal unless caught early enough. I was told that this was a common problem with certain large breeds.

It hadn't yet dawned on me that the type of food and particularly the amount of it could be the cause of this problem. There was no reason to make these connections or draw any conclusions. None of the professionals, from veterinarians to dog food companies, did. And some still don't today.

How many times do we instinctively feel that we know something, although we let conventional wisdom and practice influence us into thinking we're wrong. When I calmed down, I thought about the whole incident, and especially about that food. All that food, all over my car. My instincts told me that this condition had to be food related; no way it could be otherwise. But I didn't believe my instincts. It just couldn't be.

After the emergency, I was instructed to treat this condition by feeding my dog prescription-type canned foods (which are of a heavier consistency than the commercial canned foods) and smaller meals. To make up for the smaller meals, I was to feed him more times each day. I was told that this type of feeding would hopefully prevent his stomach from stretching, or at least lower the chances of Plum bloating again.

Bloat can be described this way. A balloon will weaken if you blow it up and deflate it over and over again. If you fill it up with water, it weakens even faster. So would a large dog's stomach when it's been stretched continuously.

I followed the feeding instructions and he was fine, and we fell into our usual routine. After a few months, the entire incident became just a bad memory.

Then one day, I fed him at four-thirty in the afternoon and left the house to run some errands and then to see a client. I got home at about eleven-thirty that night, opened the door, and was faced with a terrifying scene. Plum had bloated again. It was horrible. I picked up the phone, but all I could hear were taped referrals as to where to take my dog. Why do all emergencies happen late at night and on the weekend when you can't get help? This happened to be late on a Saturday night and I couldn't reach anyone. I hung up the phone.

I remembered being told to try antacids and if they didn't work then to try slipping a tube down his throat. From the look of my dog, I figured this was beyond antacids, but was I able to take the next step? Let me tell you, I'm a professional, but still my hands were shaking at the prospect of what I had to do next. I didn't know if I would be able to put a tube down my dog's throat. I didn't know if I would be hurting him or causing even more problems or damage. But I had to do something. This was a matter of life and death. He was in pain. A dog in pain isn't just sitting around calmly waiting to play. He was frantic, moaning, pacing, running in circles, trying to throw up, as if he were choking. It was a frightening scene. But I knew what it was, and I knew he could die. I had no choice.

I had two large saltwater fish tanks and I kept some half- or three-quarter-inch plastic tubing. I'm not exactly sure of the size, it doesn't matter. They were for siphoning water from the fish tanks. I cut a length of this tubing, about three or four feet, enough to put into his mouth, down his throat, and into his stomach.

This procedure works best with two people (I was lucky I had a friend with me), one to put and hold a roll of adhesive tape in his mouth to prevent him from biting down on the tube and to keep his head straight up, so the hose could go unblocked through the hole of the tape roll in his mouth, down his throat, and into his stomach. The other person controls the movement of the hose and gets it down into the stomach to release the pressure so the food, water, gas, or all three can come up and out through the tube.

This has to be done before the dog's stomach totally flips; if it does flip, this is now gastric torsion. Visualize holding a plastic bag by the two opposite corners; this would represent a dog's stomach. If you flip the bag over it becomes airtight. The stomach totally closes in the same manner, with no way for the food to come up and out of the dog. At this stage, your dog will die if you don't get him help in time.

We succeeded in getting the tube down into Plum in time. The food came up like oil from a well, all over my living-room floor. Lots of food and lots of water.

Subsequently, when I took Plum to the veterinarian, surgery was recommended as a maybe permanent solution for this problem. The surgery was to tack his stomach down. I didn't do it.

The first time this had happened to him I remembered how the food that came up seemed to be much more then I had fed him. The gears started turning. Now, I realized that my initial gut instinct had been right. Food was the problem; all the signs pointed in that direction. These episodes always occurred just after I had fed him.

Plum had been on dry food for six years when he'd had his first bloat problem. So I looked at that first. When I gave him his dry food he wouldn't want it; he hated it. So I had to mix it with a canned food or a chicken or beef gravy to give it some taste. Even then it seemed that he didn't enjoy this food. This was obvious from the way he picked at it. I guess I thought that was normal. Most of my clients' dogs who ate dry food didn't enjoy it either. But you are given the argument that some dogs are finicky eaters. And you shouldn't spoil them. And they have to eat it because it's good for them. People just leave it around all day, figuring the dog will eat what and when he wants. And the dogs eat so they won't starve; they want to live. A starving dog or person will eat anything.

I know when I like certain foods I eat them with relish, digging in because one of the great pleasures in life is eating and enjoying food. And good food in my house is never around for long. Obviously, Plum never enjoyed his dry food by the way he ate it. When I gave him some of my food, like a nice taste of my strawberry shortcake or some of my roast chicken, or even a slice of pizza pie, that food would go down like he was a vacuum cleaner.

But why did dry food cause this bloat problem in the first place? My first experiments were simple. I would add water to a cup of dry food; it swelled up to at least twice the size. When he ate this food he would drink huge amounts of water. This meant more weight in his stomach. You remember I compared bloat to a balloon that is constantly being inflated and deflated. The constant stretching of the stomach, with too much food or water, causes it to stretch and weaken. I'm not certain if this condition is reversible on its own, but I do know that dogs' stomachs are tacked down as part of the procedure when gastric torsion is operated on.

I was now feeding my dog prescription canned food and in smaller amounts, so why had it happened again?

My answer to this question is that the prescription canned dog food was a denser food than the ordinary commercial supermarket canned dog foods, and although it didn't swell up in a dog's stomach, it created, just as the dry foods did, an insatiable need for water. And this added weight to his already weakened stomach.

I switched to plain commercial canned dog foods from the supermarket, which were lighter in consistency, and I also fed him people food. Small meals at first, then down to one meal a day. Eventually I gave him only people food.

The changes were immediate. He loved his canned dog food and he loved his people food even more, eating it all with gusto, and he wasn't drinking much water at all. I found that the advantage of the people food was that I could feed him a lot less food and get the same or more necessary nutrition. If you didn't know Plum, you'd think he was starving the way he gulped that food down. But the best and most extraordinary changes were that his coat looked much better and his skin wasn't dry anymore. The hot spots (sores and skin rashes) that he got from time to time vanished completely. His skin and coat were so healthy that he never needed a flea and tick collar.

All of these positive benefits were because of the food changes that I had made and finally formulated to fit him. He never again suffered from any of those scary, dangerous stomach problems. Plum became a totally different dog, both inside and out.

Dog-food companies either know or should know about food-related problems and put warnings on their packaging. That way these conditions can be prevented and dog owners can be warned and educated.

When a dog suffers from bloat or gastric torsion, but he survives, you're told to put him on a canned-food diet. If that's the case, then why give your dog dry food in the first place? It's like an accident waiting to happen.

In the last three or four decades we have changed and mutated dogs into machines that don't enjoy eating but eat to live, don't eat real food, and are treated with steroids as if they were candy. In my view, as the popularity of dog foods increased, the life spans of dogs started to change and not for the better. When dry dog foods came along, dogs' health problems increased even more.

There have been dramatic changes in our human world in the area of proper diet and nutrition. It is widely known that what you eat, and how much you eat, will affect your health, well-being, and behavior. In fact, an entire health-food industry has grown up around these new ideas. And even favorite traditional foods have undergone major changes with low fat, no fat, good fat, bad fat, low salt, no salt, low sugar, and no sugar, and on and on.

If all of this good food and good living is good for us, why isn't it also good for your dog? Your dog is biologically the same as you. He needs the same elements that you need to live— good food, clean water, and fresh air. He needs proteins, carbohydrates, vitamins, and minerals to live, just like you do. Why should he have a totally different food? One that's not fit for human consumption?

In addition to the quality of food, we believe that one of the main problems with dogs' health is their intake of food. In one word, *overeating*. If you follow the instructions on dog-food labels, chances are you are overfeeding your dog. If you don't feed dry food or dense canned foods to your dog and you don't overfeed your dog, you alleviate many problems, both skin and otherwise, that are caused by overeating.

Remember, when you are feeding your dog according to dog-food labels, you are giving him incredible volumes of food. To put so much food into an animal to get the proper nutrition that he needs adds up to overeating, which then adds up to obesity. Which to us is a far greater problem than not getting the proper nutrition every single day.

With the dramatic changes I saw in Plum, I then started switching my clients' dogs to commercial canned foods and, of course, my favorite food for dogs, people food. I started my own weight charts and feeding charts so I could control proper amounts of food for all these dogs. We're talking about more than twenty-five thousand dogs in over forty years. It wasn't just Plum that was unique in these dramatic changes, but all of my clients' dogs, and I consider their dogs my dogs.

Another puff of smoke told to you by these food experts is that your dog should eat the same food every day. And, if you want to change his food, you must do this gradually or else he will get sick. We're not gradualists when it comes to switching dogs from one food to another. If you have Chinese food one day and the next day you want Italian food, would you gradually wean yourself off the Chinese food and slowly onto the Italian food? Ridiculous. It is no different for your dog. You can change your dog's food from one to another anytime you want to. Variety is the spice of life.

The diet changes that I had made for my dogs also had a profound effect on all of my work, including the solving of behavioral problems, because food is related to behavior as well as to health. I also learned to believe in myself and to trust my common sense when the health and well-being of my dog was at stake. Use your power sense, that is, your common sense, when it comes to your dog.

The list:

Is your dog an incessant and destructive chewer?

Do you find that your dog never stops going to the toilet?

Do you find your dog to be hyperactive and nervous?

Does your dog have a dry coat or skin problems?

Do you find that you're allergic to your dog? Or maybe some of your friends, relatives, or even someone in your immediate family is allergic to him?

These problems can be solved simply and quickly. They are all food related.

When It Comes to Diet, One Look at the Dog Says It All

While a dog owner is trying to tell us about the problems he's having with his dog, and suggesting to us, from books he's read and experts he has spoken to, that some of these problems might be psychological in origin, the dog is truly telling us everything we want to know by the way he looks and how he behaves. If he's overweight and his coat and skin are dry, if he's hyperactive, or if he's destructive, generally he's eating too much food or the wrong kind, or both.

There's more. While the dog owner is going down his wish list of dog wants and don't wants, all around us are the signs of his don't want list. There's that unmistakable smell permeating the house or apartment. This means they have a housebreaking problem. Then there are all the changes that the dog made when he moved in. You know, the furniture that he beautifully chewed up and changed to his liking.

His owners aren't just sitting around doing nothing; they are fighting back by throwing up gates across every entrance and exit in the house. Cages and crates keep him from roaming free and taking over the house completely. All types of dog-training paraphernalia and books are strewn around, this to try and teach him the error of his ways. There are dog chews and toys to control his teething habit and to keep him occupied.

Classic chaos for the dog owners, but plenty of fun for Fido. Oh, yes, we almost forgot. There is the mysterious water dish that always seems to be empty, and filling it becomes a full-time occupation. Last but not least, sitting on the kitchen floor, taking up one corner of the room, bigger than life, looking like a soft sculpture piece by Klaes Oldenburg, is a giant sack of dry dog food.

Many dog owners will tell us about the highly touted dry food that they give their dog. Some proudly tell us how they even buy the expensive designer professional dog foods. What amazes us about these foods are the enormous quantities of professional designer–colored dog poop that the dogs leave behind, either on the floor in the house or outside, if they can make it outside in time.

They ask. "How can a dog so small, who eats so little, go to the toilet so much?" The answer is, dry food.

It's not that we're psychic, knowing what people are going to complain about even before we get there; it's that this is the classic situation most owners experience when they bring a new dog or a puppy into their home. Because along with the new dog comes what appears to be a lifetime supply of that ever-expanding dry dog food with an incredibly long shelf life (several years) and it's not even vacuum sealed. It must be magic. Or maybe there are preservatives in there? Just think, Napoleon could have conquered Russia if only he had had bags of that well-preserved dry food.

Dry Food: The Best Food for You! But Not for Your Dog

This is the most popular and most profitable dog food on the market. It's also cheaper. Marketing and advertising make you believe that it's the best for your dog. But no matter how much money is spent on publicity it still doesn't change the quality. Dry food has been promoted as healthy for your dog, good for your dog's teeth, and a good solid stool for an easy pickup. Actually, this food is made for your convenience, not for your dog's benefit. It's easy for you to store, easy for you to serve, and easier for you to pick up.

It Seems There's Never Enough Water

If you feed your dog dry food, he will drink excessive amounts of water all the time. The dry food will swell up in the dog's stomach, making him full and uncomfortable, like eating a piece of pizza that becomes three pieces of pizza in your stomach. You might think you're giving your dog a little dry food, but with all the water he drinks, it becomes a lot of food and a lot of weight in his stomach. In large breeds this could even cause bloat, or gastric torsion. However, if your dog can't get to water, or get enough water, then the dry food can cause the body to supply the moisture, which means a dry coat and a dry flaky skin, which could mean lots of scratching, chewing, and self-mutilation.

In Pursuit of the Perfect Stool

Some owners are preoccupied with the size and texture of their dog's stool. They feel that if the poop is not rock hard there must be something wrong with their dog. Of course, it's easier for dog owners to pick up after their dog when the stool is rock hard, but then, that's good only for the dog owner, not the dog. These people are not thinking about how uncomfortable rocks feel to their dog. Because while in pursuit of the perfect stool, remember that a rock-hard stool is constipation and constipation is a hurtful experience, universally.

If a dog-food company could invent a product that would reduce a dog's stool to a small pellet all wrapped up and completely sealed in plastic, they would do it. Or if they could devise a way for your dog not to go to the toilet at all, they would do that too. For that matter, why not just add some plaster of Paris or concrete to his diet. That would give a dog a "perfect" stool, but no more dog. None of this makes sense, and neither does this firm-stool reasoning make sense. Don't be so concerned with this perfect-stool syndrome, or the nonformed-stool syndrome. A proper stool should be soft and ploppable, for lack of a better word.

What dog owners should be concerned about is diarrhea, which can be an indication that their dog is sick. At this point, the dog should be looked at by a veterinarian and a stool sample checked for parasites or worms. Diarrhea can also be a sign that your dog is eating too much food, and it's his body's way of getting rid of the enormous volume of food that he's taking in. The amount of food you are directed to give your dog by dog-food companies feeding guidelines is usually far more than your dog should have, and this can also cause diarrhea.

Allergies

We love our dogs. Oh! how much we love our dogs! But all of a sudden you have developed a bad skin rash, or your sinuses are all messed up. What happened? Did you become allergic to your dog? How can this problem be prevented? Why does it happen? When I was a child these allergies were unheard of, or very rare.

Years of working with animals have convinced me that diet plays the major role in allergies. Just as in the people world. It can be the wrong food or too much food, or both. It isn't the hair or saliva that causes these allergies but the dander or dry skin flakes. You can end these allergies by feeding your dog only canned food or people food and by controlling the amount of food your dog eats. Then start vacuuming your house more than normal, especially in the areas where your dog frequents. It will take a few weeks for you to get all the dry skin flakes and dog hair out of the house. However, after only a short time on his new diet you'll see your dog's coat come alive again and you'll be able to enjoy all the good things you want from your pal, without the anxiety of an allergy attack.

Steroids and Dry Dog Foods— A Symbiotic Relationship

You start with a dry food, then come skin problems. The dry skin and coat can get so bad at times that the animal can chew himself raw, causing hot spots, or lick granuloma. The dry skin is also a welcome mat for fleas and ticks, whereas the natural body oils would give some protection against them. Telltale signs of poor nutrition are always bad skin or a dry coat.

Your veterinarian gives your dog steroids, a cortisone product of some sort, and you add various oils to the food. The problems go away but come back again another day. This becomes a vicious cycle that goes like this: dry food, dry skin, hot spots (skin sores), steroids, oils. Pretty soon your little guy will always be loaded with steroids, which will increase his need for food and water. You get to pay the veterinary bills and pick up the mess because while your dog is on steroids he will need to pee a lot, so be prepared to take him out more often.

The steroids solve the problem temporarily, but they could cause major problems later on. It is a known fact that repeated use of steroids is harmful, damaging the kidneys, liver, and nervous system. The oils that you add to your dog's food for his coat do nothing. Instead of all that medication, why not try changing the food that your dog is eating. Or, you might think about taking him off dog food altogether and giving him our choice, people food.

Some Dog Food Makers Claim That Their Food Cleans Dog's Teeth

As soon as we suggest taking the dog off dry food, the horrified dog owner turns into a professional dentist. "But," this dentist says, "the dry food cleans my dog's teeth." Maybe we don't have to brush our teeth either? All we have to do is eat dry dog food. I asked my own dentist if there were any foods that I could eat that would possibly keep my teeth clean so I wouldn't have to brush them. He laughingly threw me out of his office. Why?

Many experts say dry food is good for your dog's teeth, that it helps keep them clean because it's crunchy and rubs off the tarter. If we asked you, "If you chew something crunchy, would it clean your teeth?" the answer would be no. If we asked you, "What teeth do you chew crunchy food with?" you would say, "My back teeth." There are forty-two teeth in an adult dog's mouth. He uses his back teeth to chew his crunchy food and that leaves thirty teeth that do not get cleaned at all even if this theory were correct. What about those teeth? If we asked you, "When you chew a crunchy food does it often get stuck between your teeth?" Your answer would be, "Yes." "How do you get these stuck food particles out?" "With floss, a brush, or using a toothpick." "When was the last time you saw your dog flossing, brushing, or using a toothpick?" Okay, then, so much for the cleaning teeth theory.

The only way to clean your dog's teeth is the same way we clean our teeth. Brush them with a toothbrush.

Rub your fingers over your dog's teeth and when he gets used to that, get a toothbrush or a small cotton ball and either wet it with plain water or use a little mouthwash, then brush or rub your dog's teeth. Presto, they're clean. No muss, no fuss. Don't use a toothpaste of any kind because you will see the dog's mouth full of foaming toothpaste and the dog can't rinse his mouth the way you can. If your dog won't sit for a brushing, then put the brush down and tell him in no uncertain terms to stop fooling around. This is done by taking hold of his collar and giving him a good shake or a light cuff. Repeat this procedure until he stops fighting getting his teeth cleaned. Then tell him how good he is for letting you clean his teeth. When your veterinarian cleans your dog's teeth, you should be aware that the dog is knocked out with a general anesthesia. To us, this seems a drastic way to go to the dentist.

Your Dog's Chewing Problem

Do you know why your dog chews up your house, including your favorite shoes or maybe that beautiful tapestry couch? It's not because he's teething. At four and a half months his puppy teeth are falling out and the adult teeth are coming in, pushing through the holes in his gums. Just like with young children getting their adult teeth, there isn't any pain or discomfort.

Chewing is not caused by an acute separation anxiety complex either. Experts have used this very popular "complex" excuse for every behavioral problem from A to Z, especially the ones they can't explain.

A dog's chewing is a nervous habit. Like a person biting their nails, he chews things, including himself, when he is nervous. And having to go to the bathroom or wait for you to come home to take him out makes him very nervous. When you gotta go, you gotta go. He has to go to the bathroom all day long when he's eating all that dry food and drinking all that water.

Your hyperactive dog will calm down, your destructive chewer will stop chewing, and that complex will miraculously disappear without any therapy once you change his diet. Unless, of course, your dog has parasites or worms. In that case, he will chew nervously because the discomfort will bother him the same way a headache or a toothache bothers the hell out of you.

If you are what you eat, then dry food means dry skin and a dry coat.

Too much of a good thing is not always good either.

It seemed that Herb wanted his dog, Louis, to be a giant yellow Labrador retriever. He felt that by feeding him lots of food he would grow up to be this great big, strong dog that Herb had always wanted. So Herb fed Louis lots of food. Herb wanted the biggest and he got it. The biggest dumps, and a lot of them. He also got something else, a fat dog that chewed everything in the house, including himself.

We explained to Herb that if Louis's genes told him he would be a giant Lab, then he would be that. But his genes told him, "No way, Louis." So Louis is a beautiful, well-behaved dog, just small. We also convinced Herb to cut back on Louis's food. He did, and we were able to solve that other *big* problem.

Canned Foods

The basic supermarket commercial canned dog foods are the next best food to people food. Just get the simple formulas, either chicken or beef, and look for the brands that don't contain corn. Corn tends to promote gas and excessive drinking of water. Even farmers don't give their animals a steady diet of corn; it's given as a treat.

Your dog will enjoy this food and eat every bit of it. You will see improvements in his coat and skin very quickly (within ten days to two weeks). It will also help you housebreak your dog much faster, and will help solve destructive chewing. He will calm down dramatically and stop being a nervous wreck.

If you're going to feed your dog dog food we feel that canned food is the way to go, but even as we are writing this chapter the amount of food in a can has shrunk from fourteen ounces to thirteen ounces. We don't know what other economic changes are being made in the quality. The way to make sure your dog is getting what he needs is to remember that one fourteen-ounce can will sustain a twenty- to twenty-five-pound dog, as our food chart will show you in detail. So if you are buying these incredible shrinking cans, make sure you compensate by adding the extra ounce.

Also, to supplement any hidden nutritional changes, add people food to his diet. Proteins, like beef, chicken, fish, cheese, or eggs, and for carbohydrates, bread, pasta, rice, and potatoes. And then include steamed vegetables along with everything. Then you can feel more confident that your dog is getting what he needs nutritionally. You can also control his weight much easier by feeding him canned food supplemented by people food.

Mac called the other day and he told us we were "all wet" with our diet program. He said he was giving Maggie, his fifty-pound collie mix, the four cans of dog food we had suggested. I told him that I had said two fourteen-ounce cans, not four. Without listening, he continued on and told me his dog was losing weight, and that she was now under forty pounds. I couldn't believe my ears. This was impossible. "You're feeding your dog enough food for a hundred-pound dog. I think your

Maggie must have a tapeworm or else your scale is broken." Mac told me I was wrong on both accounts, his scale worked, and his Maggie had been to the vet yesterday. I didn't wait to be invited but went right over to his house. He let me in and greeted me by tossing the dog-food cans at me. I caught two of them and had the answer to this great mystery right in my hands. Disbelief turned to laughter when I saw that these cans, these same cans he was feeding his dog, weren't fourteen-ounce cans at all, but six-ounce cans. Only enough to sustain a thirty-five-pound dog. Some people just don't listen. Mac said, "What?"

When Your Dog Gets Sick (the Quick Fix)

One client told us how her dog was always sick no matter what dog food she would feed her, until she finally had to buy a special prescription food. It was very expensive. She went on to say, "It looked like hamburger, smelled like hamburger, and even tasted like hamburger."

One day her father went into the kitchen looking for something to eat and ate the dog food by mistake. Now he always makes it a point to ask which food is for him. Why put yourself through all of this aggravation? Give the dog a real hamburger and be done with it. Then you can all eat the same good food at the same time and everyone can be happy, including our client's father.

Marcia has a beautiful bearded collie named Bessie. Marcia also spent thousands of dollars at the veterinarian's office. Seems her dog was always getting sick. They ran a lot of tests on Bessie trying to find out what was wrong with her. Eventually Marcia was told that they could find nothing physically wrong with her dog and they figured maybe it was the food. So they went about trying to find a bland prescription food that her dog could tolerate. We put the dog on a plain commercial canned dog food and cut down on the amount of food the dog was getting. We also changed Bessie to people-food treats, contrary to what Marcia was told. Now Marcia's Bessie has no food-related problems. Bessie and Marcia can both enjoy having breakfast together every morning, hot cereal with milk on a cold day or cold cereal with fruit if it's a warm day.

When your dog throws up or has diarrhea, your veterinarian will tell you to feed him chicken and rice. When your dog has skin problems you're told to switch him to canned foods and add special oils for the skin and coat. When some show breeders are about to show their best dogs, they switch to canned foods or add oils to the diet or even switch their dogs to people foods.

Why wait for problems or big events to give your dog a decent meal? Switch before the problems, or the shows. If you give chicken and rice to your dog and just add steamed vegetables, it becomes a perfectly well-balanced and delicious diet, with all the amino acids and carbohydrates and all the necessary vitamins and minerals. And you can give your dog less food and control weight problems.

You Can't Fool a Good Nose

That dog of yours has a sense of smell that is mind-boggling. It varies from hundreds to thousands of times more sensitive than ours, according to which expert you talk to. Just stop and think for a minute what it would be like if your sense of smell was that sensitive. Good Lord! Think about your favorite ice cream or that great-smelling hot dog, or for me, I wonder what Gorgonzola cheese would smell like. I would probably love my favorite foods thousands of times more if I had my dog's sense of smell. Common sense will tell you that your dog will appreciate human food just as much as you and probably even more. Contrary to the accepted wisdom, he knows all about what we eat because he smells it all around him. He probably wonders why you won't give him what you eat. I know his mother wouldn't have denied him her food.

Don't Always Believe What You're Told

You are told not to feed your dog people food, that it isn't good for him, you will have a "beggar" on your hands for the rest of your life, and he won't eat his dog food. Try explaining that to your dog. All that good food he smells isn't for him, and the only food he can have is dog food, which he doesn't like. Of all the adjustments dogs have to make to live in a people world, the most difficult has to be eating dog food. Dogs don't like dog food, especially dry dog food, no matter how many food enhancers are put into it.

We believe dog food isn't as good for your dog as people food is. It might be cheap and convenient for you to feed your dog dog food, but I don't think you'll make that a very convincing argument with your dog.

Yes, you can feed your dog from the table as long as he listens to you when you tell him to leave or just not to go near the food until you say it's okay.

Take something your dog really likes—chicken, cheese, a piece of cake, or some ice cream—and put it on a plate either on a coffee table or even on the floor, but within your dog's reach. When he goes for the food, either use our throwing technique or give him a tap on the nose with one or two fingers. Not a push, but a tap. To push him only makes him more determined to go around your push because he can, but if you tap him he can't learn that so he can't compete, and he will listen to you. *Don't say anything to him* until he stops going for the food. When he stops, then tell him how good he is not to touch the food. This message might take you a few times to deliver, but he will stop. When he does stop grabbing or begging, then you can take some of that food and give it to him. It isn't confusing as some will say; rather, it's simple and direct. He will learn only to take food when it's offered to him, even if it's in front of him.

Positive Reinforcement

This is called positive reinforcement, and that is praising him for not taking food. No "nos" to be said, no "bad dogs" to be said, and no practice sessions are necessary. Just like everything else you've been taught. Every behavior in this technique is taught for real. Just a little reminder from time to time if he forgets. If you keep practicing, your dog will be good in practice. If you just tell him that you're not going to put up with any nonsense every time he tests you, then he will learn not to test you and you will have a perfect dog.

Your dog should only eat our balanced diet, or else. Sounds like a theocratic message, delivered by divine authority.

Dog food is said to be a completely balanced diet, and all that your dog will need for the rest of his life. This message is delivered by the dog-food industry and the veterinarians, who get their information from the dog-food industry. What this message does sound like is a divine message coming from above. Probably from a marketing company on a high floor. How can that be when there's a lot of "approximates" printed on those labels? There's no way to know exactly what's in there. You should be the last word on diet and nutrition for your dog. You should educate yourself and ask questions, just the way you do about your own diet. Don't rely on a company that wants to sell you a product at a high profit to give you the best information for you. But to sum it all up, it does take two to tango.

We believe in a balanced diet for both you and your dog. Many people feel a balanced diet is very difficult to follow and some feel it is impossible. If they feel this way about their own diet, think how helpless they must feel about their dog's diet. Most people don't eat a completely balanced diet every single day. And still they manage to live through the day and evening and stay healthy. What they do is try to eat right and complain when they are eating wrong. Have you ever missed an occasional balanced meal? Ever? Are you close to dying or are you dead yet? When you miss a balanced meal, does it have a permanent effect on you?

People Food: The Right Source and Easier Than You Think

If you want a true, honest, balanced diet, and something that your dog will love, it's people food. This way you'll know exactly what he's eating. Don't take our word for it. Think about this. Is the chicken in dog food better than a fresh piece of chicken? Are the carbohydrates in dog food better than fresh pasta, rice, potatoes, or kasha, and so on. And for the rest of his balanced diet, vitamins and minerals, are the supplements in dog foods better than steamed fresh vegetables? We don't think so. Use your eyes and your common sense and you be the judge.

A simple way to balance your dog's diet is to take an empty fourteen-ounce can and fill it with one-third protein, that is meat, chicken, fish, or any protein you want. The next third fill with carbohydrates — pasta, rice, potatoes, and so on — and the last third with steamed vegetables (steamed because they are easier to digest, same as with humans). You now have a balanced can of food, and good food. Now follow a feeding schedule of amounts and times. An added benefit of the green vegetables, in addition to their vitamins and minerals, is that the chlorophyll helps keep your dog's breath kissing sweet.

Get into the habit of weighing your dog frequently so you will know how to adjust his diet accordingly. If you are a yo-yo dieter and always think you're either too heavy or too skinny, don't read your weight problems into your dog. Don't look at him and think he's too fat or too thin. You're generally wrong and you could be causing him a weight problem. Weigh him and that way you'll know for sure.

The Real Thing Is Better Than a Look-alike

In addition to your dog's regular meal you can give him treats all day. People-food treats. Whatever you're having, give him some. Not a lot of it, some of it. Real bacon is better than fake bacon. Roast pork is better than pig's ears. Real beef is better than cow's hooves and treated rawhide skins. A real biscuit and real bread and a real cookie are all better than a dog biscuit. Chopped liver is better than dog liver snaps. Real steamed fresh vegetables are better than dog veggies. And so forth and so on. Use your common sense. Your dog knows the difference with his senses.

The Ritual and Spiritual Side of Food

We prepare candlelight dinners for romance, we have festive dinners for holidays, the whole family comes and partakes and enjoys lots of good food. Food is the social bonder used for all special occasions. The preparation is carefully thought through; we make special dishes for those we love and sometimes for those we hate. Of course, those hateful dishes are different. Food provides all the psychological benefits of sharing, warming the heart and soul, like a hot bowl of soup on a cold winter's day. Parents make good food for their children. Food can provide emotional nurturing. Why, then, do you just plop down a couple of handfuls or open a can of not-fit-for-human-consumption food for your dog, who is one of the family members? Feed him what you eat. He will love you even more.

The Successful Dog

The continuation of a species depends on its adapting successfully to a changing environment. If it doesn't, it ceases to exist. Man and dog have been living in the same environment and eating the same foods for a very, very long time. Probably since they first met on this planet. When man was able to get up on his own two feet, it was probably a dog that helped him get up. If the dog could have foreseen the future, he wouldn't have helped man so quickly; he might have "ate" him.

The human animal has a more varied diet than any other species on earth. This helps make him the most successful animal of all, and running on four legs closely behind him should be his dog. We know that's the way it is with many of our clients and their dogs. And in some ways, the dog is more successful because he doesn't have to pay the rent, doesn't have to pay for health insurance, gets his food for free, and most importantly, he is excluded from paying taxes.

Some of us eat meat diets and live long lives. Some of us eat vegetarian diets and live long lives. We have a long intestinal tract, which some say is for a vegetarian diet, but we do very well on a combination of both. If the size of the intestine is the indicator of the vegetarian or the carnivore and what we should eat to live, why are we all here today? Our species should have been long gone and history might have been written by Orwell's pigs.

Some experts speculate that the short intestine of a dog makes him a carnivore. As an example they use the dog's nearest relatives, the wolf, the wild dog, and the coyote. However, these animals hunting in the wild are getting their vegetables, although partially processed, by eating the stomachs of their kill. And they eat vegetation when they want to.

These experts then conclude that because the dog is a carnivore that he should eat only dog food. This is an oxymoron. A representative sampling of the protein content in many popular dog foods, the labels listing only approximate amounts per can, will read: 11 percent or 9 percent or 5.50 percent or 8 percent, which means it's mostly something else, not meat. So if a dog is a carnivore, then why so little meat? Where's the beef?

Our people-food diet calls for at least one-third of the dog's diet to be protein. If he is a carnivore and should eat meat, he's getting more with our diet than he is getting in any dog food. Some dog foods, like anything else in life, are better than others. But still, fresh, real food is always better then processed dog food.

We have the ability to balance our diets in many different ways and we can and should do the same for our pets. This isn't difficult to do. You could bring up a lion cub as a vegetarian. But you would have to make sure the lion got a balanced vegetarian diet. We can even feed our dogs full vegetarian diets, but that could be difficult for people not experienced in this area.

Some people don't eat meat for psychological reasons. Paul stopped eating pork, his last occasional meat, after seeing the Bertolucci movie *1900*. Gerard Depardieu slaughtered a pig in this movie. Now Paul won't eat pork, and he also doesn't like Depardieu anymore.

However, we don't recommend a 100 percent vegetarian diet for your dog unless you are really good about making sure he's getting what he needs. A people-food diet containing a combination of meats, grains, and vegetables works very well.

Certainly if you have a taste for meat, the length of your intestine seems to be the furthest consideration on your mind if you are a hunting animal.

Chimpanzees, who are the closest relative to man biologically, have always been thought to be peaceful vegetarians.

Not so. Jane Goodall was one of the first scientists (primatologists) to show otherwise. A recent article in the *New York Times* (June 27, 1995) called "Meat Viewed As Staple of Chimp Diet and Mores" shows that "these able hunters forage for meat with a passion and motivation not chronicled until recently." They "hunt with such gusto in Gombe National Park in Tanzania that each year they lay waste to one-fifth of their territory's population of the red colobus monkey, their preferred prey." The 45-member Kasakela chimpanzee community "eats one ton of meat on average each year," consuming "up to a quarter pound of meat a day when they hit their hunting stride."

Humans and chimps both have a long intestine. Dogs have a shorter intestine. But you eat what you can get. If you can get a lot, then you eat what you like.

If you are living in the wild, and a scarcity of food exists due to environmental changes, you will have to find and eat other foods in order to survive. Simply put, if you are a meat eater, and if you can't get meat, you'll eat something else or cease to exist. If you are vegetarian and can't find vegetables you might have to eat meat to survive.

We know that bears eat a diet ranging from berries and vegetables to meat and fish, and even human garbage. They're omnivorous. The panda, a bearlike mammal, eats mainly bamboo, but will eat meat if he can find some. They eat what they can get to survive. These are all evolutionary and practical adaptations.

There is so much conflicting dietary information around today that at times it's confusing to know what to eat and what not to eat. Our dogs live in our world—the house, the home, the apartment, or wherever we choose to live. That's the natural environment of the domestic dog, approximately sixty million of them living with us in this country alone. We feel very strongly that they should eat what we eat.

Dogs don't obsess about their looks, their weight, or what they should eat. They don't think about a food's nutritional content, the cholesterol count, the amount of fat or sugar it contains. They just eat what tastes good to them. And enjoying food is a very important part of life. So give them plenty of enjoyment in the form of good food, including plenty of fruits and vegetables.

Food Chart

Dog food amounts can only be approximated. Vary amounts according to your dog; use your common sense. Some food companies reduced their cans of food from 14 oz. to 13 oz., so add a little extra food if that's the case.

Size Chart
Small dog, up to 19 lbs.
Medium dog, 20 to 49 lbs.
Large dog, 50 to 89 lbs.
Giant dog, 90 lbs. and up

For the ADULT DOG: One Year and Up
For a 6 lb. dog, ¼ to ⅓ of ONE (14 oz.) can, ONCE a day.
For a 10 lb. dog, ⅓ to ½ of ONE (14 oz.) can, ONCE a day.
For a 12½ lb. dog, ½ of ONE (14 oz.) can, ONCE a day.
For a 15 lb. dog, ½ to ⅔ of ONE (14 oz.) can, ONCE a day.
For a 20 lb. dog, ⅔ to ONE (14 oz.) can, ONCE a day.
For a 25 lb. dog, ONE (14 oz.) can, ONCE a day.
For a 50 lb. dog, TWO (14 oz.) cans, ONCE a day.
For a 100 lb. dog, FOUR (14 oz.) cans a day, 1 in the morning, 3 in the evening.
NOTE: *The cans of food in the morning are only for dogs weighing in at 100 lbs. or more. (For dogs weighing more than*

100 lbs. increase the morning meal according to chart. Example: For a 125 lb. dog three cans in the evening and two cans in the morning. Never give a giant breed more than three 14 oz. cans at any one meal.)

If you choose to use dry dog food, then substitute an 8 oz. cup in place of a 14 oz. can. Example: one 8 oz. cup = one 14 oz. can. Be careful, overfeeding can cause bloat, gastric torsion, diarrhea, or skin problems.

Guidelines for a PUPPY Are As Follows

Use adult dog chart above for all weights and amounts.

Up to 4½ Months
Small dogs: TWICE a day, morning and evening.
Medium dogs: TWICE a day, morning and evening.
Large dogs: TWICE a day, morning and evening.
Giant dogs: TWICE a day, morning and evening.
Example: If your puppy weighs 15 lbs. feed him the amount for a 15 lb. *adult dog* TWICE a day. Once in the morning (½ to ⅔ of a can) and again for his evening meal (½ to ⅔ of a can).

4½ Months to 6 Months
Small dogs: DECREASE morning meal by ½. Evening meal follow adult chart above.

Medium dogs: DECREASE morning meal by ½. Evening meal follow adult chart above.

Large dogs: DECREASE morning meal by ½. Evening meal follow adult chart above.

Giant dogs: Twice a day morning and evening. Follow adult chart.

Example: If your 4½-month-old puppy weighs 15 lbs., he now gets ¼ to ⅓ of a 14 oz. can in the morning and ½ to ⅔ of a 14 oz. can in the evening.

6 Months to One Year

Small dogs: One meal a day in evening; follow adult chart for amount.

Medium dogs: Decrease morning meal by ½. Evening meal follow adult chart above. Go on one meal a day at 9 months. Feed in the evening, follow adult chart above.

Large dogs: Decrease morning meal by ½. Evening meal follow adult chart above. Go on one meal a day at 1 year. Feed in the evening, follow adult chart above.

Giant dogs: Don't go more than three cans in morning. Evening meal follow adult chart above. At 1 year go to adult chart above.

At 1 year we consider dogs to be young adults and they should be fed as adults; follow chart.

Food snacks can and should be given all day but in small amounts. We recommend people food as the food snacks.

THE OPTIMUM IN NUTRITION FOR YOUR DOG BOTH FOR HEALTH AND PURE ENJOYMENT IS OUR DIET. *The people food amounts are close to perfect!*

People Food for Dogs

Using an empty 14 oz. can fill one-third of the can with protein: fish, meat, or chicken. One-third with carbohydrates: pasta, potatoes, rice, bread. And the last third with steamed vegetables: carrots, spinach, peas, broccoli, zucchini, lettuce, avocado, green pepper, tomato, and so on. Raw vegetables are sometimes difficult for your dog to digest, just as they are for humans. Feed as described in our food chart.

Example: The above recipe is for one can of food; that's enough for a 25 lb. dog. If you have a 50 lb. dog then give him two cans of this formula, follow food chart.

For adult dogs on one meal a day or even giant dogs eating two meals a day, it would be nice to give them a piece of toast with butter, a roll, a bagel, a part of an egg, or even some of your cereal for breakfast. But please, small amounts; we believe in moderation.

We emphasize that treats, in small amounts, can be given at any time during the day, including fruits and vegetables. But just as in your diet, watch the rich, fattening desserts.

Don't take our word for the food changes. Try it for ten days and see. You'll be pleasantly surprised.

CHAPTER 4

Communication Line

Teaching Your Dog to Walk with You

Little Billy and Big Nose

A friend of Billy's recently died and left him an inheritance. Oh, boy, and was it ever a large one. Billy now has a four-year-old, 180-pound, giant, massive, Great Pyrenees dog named Big Nose.

Big Nose was never taught to walk on a leash. He didn't know what a leash was, for he was a country dog, who loved to roam free in the mountains and the ski areas around Stowe, Vermont, generally with a keg of warmer hanging from his neck.

This dog's new mountain home was a one-and-a-half-room studio apartment on the thirtieth floor of a high-rise apartment building on the East Side of Manhattan. He and Billy were now roommates.

Billy, a forty-year-old bachelor shoe salesman who had never had a dog in his life, made up for this deprivation by having a lot of dog all at once. Billy's five-foot one-inch frame and his 120 pounds were dwarfed by Big Nose, who when standing up on his hind legs reached a towering seven feet.

It was no surprise that Billy would have major problems walking Big Nose. But the Nose knew no problems towing Billy along for a walk.

Billy complained that the main reason he was always late for work now was that he couldn't control Big Nose, and to take him out in the morning was a three-hour proposition. His boss, who was a weight lifter, jokingly suggested to Billy, "Why don't you borrow my weights and maybe wearing this extra weight on your body might help you keep your dog from dragging you all over town."

Billy took this suggestion seriously. He went home and donned twenty-pound ankle weights, ten-pound wrist weights, and he also fashioned another thirty pounds of weight that he wore around his waist. Now fully loaded, and weighing almost a hundred pounds more, he took his big dog out for a walk.

Billy got stuck in his elevator. He fell down and couldn't get up.

The leash should not be the reason your dog walks alongside you; he should do this because that's where he belongs.

Walking your dog can be one of the great pleasures in life, or it can be one of the worst depending on your dog's social graces, or lack of them. You all know what we're talking about because walking the dog happens usually three times a day, every day, for fifteen years. That means approximately 16,425 dog walks.

Once you've taught your dog to come to you indoors with our Magic Touch, you have established control. However, even if he's incredibly well behaved at home, it's more important that you make certain he listens to you outside. That's where all the major distractions are and that's where you will be walking and exercising him. As long as your dog has been taught to come to you and to stay with you, then walking with you outside should become a simple matter of transference.

Your dog will feel that outside on the city streets or out in the country, everything is fair game for his curiosity. His brain will pick up information like a sponge picks up water. Everything is a learning experience, so make sure he learns in the right way. If left to his own devices, his devices probably won't be the ones you would approve of.

Your dog will react to every dog and every person who walks by. Every noise will get his attention, and unless he can look to you for direction he'll drag you down streets, checking things out, jumping on people, wanting to get his head or his butt scratched, playing or fighting with other dogs, peeing on every pump, car tire, or tree, claiming his territory everywhere, or imitating other dogs.

He's either pulling you to where he wants to go, or you are pulling him where you want to go. We call this a pull-pull relationship.

If you think your dog is pulling you just to pull, or that it's aimless pulling, you're wrong. A dog pulls to make certain that you are behind him; as long as there is tension on that leash, he knows where you are. That way, he can concentrate on all the more important things in his world.

What this really means is that your dog doesn't trust you with his total security. Oh, yes, he knows you'll feed him, but that's all. If he did trust you, then he would be right by you, depending on you for leadership and for guidance, and not running off to every other dog or person he sees. If he knows you are capable of handling things out there in the world for him and that he can depend on you for his safety, then he will. He'll trust you to make all the decisions.

When your dog is approached by another dog or by a strange person, if he is not certain of what to do he will look to you for guidance. Should the situation get out of hand, and if you don't step in and control it, then your dog will feel he needs to do your job for you and he will learn how to fend for himself, developing his own habits. These habits are generally not ones that you might approve of, and could even become major problems for both of you.

Part of your dog's pulling and barking is to alert the rest of the world that he's here and can take care of himself and take care of you, because as far as he's concerned, unless you establish yourself as a strong, capable leader, then you are only the other end of his leash, and not his security blanket. You're not doing your job being a parent figure.

Make no mistake about it, your dog will and does interpret kindness for weakness. Not that you shouldn't be kind to him, or that he doesn't want to be treated with kindness, but make sure he doesn't take advantage of you. You could lose total control of him. By this we mean letting other dogs or other people have their way with him, and not protecting him from them if he doesn't want to be bothered with them, or not correcting any of his unacceptable or unruly behavior from the very beginning. It's not a kindness to make your dog feel that you're not a parent figure capable of protecting him from harm or capable of teaching him right from wrong. You will make him feel totally insecure in your world.

It didn't start out that way. When he was a puppy he only wanted to be with you, and learn from you, but when you allowed other dogs to push him around in the name of play, he learned to push back in the name of play. When you let people pick him up, take him away from you, and play with him, whether he wanted to be played with or not, you compromised your bonding with him. How was he to know what to do, or what you wanted him to do? He wanted you to step in, protect him, tell him what to do, and control the situation.

Obnoxious behavior can also be a test to see how far your dog can push you and find out who's in charge. You have to stop him wherever and whenever he starts this testing. You have to stop him when he wants to go to other people or to other dogs, until you have total control of this guy and he learns to wait for your permission.

In fact, before you even leave your house or apartment, if he's pulling you, stop him. If he pulls you down your hallway, into an elevator, or even down your front steps, then that's where you stop him. The first time he pulls you or becomes wild, that's when you stop him. If he's not under your control at the beginning of his walk, then chances are he's not going to get any better as your walk continues.

As he learns to walk nicely with you, you can give him more freedom because you know he's learning your rules. This is called communication, and that is what we are looking to achieve.

Two artists, Leon and Nancy, had a major problem with Prax, their five-year-old briard. He was impossible to walk. One afternoon when Nancy was taking Prax out for a walk, he saw a cat in the hall and took off after it, pulling Nancy behind him. He ran down a flight of stairs. Nancy, still attached to the leash, fell down the stairs, breaking her shoulder. This incident kept Nancy away from her work for three months.

A month later, I used the same dog in an FTD Florist commercial on national television. He was walking beautifully with a little six-year-old girl. Prax walked calmly down a flight of stairs and over to the little girl's grandparents' house to deliver flowers.

If you are relying only on your lead for control of your dog, you are going to lose. Your dog should be listening to you with or without the lead; your lead should be just an extension of you. It's nice to feel that you have the security and control of your dog while he's on a lead, but it's a false sense of security. You have to be sure that if the leash falls, breaks, or is pulled out of your hand, you still have a dog.

If you see a person walking their dog, and their jacket pockets are ripped, you can be sure that their dog pulls on his leash. People generally keep the handle of the leash on their wrist, and their hands in their pockets when walking their dogs on cold days. Generally, if the pockets are ripped, the dog is a puller.

I don't believe it!

The Setup—Manhattan

Arlene and Steve called us, saying they had a problem with their dog. They said, "A friend of ours whose dog you trained about five years ago suggested that we give you a call. She said you might be able to help us." Arlene was asking for help, but Steve was skeptical and felt that he had every reason to be. He said, "How in the world can this guy come over to our house in Manhattan and teach our dog, Leo, not to run away from us and jump into a lake on someone else's property in Massachusetts? That's a couple of hundred miles away. We've already had Leo trained and it didn't work. Leo is still running away and still swimming in the muddy lake with his pals."

The Confrontation

We met this Leo, this seven-month-old wayward wheaten terrorist. At first he didn't like the fact that he was being made to follow some new rules, rules much different from the usual stuff that he had already masterfully manipulated. This canine cunningly came when called. But the wily wheaten wasn't worried and willingly waited. He figured he'd beat this new game at the right time and the right place. The right place was his muddy Massachusetts lake.

Steve, still skeptical said, swell, he's perfect here and now, but . . .

The Resolution—Massachusetts

Preparation. Steve, with a book in his hand, stood outside the open front door. Arlene stayed in the kitchen with Leo. Steve, stepping out of sight, rang the doorbell. Leo charged the front door. Seeing it open, he picked up speed and bolted for freedom. Steve, hearing the paw steps approaching, threw the book down as hard as he could just before Leo got to the door, making sure not to hit Leo with the book. Leo stopped in his tracks, turned around, and ran back to Arlene. They both told Leo how good he was for not running out the door. Leo now doesn't run out the front door anymore.

Step two. Arlene and Steve took Leo for a walk without his leash. They stopped every so often, called Leo back, and when he came they told him how good he was.

Step three. If Leo didn't come back, they threw the leash at him. When it made contact, they would call him. When he came back, they told him how good he was.

Final step. They threw the lead at him and didn't call him. He stopped, looked at them, thought it over, and came back to them.

They called it the big muddy, but Leo isn't in it anymore. He doesn't run out the front door to get in it. He doesn't run away and join his pals to get in it. And when walking with Arlene and Steve, he doesn't leave them to get in it. He will only get in it with permission.

I'm in it. In the tub, that is, trying to relax, when the phone rings. It's Steve, the now believer, telling us how great Leo is and that geography is not a problem anymore. " Massachusetts, New York, wherever we are, he listens."

Leo is now imprinted to his owners. Not to his collar, not to his leash, not to his crate, not to his house, and not to geography.

Dumbo's Feather

The leash should become superfluous—outside or inside—because your dog should really be listening to you. The leash is like Dumbo's feather; you think it's something you need for security, but you don't. It's there because you're not certain you can control your dog.

The mothers of pups or cubs living in the wild never use a leash. All the little ones follow her around without question. Do you think maybe she whispers something in their ears? Like the threat of taking away their phone or television privileges?

Teaching your dog to walk on a leash and then to walk without a leash can be done, and it will be done. You will have an invisible, magic leash—we call it the communication line.

In Europe, dogs are allowed into restaurants, and a leash is used almost as if it were a social accessory. It's similar to your walking into a restaurant and the maitre d' asking you to "please wear a tie or a jacket." Or he might ask you to "please leash your dog."

You use a leash if the law requires it; you use a leash if you're not certain you can control your dog; you use a leash when training a new dog, and sometimes if you are in a situation where using a leash is the most expedient thing to do, in large crowds, or around people who aren't comfortable around your dog.

But you must teach your dog to stay with you without a leash.

Type of Lead to Use

We like to use a six-foot cotton or nylon training lead. Anything longer isn't necessary and anything shorter is too restrictive for both you and your dog.

Fancy, flimsy jeweled leads with matching collars are great-looking stuff, but I've seen these trinkets hanging from dog owners' hands while they went screaming and running after their dogs, crossing streets and avenues, down roads and onto highways and byways, stopping lots of traffic, trying to get their dogs back, and sometimes never getting them back. These dogs were never taught to stay with their owners.

If you want your dog to wear a fancy jeweled lead, that's fine. You can even walk him with a cotton string if that's what you want. But he must learn to listen to you first.

I once used a six-foot cotton string as a leash on my dog Plum during an obedience trial competition. There were a few sour-grapers screaming, "He shouldn't be allowed in with that piece of string!" But most of the people loved it; everybody loves a well-behaved dog. I was allowed to bring Plum in with his cotton string on and he took home first prize.

Eden wanted a small black poodle. She bought one and named him Higgins. The pet shop from whence he came said that the puppy Higgins was a pocket poodle and would weigh no more than three pounds full grown. I guess that would have been true if Eden had had giant pockets because Higgins, now four months old, weighs a hefty twelve pounds.

Eden had also bought a three-foot leash, thinking, we guess, that this little pocket dog should have a little leash. Standing six feet tall in heels, Eden, when she would walk Higgins, found to her surprise that his short leash caused her to walk bent over. If she walked upright, Higgins would be pulled along on his hind legs, or inadvertently be hanged. No wonder Higgins would put up a terrific fight to keep Eden from putting his leash on. And when she finally got the leash on him, he would sit down and refuse to move. Eden couldn't understand this.

Without his leash, Higgins would walk perfectly because all of his four feet would be on the ground. When she changed to a six-foot lead it gave both Eden and Higgins enough slack to walk normally. Higgins on all-fours, and Eden upright on all-twos.

Chain Lead

If you use a chain lead it adds an unnecessary extra weight for both you and your dog when walking. It's uncomfortable. Also, the chain will hurt your hand if and when your dog pulls you. The chain isn't any stronger than the nylon lead. The only reason that we can see someone using this type of lead is if they can't stop their dog from chewing up the softer nylon, leather, or cotton leads. So rather than using a chain, teach your dog not to chew on his lead.

Expandable Lead

Thirty-foot clothesline leads, or expandable leads, as they're called, are a menace to society. Anyone who gets within their reach can and will trip over these tangling tentacles.

Collars: The Good, the Bad, and the Ugly

We like to use a regular buckle collar. If your dog is uncontrollable when you first start teaching him how to walk on a leash, then make certain that the buckle collar is on tight enough so that he won't slip out of it.

There are many different kinds of collars and walking devices around today to teach your dog how to walk. Many profess to be humane. But most of them are restrictive, very uncomfortable, and not so humane for the dog.

A collar that's designed to pull a dog's head around isn't so humane. A collar that's combined with a muzzle that's designed to prevent a dog from pulling, biting, or picking things up off the ground isn't so humane.

Harness

A harness is primarily designed and used for pulling. It's generally worn by a dog when he is pulling something, like a sled. It is also used for guide dogs and companion-aide dogs. Its main purpose is to give the dog better leverage when he is pulling. Even when he's on a harness you have to teach him not to pull until you tell him he can, because even on a harness, a pulling dog that's out of control can be a danger to you or to himself.

We can understand a harness for working dogs such as seeing eye or companion-aide dogs for the physically challenged or the sled dog, but not just for walking your family pet. If your dog pulls and you want to stop the pulling, why use a harness that encourages him to pull? You will never be able to stop a dog from pulling if you try to teach him with a harness.

From the dog's point of view it's like wearing a girdle. It's very uncomfortable and restrictive for him to be wearing straps under his legs. If you put on these straps and belts, I don't care if it's under your arms, under your legs, around your waist, or on top of your head, you would be very uncomfortable unless you enjoy that sort of thing. Your dog will wear these things because he has no choice. The harness is not as humane as a plain buckle collar.

If your dog has a problem with his neck or throat, then it's okay for him to wear a harness temporarily until the problem has been taken care of. Then put him back on his collar. It should not be worn for just walking or for teaching how to walk.

Choke Collar

We ran into Keith, a dog walker we know. He was walking a small beagle for one of his clients. Keith had mentioned that the dog was terrific with his owner in every way except when she had to put the dog's collar on to take him for a walk. He would try to bite her. The collar was a choke collar. For some reason the obvious seemed to escape both Keith and this dog's owner. The dog hated that choke collar because it hurt him. And he would try, in his own way, to tell his owner by biting at her when she would make him wear it that he didn't like it.

One of the most popular collars seems to be the choke collar, sometimes called a "release" collar for public relations purposes. But it still is a choke collar because it's designed to choke your dog. We don't use choke collars, but they may be necessary when working with large dogs that are out of control. Then you use a choke until you can control him and teach him not to pull you. Again, it should only be used as a temporary learning tool.

If you feel that you need a choke collar, remember that long-haired dogs, such as sheepdogs, could get their hair tangled or entwined in the collar, so check the collar on the dog frequently.

Prong Collar

Also named a spike or pinch collar. Many trainers tell you that this collar doesn't hurt your dog. It does. Don't just take our word for it; put one of these collars on your neck or on your arm and pull it. Does it hurt?

By using these training devices, what will ultimately happen is that your dog will behave only when wearing one of them. These should be temporary training tools until he learns what you want. Then get rid of it. But unfortunately many dog owners use them for the life of their dog.

Shock Collar

An electric shock collar, both the barking kind and the distance control kind, including an electric fence, will keep your dog under control but at an incredible price to your dog. An electric shock hurts. Put your finger into an electric socket while changing a bulb, or touch an exposed wire. But to put an electric current into your dog to shock him, and to do this deliberately, to us is incredibly inhumane. In some cases, where the choice is either the collar for control or getting rid of the dog, then perhaps it's the lesser of two evils. This we understand. Seriously think through what you're doing. Try these devices on yourself and see what you are asking your dog to go through.

The most humane collar and the least restrictive for a dog as far as we're concerned is a plain and simple buckle collar made of nylon, cotton, or leather. Oh, yes, and your dog knowing how to walk with you.

If you feel that you must use one of these torture collars or you can't walk your dog because you can't control him, then you are probably right. Whichever collar you decide to use, remember, your dog will be wearing it and subjected to it a minimum of 16,425 times in his lifetime.

Just as we want you to become the leash, we also want you to become the collar, so to speak. By using these artificial control contraptions, your dog doesn't listen to you, he listens to the artificial control devices, and you will need to use them for the rest of his life. One way to transfer that control to you is to use our throwing technique; the other is to give your dog a slap on the behind when and if he needs one. This way he listens to you instead of to a collar or a leash. You will control him all by yourself without needing any of these permanent aids.

You would be very surprised at what a well-timed and strategic slap on the behind can accomplish. It can instantly reverse years and years of bad behavioral imprinting, and you suddenly have a well-behaved dog who walks beautifully with you, listens to you, and who allows you to control the environment and protect him, so he doesn't have to.

Just one well-placed, thoughtful slap on the behind could mean that the problem is over with, once and for all, and you will never need any of those painful collars or contraptions for your dog again. Think about it. Walking your dog 16,425 times with a painful and inhumane collar or a pop on the behind, and you have a happy walking dog forever.

Compare. Give yourself a slap on your hand, or on your arm, then put a choke collar, a prong collar, an electric collar, or a harness on yourself. Use these devices in the way their instructions advise you to. Which hurts the most? And which hurts the least?

If you are concerned that to slap or to cuff your dog will make him vicious, or afraid of your hand, don't worry. It won't.

Because if that were the case, your dog should become vicious every time the veterinarian sticks one of those big bad needles into his butt and he should shy away from the hand that wields the needle. I guess the treat that's given to your dog after his injection makes everything all right in your dog's mind. If you believe that, then you should probably believe in the tooth fairy.

The truth is an injection hurts, but your dog does not become progressively vicious each time he goes to the veterinarian. If he did he would be a monster by the time he's a year old.

Compare. Go to your doctor for an injection, then also ask him to give you a slap on the behind. Which hurts more? We bet the least painful will be a slap. You be the judge.

Any dog mother or wolf mother knows that when her puppies sharp teeth are biting at her nipples and hurting her, it's time to wean her babies to solid food. She doesn't do this by kindly saying to them, "Darlings, please stop, you're hurting my nipples with your sharp little teeth, it's time you stopped having my milk." Instead, she bites them and chases them away. It's a hard lesson and it's quite scary to those little puppies because the milk is their only food source. They don't realize that mom is going to teach them to eat solid food. But they listen and learn quickly. The mother dog teaches her babies *physically, and not always gently.* They still love her and trust her 100 percent and she will protect them with her life.

When dogs are pulled on a choke, when they are pulled on a pronged collar, when an electric collar is used, an electrified fence is used, or even when they are put in a crate all day without water, to us that is cruel. None of these are nice, but the least offensive of all and the most effective is a good slap on the behind when and if your dog needs it.

Don't worry, if you slap your dog, he won't run away from home, join a drug culture, or marry wrong, and he won't hate you. He will only behave himself.

Let us make it very clear: A slap is a slap and only a slap, and abuse is something else. There is a world of difference between abuse and a well-meaning, well-placed slap on the behind.

A slap uses the same principle as throwing. It's a contact that he can't duplicate. He can pull you, push you, bite you, piss on you, jump on you, and all of these things he can do better than you can. But he can't slap you, thank God for that! If he could, he would do it for everything. Every time he wanted things his way. If he didn't get it, he'd slap you for his breakfast, his lunch, his dinner, to take him out, to take him back in, to read him the newspaper, and maybe even to stop you from snoring.

You can either choke, prong, twist your dog on each of his 16,425 walks. Or you can give him a slap on the behind once or twice and it's over. Then the next 16,423 walks will be tug free, without artificial control, and with only a plain and simple, collar au naturel.

What Side Should He Be On?

If you are going to teach your dog to walk properly with the idea of entering him into obedience competition, then he should be taught to walk on your left side because that is the side that competitions require.

If that's not what you need or want, if you just want a dog that fits into your lifestyle, then you should train him to stay on the side of you that you feel most comfortable with.

We like to teach our dogs to stay on the side opposite their owner's active side. For example, if you are lefthanded, the dog should be on your right side, and vice versa. There is a very good reason for this. Once your dog is trained to walk with you both on and off a lead, you'll want to keep your more active side free for more active movements, important things like opening doors, using keys, writing something, putting money in a meter, whatever. You want to be free to do whatever you have to do without getting tangled up with your dog. This frees you.

Snapping the Lead Is Effective, Pulling Is Not

You pull him or he pulls you; either way you're teaching your dog to pull. If you want to stop the pulling, break the pattern. You must learn to snap your dog's lead. The snapping of the lead will have approximately three times the effect in strength as pulling on his lead. It is the same principle as throwing; he can't copy your snapping of the lead, and he can't find a way around it, so he learns not to pull you.

How to Walk Your Dog

Put a six-foot lead on your dog's collar. Place him at your side. If he's on your left side, his right front leg should be in line with your left leg. That's the perfect place to have him. If you want him on your right side, vice versa. We're going to teach your dog to walk as if he were on our left side. Hold the middle of the lead in your left hand. Make sure there's some slack in it—not much, but some. The handle of the leash should be on your thumb in your right hand. Don't bundle it up in your right hand and don't wrap it around your wrist. You need to be able to take slack in and let slack out when necessary.

Take a couple of steps forward, snap the lead forward, and tell your dog, "Let's go," or "Come on." Then stop. He must stop with you. If you stop and he doesn't, snap the lead back a few more times until he comes back to you. Remember, he must come back to you on his own. Give him some time, six to ten seconds, to think through what you want. If he looks thoroughly confused, reach down and place him on your left side, then praise him. Repeat this move until your dog gets the idea where you want him to be. Then praise him only when he is there. His front leg at the side of your front leg. If he isn't there and he is in front of you, then snap him back until he is back at your side. Then praise him again. If he is lagging behind you or he refuses to walk with you, then snap him forward. When he gets to where you want him, praise him. Only praise him when he is perfect, when he's done exactly what you want. Get into the habit of expecting him to be perfect from the very beginning, even if perfect means picking him up and placing him exactly where he should be. Then give him the world.

After he's got the idea, take a couple of steps backwards. If he comes with you, praise him when he is exactly where he is supposed to be. Again, give him time to think this through. If your dog doesn't walk back with you, snap the lead until he does. Let him understand that you can walk backwards as well as forwards. You don't want him to think you're an animal only capable of going in one direction. This also teaches your dog to keep you in his peripheral vision, meaning that whether your dog is on or off a lead, he will make it his business to always know where you are and where he has to be. And this will be paramount for on- and off-lead control. When he learns to keep you in his peripheral vision, then he will always look to you for guidance. Then he can explore the world around you with you.

This is a much more effective way of teaching your dog to walk with you than the traditional turning techniques. With this turning stuff you're supposed to walk your dog and surprise him with sharp turns until he never knows what you want of him and never relaxes on any of his walks with you.

You usually walk forward and in a straight line much more often than you make turns, and very rarely do you make abrupt turns, so you are better off teaching your dog to respond to you in the way you normally would walk. Unless you are a left-foot Louie who only walks to the left.

Now you can start walking your dog. Here's how to talk to your dog while walking.

We don't like to use the word "heel." We like to ask our dogs, "Let's go," or "Come on." You can say anything that makes you comfortable. But speak to him in your language, not with one-word commands. Remember, how you talk to him now is what he is going to expect from you for the next fifteen years or so. Only ask him to go with you once. Do not repeat yourself.

Another exercise is to normally walk with your dog snapping the lead. Do not tell him to "heel"; do not say anything. If you start saying "heel," you'll have to continue to tell him "heel" all the time you are walking him. Who wants to go through life saying "heel"? You're better off saying nothing except "good boy" when he's good, stops pulling, and walks nicely with you.

You can clearly get your dog's attention by popping or tapping him in the behind, using your foot while walking. This will work very well if done properly. And if he is a larger dog, nudging him with your knee or pushing with your hand will remind him that you are still there. If your dog pulls out in front of you, give him a tap on the behind with your foot. He'll stop pulling and look back at you to see what else you want. Tell him he's very good for acknowledging you and good for not pulling you. Tapping, nudging, and popping are definitely not kicking. Please, don't mistake it as such. Don't kick your dog.

Turning Left and Right, or in a Circle

If you are walking with your dog on the left side, and you want to make a left turn, snap the lead. This makes him stop walking forward. Then make your left turn in front of him so that you lead. Snap the lead forward so that he comes along with you. If you are making a right turn and he's on your left side, then you use a series of small snaps in quick repetition until you make your turn, making him turn with you. Then release the pressure on your lead and continue walking. Remember, don't give any verbal commands. Praise him after he does what you want. And always give him time to think.

Stopping at the Curb

For the city dog, the suburban dog, or the small-town dog. When you get to the curb, snap the lead and stop. If he's good and stops with you, tell him how good he is. If he steps off the curb, snap him back sharply and firmly and take a few steps backwards. Head for the curb again, fast. Stop. If he stops with you, praise him. If he doesn't, repeat this procedure until your dog does stop. Then praise him, as if he were perfect the first time. Don't say anything to him until he does what you want, then praise him verbally.

This could save your dog's life, and maybe yours too, so be firm. Once he's got the idea, walk to the curb again, but this time walk quickly. He still has to stop at the curb with you, even if you are running to it.

Bella Chases Cars No More

Sounds like a song. Bella, the border collie, had no borders. She loved to chase cars. Whenever she saw a car, it didn't matter what her owner said or did. If Bella wasn't held tight on her lead, and even if she was, if her owner wasn't alert, Bella would pull free and enter into this dangerous chase game.

Not realizing she could get hurt or killed, Bella was having a great time barking, yelling, and jumping at these moving vehicles. Her owner, Fay, was terrified. She thought her dream of enjoying long walks with her dog was never to be.

We spent an hour working with Bella inside at first, teaching her to stop running and to come to us and stay with us, using the Magic Touch. All the while Fay complained about her terrible aim and that she would probably miss Bella the first time she threw something at her. In Fay's apartment we were successful. Fay was able to throw a magazine at Bella and hit the target. Bella came right over to Fay. Then it was easy; every time Fay threw something at her dog, even a pair of socks, it worked. We wanted Bella to know that Fay could reach her from any distance.

Fay kept telling us that outside, because of her bad aim, she thought it would be a different story. Bella would be long gone and she wouldn't be able to reach her with anything. We made sure Fay held her six-foot cotton lead in her throwing hand. So when she threw it at Bella, it would spread out and at least, we hoped, maybe part of it would make contact.

Sure enough, Bella ran, Fay threw. The leash sailed through the air and made contact. Lo and Behold, Bella stopped in her tracks and looked back at Fay. Maybe she didn't believe her owner's aim was that good; hey, the toss was all of five feet. But more realistically, Bella thought back to the apartment where we had worked out the throwing behavior. It doesn't matter what she thought. What mattered was that Bella stopped and came back.

Bella stopped chasing cars and would walk and stay by Fay. It was that simple. Fay now was able to take those long walks with Bella that she thought weren't going to be possible. Now Bella has borders

Fay, then armed with this great information, told all of her friends who own dogs about the throwing magic. Some tried it, and their dogs ran off in the opposite direction. I guess Fay forgot to tell her friends that the dogs had to be taught first that the throwing means to come back.

Walking Your Dog Without a Leash

Once your dog learns to stay with you while walking on a leash, and he comes back to you when you want him to, then you won't need a leash on your dog. Then, teaching him to walk without it becomes a simple matter of transference. Now you can really use our throwing technique to great advantage. Instead of snapping the lead for control, you can now have this same control by throwing.

Take the lead off your dog and start walking with him. When you stop, he should stop with you. If he doesn't stop with you, then call him back to you. Give him the six- to ten-second time frame to do this. If he comes back to you, tell him how good he is. If he doesn't come back to you, throw something at him. Don't move and don't say anything. He should come back to your side.

If your dog's out in front of you, or wandering, or playing with other dogs, and you want him back, throw something at him, your keys or your lead. He will come back. That's what he was taught. The throwing becomes an extension of you.

If you find that you are calling your dog too often and too loudly, then you're being tested by him. At this point, don't call him at all, just throw something at him. Remember, by throwing and not saying anything to him, he will learn to come back to your side automatically and stay with you. If you throw and are always calling him, he will come back to you, but then he will leave again. This gets to be annoying after a while. You always seem to be telling him what to do. He always does it and then he leaves. But if you throw and don't say anything, he will think it through, come back to you, and stay with you. Remember to always touch him or hold his collar when he comes back before praising him.

If you throw and your dog still doesn't come back to you, then go after him, get him, take him by his collar, and pull him all the way back to where you first were when you called him. Then, even though you had to pull him all the way back, tell him how good he was. If all of this sounds similar to teaching your dog to come to you indoors, you're right. The only difference here is that there are no walls. That's why your dog should be perfect inside before you do this outside.

Backing Up Without the Lead

Just as we did with the lead, to stop your dog from anticipating your always walking forward, every once in a while take a step backward from a stationary position and give him those six to ten seconds to figure out what you want. If he makes the wrong decision, throw something or tap him with your foot. He should come back to you. This will remind your dog to keep you in his peripheral vision when walking next to you without a lead.

Turning Without the Lead

There's no lead to tell your dog when to make a left or right turn, but since you have taught your dog to keep you in his peripheral vision, he will turn with you as if he were on a magic, invisible lead.

Walking the Puppy Without a Leash

When you teach your puppy with our throwing technique, to come to you and follow you, then he is already going to naturally want to walk with you outside, just like he would with his real mother. The big advantage with training a puppy is that you can pick him up and place him at your side without a lead, and start walking him. You don't have to worry about him running away; he's too slow and you can catch him, no problem.

With a puppy taught this way you can start walking without a lead first, then teach him to walk with one. All you have to do is get him accustomed to wearing a leash when he follows you.

Grabbing and Chewing on His Lead

Whenever your dog grabs his lead in his mouth, he is doing it for either of two reasons. He is learning to hold his leash; in this case he is imitating you. Or, he wants to bite it and pull it loose from your hand so he can run free and not listen to you.

Remember your dog uses his mouth not only to eat and to talk but also in the same way you use your hands: to hold something, to feel texture, to carry, to pull, to catch. I'm sure you have played tug o'war with your dog. In the wild, dogs use their mouth to carry their young, hunt and kill, or to defend themselves.

To stop your dog from grabbing and biting on his lead is simple. When he has the lead in his mouth, you just snap hard on the lead a couple of times. Don't say anything to him. The snapping will tell him to stop, and he will. You then tell him how good he is for not biting on his lead.

If he is free, off his lead, and wants to carry it, or you want him to carry his lead, as some dogs like to do and some dog owners like them to do, then just encourage him when he takes hold of his lead. But not when you are using it to walk him.

Lucky Sandy

A young couple, Marilyn and Alan, had purchased a small but comfortable beach house on Fire Island. The house had a deck in the front, facing the ocean. What a great view! The house and deck, five feet off the ground, had four steps descending to a path that led around to the back of the house where they parked their cars.

They didn't have any children as yet, but they did have a wonderful nine-month-old King Charles spaniel. Her name was Sandy, but not because of the color of her coat, which was red and white, but because this dog loved the beach and would bring much of it back into the house. This aggravated Alan because it was his job to do all the vacuuming, and because of Sandy, it was becoming a major, time-consuming occupation.

Sandy was a very energetic dog and a very trusting one. So trusting that when Alan would stand on the beach a few feet away from the deck of the house and call to Sandy, she would run as fast as she could and jump off the deck right into Alan's arms.

She was very attached to Alan and Marilyn and wanted to be with them all the time and wherever they went. Many times, Marilyn and Alan had to leave Sandy at home alone. Sandy didn't like this. Feeling guilty about leaving Sandy home alone, they decided that on nice days they would leave Sandy out on the deck instead of in the house.

So, one day, they tied Sandy to a six-foot lead outside on the deck, and went around back to their car. No sooner did they get out of the dog's sight than they heard a bloodcurdling scream. Racing back, hearts pounding, they found Sandy hanging by her neck choking and struggling to get free.

Marilyn hysterically ripped the lead out of the wall where it was tied, while Alan, holding Sandy in his arms, was doing everything that he possibly could to help. The three of them were frantic. It turned out that except for a sore throat and a bruised neck, Sandy was all right and this story ended happily.

Apparently what had happened was that Sandy had jumped off the deck not wanting to be left behind and had almost hanged herself. Be aware that the leash on your dog, yes, can keep him secure and prevent his running away from you, but at the same time a leash can be very dangerous if not used correctly. Don't tie your dog up anywhere and then leave him.

Remember:

1. Ultimately your dog has to walk for you, not because he's wearing a leash or any other training control device.
2. Make sure your dog learns to keep you in his peripheral vision when he is walking with you.
3. He has to look to you for all guidance, security, and direction.
4. He must listen to you 100 percent of the time before he can be taught to be leash free.
5. Give him ten seconds to think over and respond to what you ask of him.
6. Be a strong but fair teacher; your dog will test you and could mistake kindness for weakness.
7. The younger your dog is, the easier it will be to teach him to walk off a lead.
8. Don't let your dog socialize with other dogs or people until he listens to you 100 percent of the time.
9. Don't leave your dog tied up on a leash unless you have made sure he will not be in any danger.
10. If your dog must wear a choke collar, make sure he doesn't wear it in your home.

CHAPTER 5

To Have and to Hold Overnight

Housebreaking or Paper Training

It's in the Bag

Lost or forgotten civilizations are sometimes discovered by surviving artifacts. Objects that haven't disintegrated or eroded over time leave clues telling us about the way things were then, and how these societies flourished and eventually died.

Approximately sixty million dogs live in the United States alone. A dog lives approximately fifteen to sixteen years. And some do live to twenty years.

A dog poops approximately three times a day, which means that approximately three nonbiodegradable plastic Baggies are used. We're saying approximately because not everybody uses plastic to pick up after their dog. And not everybody picks up after their dog. Shame on the latter.

Three plastic Baggies a day, seven days a week, four weeks a month, twelve months a year, times sixty million dogs equals what? Nine hundred eighty-five billion, five hundred million plastic Baggies. Approximately one trillion plastic Baggies filled with doggy doo that will last forever and ever.

Can you imagine ten thousand or so years down the line, after our civilization has disappeared, completely turned to dust—and it will one day, nothing lasts forever—discoverers in the future might find what's left of our civilization? Some of the remains that will be found for sure will be the billions of doggy poops, encapsulated in their nonbiodegradable plastic bags. And remember, this is just in the United States alone.

When all of this stuff is found, and because there is so much of it, who knows, it could even be mistaken for our monetary system.

Midnight Surprise

Have you ever gotten up in the middle of the night thirsty, your mouth dry, full of sand? And you just had to have a drink of water or die of thirst. Maybe you had to get to the bathroom fast, because if you didn't, you were going to explode. Were you ever surprised by the something that your foot discovered? I guess the dog had to get to the bathroom also.

A Piper Puppy Love Story

They fell in love with my dog Plum as soon as they saw him on the *Tonight Show*. They begged me to give them a puppy if Plum ever had kids.

I told Pam and Andrew that Plum had become a father about two months ago. His girlfriend had had six beautiful puppies, but they had all been given to friends. Given with the promise that if for any reason any of the puppies were a problem, that puppy would be returned to me.

Piper did come back, flown all the way back from California. Piper's owner said she was getting married and that her fi-

ancé was allergic to dogs. I suggested she get rid of her fiancé
and keep the dog. She didn't.

When Piper came back, she was wet and wild as some
would say; others would say extremely destructive and not at all
housebroken. She was a seven-month-old, out-of-control, gor-
geous taupe-colored devil in dog's clothing. But I loved her.
Hey, I had to, she was my granddaughter.

Pam and Andrew lived in Detroit, and as it happened, I was
going there to do some radio and television appearances to promote a new book. I called them and explained that if they still
wanted one of Plum's pups, I had one for them. The phone
went silent for a minute or so, then a resounding yes! Piper
came to Detroit.

They fell in love with her instantly, and Piper fell in love
with their Persian rug instantly. And she went on it, instantly.
Pam and Andrew looked the other way. "She's just a puppy,
what does she know?" Changing the subject, Andrew showed
me two very beautifully hand-carved doors he and Pam had
bought from a well-known singer-actress.

The doors were magnificent, a work of art. I went over to get
a closer look and to touch them. Piper came over to see what I
was doing, looked at the door, then put her nose to it. Pam
reached down and rubbed Piper's head and jokingly said,
"Piper you have good taste." Pam told me that it had taken the
artist years to carve them. These French doors were the cen-
terpiece of their apartment.

Before lunch, during lunch, after lunch, I kept trying to explain to them how to take care of their dog, how to feed their
dog, and how to housebreak their dog. They kept smiling, they
kept agreeing, and they kept saying, "No problem, don't worry,
we've had dogs before and we know what to do."

I finally wished them luck with their new dog and left. I took
care of my business in Detroit, then flew back home.

Well, the first day Piper was alone, she was left in the great big kitchen as part of their training plan. There was plenty of water available for her in case she was thirsty, and also some soothing music so she could relax and wouldn't get bored. Pam and Andrew told her they would be back as soon as possible, asked her to be a good girl, and then they both left and went off to work.

Pam and Andrew couldn't wait to get home. They called each other all day from work, nonstop. It got to be too much for them, the thought of Piper being alone in her new environment, so they left work very early and ran home to be with their dog.

When they opened the front door they listened for a greeting from Piper, but all they heard was the soothing music that had been left on. They went into the great big kitchen where they saw Piper stretching out after a pleasant nap. They both went over to hug their dog, when to their surprise they saw a large hole in the kitchen wall. They looked through the hole, into the living room, but everything seemed okay.

But when they went back around to the foyer, there they saw a large poop pyramid on the precious Persian. At first they couldn't understand how it got there. Then they saw the answer. Oh, boy, did they see it. Their Piper had chewed and clawed her way through the kitchen into the living room, and then chewed and clawed her way through those pulchritudinous doors, the doors that had taken a lifetime to carve. She had altered them to her satisfaction in minutes, to get into the foyer where she had left her mark on the Persian she loved so much. Piper then backtracked into the kitchen, went to sleep feeling very good, quite relaxed, and soothed by the music.

"Agreed" and "Don't Worry" frantically called me in New York. I went back to Detroit and taught them the right way to live with Piper. She was "No Problem" after that.

Control Yourself

Two of the main reasons why people give their dogs away are that they haven't been able to housebreak their dog or the dog is destroying their house. (There are other reasons we will cover later.) Housebreaking and destructive chewing are problems that can be solved very quickly, and at the same time, because these two problems are related to one another. Dog owners will put up with almost anything when it comes to their dogs, except for the two big headaches mentioned above. When it comes to these problematic areas, they can and will lose their patience.

Don't lose your temper when working with your dog. Don't show uncertainty. Don't yell or scream at your dog. Remain calm and clear when teaching him anything, and that includes housebreaking. Think things through, use your common sense. You will make things easier for both of you. He will learn the right things from you, and learn them very fast, and you won't confuse his learning process.

You Are a Parent Figure

Your dog will have to learn from you because he lives with you. You are a parent figure to him. He will pick up his habit patterns from you. We're not saying that your dog will part his hair on the left side or imitate the way you walk. Maybe he will, but we've never seen that happen. But he will pick up the following: If you are hyper, he could become a hyper dog. If you are angry and lose your temper he could do the same, or he could become frightened, intimidated, and cower all the time, which is just as bad.

When to eat, what to eat, where to eat, these are all habit patterns he will learn from you. At times, your dog will even try to imitate you. You hold a newspaper, you wear a watch, you put on your shoes and socks—this is all done with your hands. A dog will use his mouth in the same way you use your hands. So, it makes more sense for him to chew the newspaper, chew the socks, chew the shoes, or chew the watch. If you don't teach your dog when and where to go to the bathroom, he will develop bad habits, because he will go when and where he wants to go.

Did He Learn from His Master?

We had a client who was a very successful real estate broker. He had an English bulldog named Swifty.

This dog would never use his house as a toilet; he was a very nice, very thoughtful, and very clean dog. But when Swifty would go out on the street, everything about his personality would change. He wouldn't talk to people. He became focused on his job. He would lift his leg very carefully on buildings of great value, thus marking them off as his territory. He would only want to walk on the better streets in town, I guess to enhance his social image.

As Swifty grew older he grew smarter. He developed an ingenious method of increasing his claims on real estate. He would pee only on automobiles with out-of-town license plates. This way he could claim his territory all across the United States, and who knows, maybe even abroad, since cars are shipped out of the country all the time. Swifty was able to accomplish this great feat from the comfort of his own toilet.

Now, we don't know the personal habits of Swifty's owner, but I'll bet our client the real estate developer made some big deals from this toilet as well. What a dog, that Swifty!

Food, Glorious Food

Some people feed a fifteen-pound dog three cans or three cups of dog food a day and then wonder why he has seven or eight humongous poop-a-doops in a day, and in between leaving all these piles, he chews their house down to boot.

My parents felt that by feeding me every time I had a problem, the food would be the cure-all. If I came home from school and I was in a fight or I got bad grades, or had any problems anywhere in my world, my mother would tell me to eat, and eat a lot, and I would feel better. My mother's philosophy of feeding me for every problem opened up two doors in my life, the refrigerator door and the bathroom door. Your dog might not be able to open the refrigerator door—we don't know, maybe he can—but for sure his bathroom door will be wide open all the time.

Keep in mind what goes in one end of your dog must come out the other. Additionally, a dog that has eaten too much and has to go to the bathroom, and has to wait for his owner to take him out, may well be a good dog and hold, but there's a better than good chance he will compensate by nervously chewing. This could mean the destruction of your couch, your shoes, and so on. And then when you come home and see what your dog didn't do and did do, you may praise him for not going to the bathroom in the house, and you may have a nervous breakdown over what's left of your house.

Feed your dog the appropriate amounts of food for his age and size. Some dogs, just like some people, will eat until they bust. If your dog wolfs down his food and looks to you with those big hungry eyes for more, don't give in. Overfeeding leads to obesity, which leads to major problems in the long run, and you will never housebreak your dog and he will redecorate your house in the short run. (See our Food Chart.)

The Tooth Fairy Teething Theory

Human babies cry when their first teeth are pushing up through their gums. This hurts. Puppies are the same. When their first teeth push up through their gums at three to four weeks, they are in pain.

A dog's adult teeth start coming in when he is about four and a half months old. When this happens, there is no pain because of the holes that were left when the baby teeth fell out. So it's safe to say that when a dog or a puppy destructively chews after the age of five weeks, he is not teething, as many people think. And he is not having a hunger-driven problem either. He is chewing because it's a nervous habit. Now, the two reasons that dogs or puppies chew are having to get to the bathroom and not being able to, or something else is bothering them that's making them nervous. But it is nerves, not teething or hunger.

Destructive Chewing Is Tied to Diet and Housebreaking

By asking your dog not to go to the bathroom in your house and to wait until you can take him out, you are asking him to hold. If your dog has to go to the toilet and can't, he will become nervous, anxious, and fidgety. Think how you feel when you must get to the bathroom and you can't. You fidget, bite your nails, and get anxious. That's you. But dogs will chew the house down instead of their nails, they will go to the toilet anywhere that's convenient, like the lovely rug if they can't wait, then lie down as far away from the mess as possible, relax, and go to sleep. Just the way Piper did in Detroit.

There are only two important things to keep in mind. One is scheduling your dog's diet: when to eat, what to eat, and how much to eat. The other is letting your dog know he can depend on your taking him out at certain times of the day so he can relax. By incorporating these two considerations into your daily routine, housebreaking becomes an easy proposition.

Many times dogs that have parasites, worms, or any low-grade infection will become nervous and anxious enough to start chewing on something, anything. We would love to say that a headache is making them chew, but how do we know when a dog has a headache? When something is bothering a dog, he will let us know by acting nervous and uncomfortable. Chewing is one of the ways it shows. As you become more aware of your dog and the signals he gives you, you will know more about your dog than any expert.

Ellen adopted Pebbles, a little girl dog of mixed heritage, from an animal shelter. We trained her and everything went fine. A couple of months later Ellen called us because Pebbles was redoing the couch. We first checked the food situation. What kind, how much, and when. That was fine. We then had her checked for parasites. That proved negative. Then Ellen asked us if it was possible that coming into her first heat could cause Pebbles to take on destructive habits? In this case it was. Ellen knew her dog better than we did. And she thanked us for teaching her how to read her dog. After Pebbles came out of her heat, she stopped chewing.

What to Chew On

If you want to give your dog a chew toy, hard nylon type bones, heavy woven rope toys, or anything nondestructible is fine. You can also give your dog dried fruit, carrots, hard breads, or any other healthy snacks to chew on.

You don't want to give your dog or puppy any rawhides, any animal bones, skin, hooves, things that he can chew up and swallow. These treated by-products could stick in his throat or stomach. Chicken bones, lamb bones, or veal bones, are very soft and flexible and can splinter in the dog's throat, and it's good-bye dog. If a dog swallows rawhide, or hooves or pig's ears, they can get lodged in his stomach or intestines, and might come out in a couple of weeks, or your vet would be glad to remove them for you, with surgery. Rubber toys, plastic toys, or any toy with whistles and squeakers, the dog can chew these, swallow the whistles and again your vet will remove them with surgery—providing your dog hasn't choked on them first. Use caution; think things through.

The only animals in the wild that would eat skin and bones are the scavengers (vultures or hyenas) and they will only eat these leftovers when the prime cuts are gone. And we don't think your dog is a scavenger.

Note: Animals that grind their teeth down in their lifetime will eventually starve to death when their teeth are gone. So our question is, why would you want to give your dog something crunchy to chew on? It could even chip or break their teeth. In the wild, dogs, wolves, and coyotes eat only soft meats and chew around bones. Generally, the young of these species will chew on bones, but only to learn not to after breaking or chipping a tooth.

Different Methods of Confinement

More than half the battle in housebreaking is preventing a mistake. Therefore, until your dog is completely trustworthy, he should not be allowed the run of your home. Instead, you should keep him confined. A baby is not allowed to wander at will because there is too much temptation and danger. A dog that has not been housebroken should not be allowed free run either.

Confinement is the best method of housebreaking your dog, but the accepted and more conventional ways used in the past are unsatisfactory for many reasons. A gate can injure him if he gets caught in it; a cage or crate can cause psychological problems, is difficult to clean, and is not portable or convenient; a bathroom or kitchen prison is inconvenient for you and it doesn't work well because it gives your dog too much of an opportunity to get in trouble; he could get hurt by objects that might fall on him, or he could break into cabinets and swallow something poisonous or sharp. Tying him on a leash or line is unsuitable because it is too long. Your dog can become entangled in the leash and injure himself, or he could chew through it and break free. A long line or leash will not housebreak your dog—it gives him too much room, and he will go to the end of it and go to the toilet. It might even give your dog the opportunity to do damage to himself or to your property.

Crates and Cages

For decades crates and cages have been the accepted way to stop destructive habits, housebreak, and control your dog. But you pay a big price. Instead of depending on you for his security, your dog becomes dependent on a crate or a cage. This can have an insidious effect on his well-being. In case of an emergency such as a fire, an earthquake, or any disaster, instead of coming to you when he's frightened or hurt, he will run to that so-called cave security. That means hiding under a bed, or in a closet, or running away. And you could lose him, forever.

A dog is a pack animal and so he needs contact with other living creatures. Without this contact, he may become withdrawn and not grow to be an integral part of the family, and he wants to be a member of the family. Although we know that many trainers and veterinarians believe in caging or crating a dog, reasoning that dogs are cave animals and need their privacy, we believe that's a lot of nonsense. Your dog is a social creature and doesn't want to be isolated in a box any more than you would want to be isolated in a box. You see, dogs want the same things that we want: love, attention, good company, and good food. Not solitary confinement.

Having water available for your dog at all times is very important for his health and well-being. His life depends on it. Keeping your dog locked up in a cage or crate prevents him from getting to his water whenever he needs it. Even if you put a bowl of water down in his crate, there is always a chance it will be kicked over. That's one of the reasons why we won't use a cage or crate as part of our program.

By putting your dog in a crate or a cage he's not a dog anymore, he's part of the crate or cage. You can't see him, and out of sight is out of mind. He's not bonding to you or learning anything from you. He's learning to deal with his isolation.

Housebreaking with a crate or a cage could take up to a year or even longer and sometimes forever. You will never really trust your dog not to be destructive until he's an adult and then some. Teaching him to come to you becomes a major problem because of his bonding to that crate or cage instead of to you. People get lazy and rationalize how great the cave is for their cave animal, and they can end up leaving their dog in the crate for long periods of time, too long. We don't think that a cage or a crate fits in with any interior decorator's schemes. It's an eyesore. Cleaning a crate or cage isn't a welcomed chore either.

A Better Way Than the Crate or Cage: The Tether

A tether is a chain approximately eighteen inches long. A tether affords the dog owner a housebroken dog overnight, and within two weeks, he's completely housebroken. It also prevents your dog from any destructive chewing, or it breaks the chewing habit altogether if your dog happens to have been a chewer when you first got him. While you are sleeping and he is attached to this tether, he is learning how to wear a collar and a lead because a lead, in reality, is just a longer tether.

A tether gives your dog much more room and freedom than a cage or a crate does. Your dog can survey everything in his do-

main. People look for apartments and homes with high ceilings. The tether gives your dog that, the highest ceilings, higher than any cage or crate. And most important of all it is the best way to *bond your dog to you because he is sleeping right next to you*. The way it was when he was born and sleeping next to his real mother.

I have used a tether for over forty years and with great results. I developed the idea and philosophy for my tether from a combination of common sense, learning, and the understanding of how other cultures (both past and present) interacted with and taught their dogs. Dogs have always been important to people. They warned people of enemy surprise attacks, they helped hunters hunt, gatherers gather, and helped keep people warm and secure from caves to tepees to condominiums to co-ops. These dogs were tethered to their owners' leg or hand when that person slept, or were tethered next to their sleeping owner. They were tethered next to their owners when sitting, visiting, eating, and on all social occasions. The dog was part of the family. The tether was applied until that dog bonded with that person or that family. And it happened very fast. No cages, no crates, no gimmicks.

Horses are tethered, cows are tethered, all farm animals are tethered at one time or another. When you're walking your dog and he is on a lead, he is really on a long tether. The only time animals might be caged or crated is when they are being transported, if they have been injured, or if they are dangerous.

A tether should be used in two main places in your home. One is in your bedroom, and he is only to be tethered there when you're there, sleeping, reading, watching television, or whatever else you do. If you leave he leaves with you. It is a good idea to keep your dog by your bed on a rubber mat for the first couple of nights to prevent damage from any mistakes he might make. After one or two nights, you can remove the mat because he will be holding overnight. From night to morning housebreaking happens fast.

After a couple of days when you see that he is holding from night to morning, then you can put him in your bed if you want to, or you can give him a bed of his own on the floor where he was tethered, and give him some toys to make sure he is comfortable. But make sure you keep your bedroom door shut. We don't want him wandering out of the room to explore the rest of the house unsupervised.

The other main place to put him during the day should be a common area with plenty of light so he can see everything, like your living room or your kitchen. These are also good places to leave him when you go out. If you have a study or a den that you work in, then you can take him there with you, but don't leave him there alone. Again, the living room or the kitchen are the only places to leave him when you are not home. The point of this process is to make sure that your dog bonds with you when you are around, and to your territory when you are out. This way he will feel secure with you and your environment and not locked up in a cage or crate.

Whatever area you choose to leave him in when you go out, it should be against a wall, except in the bedroom where it should be next to your bed, away from anything that can hurt him or that he can do damage to. *Don't put him near a heater, radiator, or electric wiring.* The areas you choose to confine him in should be out of the way of traffic, and we don't mean cars, *but not out of contact* with the rest of your household.

Important: A dog should never be confined on our tether or any other form of confinement for more than six to eight hours at any one time. To confine your dog any longer than that is cruel. If you want to know how he feels, you try not going to the bathroom for more than eight hours.

How to Use the Tether

Simply clip one end of the tether to your dog's regular buckle collar, not a *choke collar* on which he might choke himself. Take the other end of the tether and clip it to an eye hook you have placed in each of the spots you've selected to confine your dog while housebreaking. Or attach the tether to a permanent object, like the leg of a bed, table, or heavy chair, making sure that your dog cannot pull these things. Loop the tether around the object and hook it to itself, forming an adjustable loop.

I always liked to take my dogs with me when I went visiting, or to the park or to restaurants. I couldn't bring a crate to a restaurant, but I could always tie my dog's lead or tether to my chair or to a table leg, even when they were puppies. This was the most natural and easy thing to do when I couldn't keep an eye on them. The tether afforded me the additional security I needed when my attention was elsewhere, and it had already helped teach and imprint the dogs to stay with me, and be with me, whether I was sleeping, in the shower, reading, eating whatever I was doing. The dogs always wanted to be with me.

Because my dogs were so familiar with and accepted the tether, later, when I first put a collar and lead on them, they accepted the collar and lead very naturally. These accessories became second nature to them, like you or I wearing a watch.

The tether is the best way to teach and control your dog because it allows him to be around your household and yet remain under control. It is especially designed to allow your dog optimum security and comfort while confining him.

The tether cannot be chewed or become twisted so as to entangle your dog. The tether is made of metal and has free movement at the base of the clips at either end. Additionally, it is the ideal length to allow maximum freedom and mobility for your dog while he is restricted in a specific area. Your dog can lie down, sit down, drink, chew on toys, and in general act and move as naturally and as comfortably as possible. This keeps him out of mischief and is perfect for you.

Length of Time on the Tether

The length of time necessary to keep your dog confined on the tether may vary. A dog should be free for increasingly longer periods of time as he learns to behave himself. Overnight is usually the best time to first try your dog off the tether for four main reasons: He will be restricted to your bedroom, he will have gone to the bathroom before bedtime, there are no distractions, and he will learn to sleep through the night the same way you do because he learns from you.

Visiting

Even when your dog is perfectly housebroken, you will still want to watch him when you take him to any new environment, such as someone's house or apartment where he's never been before. Put the tether in your pocket; nothing is more portable or convenient. You will need the tether, just once, for any new experience. The next time you visit you won't need it. We call this a form of preventive medicine.

You do have another choice: You can put a crate or a cage on your shoulders and carry that wherever you go. We don't think you will go anywhere, and if you do we don't think you will want to bring your dog, because a crate or a cage become a major pain. Also, you might not be invited to too many places when you bring your cage or crate with you.

How to Construct a Tether

You can get all the necessary ingredients at any hardware store. You need a 2.5 millimeter welded curb chain. (For those of you who don't know what that means, which could be most of you, it's the same chain used to make a chain leash, or a chain choke collar.) It should be eighteen inches long, but no longer than that. Two "S" hooks—these are self-explanatory, for they look exactly like the letter S—and two swivel bolt snaps. For those of you who don't know what a swivel bolt snap is, and that could be most of you again, its the end of any leash that attaches to a dog's collar. Attach the chain to the bolt with the S hook, squeeze them tight with a pair of pliers, and do the same thing on the other end. Make sure all parts are strong because a chain is only as strong as it's weakest link. Do not use key rings because they will uncoil and the sharp edges could be harmful to your dog, or they might just break. For those of you who don't want to be bothered to make a tether, or feel that you can't make one, all you have to do is to buy a chain lead and cut it or tie it, but make sure it's not more than eighteen inches long.

The length of the chain is important. If it is too long you won't be able to housebreak your dog; he'll be able to go to the bathroom on one end of it and sleep on the other. You don't want it too short either. You want it just long enough so that your dog can sit, stand, and lie down. The eighteen-inch tether, stretched to its fullest length in all directions, plus the length of your dog, affords him a minimum of five feet in length by three feet in width, and height limited only by your ceiling. That's more room than any cage or crate. Your dog can now have a clear view of the world around him. And when your dog is tethered by your bed at night he can see you, hear you, smell you and touch you. You can also reach down and touch him. This will bond him to you, not to a cage or crate. If your adult dog is a large or giant breed, then add twelve inches to the length of the tether.

The Cardboard Match Trick

The dog's real mother teaches her puppies where to go and when to go to the bathroom by licking her puppies' behinds to stimulate them. We wouldn't do that, we couldn't do that, you wouldn't do that, and we wouldn't ask you to do that. We like to use a cardboard match as a form of suppository. Although it really doesn't work that way. What it does do is stimulate the puppy and also makes him want to push the match out in order to get rid of it. It doesn't hurt him; it is smaller than the thermometer that your veterinarian uses to take his temperature. It also will teach him to stay calm when he goes to the veterinarian to get his temperature taken during a checkup.

The match trick will help teach your dog where to go to the bathroom, and very fast. The cardboard match should be used in the morning when you get up and at night before you go to bed. Remember, it's as much for your convenience as it is a housebreaking tool for your dog. Now here's another good reason. Supposing you feed your dog, and you are going out to dinner, to the theater, or to a movie. And you are not going to be back before his last walk, at say ten-thirty. So, you match him before you leave for the theater. That way when you get home, you won't find anything unpleasant waiting for you.

Don't use the match trick in the house unless you are teaching your dog to go to the toilet in the house. Wait until you get outside. Use a paper match or two or three, depending on the size of your puppy. Do not use a wooden match because it could splinter. And no suppositories please; they can get really messy. Put the match in your mouth to wet or lubricate it, if you want, but don't try to put the match in your dog first and then wet it. An anxious and nervous client did do just this. We thought we'd pass this piece of advice on to you because that could be embarrassing if someone saw you.

Pick up the dog's tail and push the match in. It's easy, just like taking his temperature. The way this works is he will try to push the match out, and go to the bathroom. You will find that in two or three days you will be using the match half the time; in a week, only some of the time; and in a month, never. But at least your dog will be going outside, where you want him to go and when you want him to go.

How Much Room Is Enough?

Take a six-foot cotton training lead—not four, not ten—attach it to your dog's or puppy's collar, and pick a spot near your house or apartment. In the city, we like to go near a fire hydrant, because cars aren't allowed to park there, so we know there will always be a space available.

Bring the puppy to that spot. If he's made a mistake or two in the house, bring some of that paper with you; if not, don't worry. Place him down and let him use the full six feet of the leash. No more. That means he can go six feet in one direction or six feet in the opposite direction. Don't let him keep walking you. If you let him find his own spot, it might be a mile away, and then when he imprints, you might have to take him that mile even if there is a snowstorm or a hurricane. Don't use a four-foot lead because it keeps your dog too close to you and he won't feel comfortable going to the bathroom. And you will have a hard time teaching him to go outside.

We have a client who was very happy when his dog went to the bathroom in Central Park the first day he got him. But after a while this man wasn't too happy when his dog would only go to the bathroom in Central Park. You see, this person lived two miles from the park. Bring your dog as close to your home as possible, give him five minutes to make up his own mind, don't let him sit down or lie down, and keep him on his feet until he goes. If he can't make up his own mind, make up his mind for him and match him. If your dog doesn't go even with the match, then put another match or two in him. Keep in mind that what is coming out of him is much wider and much larger than what you are putting into him.

After your dog goes, clean up the mess but leave some there so he can easily recognize his turf. Praise him and bring him upstairs. If he has done both while he was out there, then you can even give him some freedom and play with him. But remember, if you play rough and get your dog excited, he's going to drink some water and want to go again. You'll have to take him out again.

Vets and experts will tell you that you shouldn't take your puppy outside until he has been fully inoculated.

A man rushed by us on the street looking anxious and upset. In his arms, tight to his chest, he was clutching a small puppy. But he had to stop at the corner for a traffic light. And he did stop, but he was still bouncing from one foot to the other. We went over and asked him if anything was wrong with the little puppy? "No," he said, "but he hasn't had all of his shots yet. I don't want to take a chance of him getting sick." The light changed and the frightened man shot off across the street with his puppy who didn't have all his shots.

Experts will tell you that if you take your dog outside before he has had all of his inoculations, he could become very ill and even die. If this were true, then you would never be able to leave your own home, nobody could come to visit you, and your dog would have to be kept away from everybody and everything in order for him to survive those first dangerous six months until he's safe to go outside. However, when you bring your puppy to his veterinarian for his puppy inoculations, you are bringing your puppy outside, and dogs at the veterinarian's office are generally getting their inoculations or are there because something is wrong with them. When you walk into your house, or anyone walks into your house, you or they are bringing things — germs — from the street home on the bottoms of shoes, or on your hands or clothes, if you've been in contact with other dogs. Not to mention dogs piled on top of each other at pet shops or bunched together at breeders. They are all in close contact with each other and they haven't all had all their shots.

You should be careful when taking your puppy outside to go to the bathroom, careful but not obsessive. If you have to wait until your puppy is fully inoculated, then you can't take your dog outside until he's six months old. By that time, he could be imprinted very strongly to going to the bathroom in your house. And in the case of a large dog, like a Great Dane or a Saint Bernard, you can have some major problems, anywhere from warped floors to ruined carpets to a smell that you will never be able to get rid of. You might even have to move out of your house. It's so easy for some expert to give you plenty of advice; they don't have to live in your house with this mess and they don't even have to clean it up.

I've worked for over forty years and with more than twenty-five thousand dogs, and by housebreaking them the way I'm showing you and by being very careful outside, you will have no problems. I've never lost a puppy yet over housebreaking, and I don't intend to either. I teach my clients' puppies to go outside immediately, from the first day they bring them home.

I'd rather you bring the puppy outside at the beginning, making sure the area that he's going to use as his bathroom is relatively clean. Remember, you want to bring him out just to go to the bathroom, not to walk all around and play. And not to be near other people or other dogs.

Just take him out and let him go to the bathroom, even if you have to put paper down in the street. It will be easier and a lot more convenient for you to teach your dog where to go outside than to let him go in your house and then break him from there and restructure him to go outside. Unless you have a small dog, and you want him to go on paper, or you have a terrace and you want your dog taught to go out on the terrace, then you teach him that way. If you are still concerned about diseases, when you bring your puppy upstairs, wash his feet off, and that's that.

Your Puppy Is Not Everyone's Play Toy

Don't allow your puppy to play or to be around other dogs until he has had all of his shots and until he is totally imprinted to you. Also, it would be a good idea not to let your puppy play with people in the street as well. If you take your child out for a walk or a ride in a carriage, do you allow every person you meet to play with your child, to hold your child, and just in general bother your child? No. We don't think so. Do not allow this to happen with your puppy. You just want your puppy to do his business and then go home.

Revenge and Spite

Charles is a small white bichon. His owner, Terry, explained to us that Charles was perfectly housebroken. Except when

Terry would leave him alone. He begged to be taken along wherever she went. But Terry used to tell Charles that she couldn't take him because she had to go to work and her boss wouldn't allow dogs.

Terry told us that her Charley basically understood but out of spite he would poop and pee at the front door, and for revenge he would climb up on her dressing table and throw everything off. Dogs don't know about revenge and spite. These wonderful emotions are reserved for human beings. All we did was change the dog food from dry to canned and reduced the amount. The spite and revenge disappeared. So did the poop and the pee.

The Scheduled Run-Through

The most practical choice in housebreaking your dog is to teach him to go to the bathroom outside. Going for walks to sniff around to see and find out what's happening in the neighborhood will be a big part of his social life. It's like you and me reading the newspapers, listening to the radio, or watching television.

A dog/puppy has to be taken out a minimum of three times a day. When you get up in the morning, between six and seven, once in the evening, around five or six, and before you go to bed at night, around ten or eleven. We don't know everyone's schedule, but this is the general plan. If you get up at ten A.M. and you go to bed at one A.M., then you should take him out when you get up. You take him out before he has his dinner. And you take him out before you go to bed. Try not to make him hold for more than eight hours at a time.

When you take your dog out in the morning, get up, get dressed, and get him right out. If he goes, fine, if he doesn't, use the match trick. Don't get up, shower, have breakfast, watch the news, then get your dog outside to go to the bathroom.

You should feed a puppy twice a day, not three times as you have been told. Once in the morning and once in the evening. Know with no uncertainty that your very young puppy will poop after he eats. For the very young puppy it will be immediately after his meals. He will go after he drinks and plays and if he is excited or frightened. So if you have been playing with him, he will want to drink some water and then go. So get him outside.

For the first few days you will have to get him out after his meals, but still get him out in the morning before he eats and before his evening meal. There is a very good reason for this. When your puppy is an adult he will be eating once a day, generally in the evening. I know I don't like to sit down for dinner and have to go to the bathroom. I like my meals in comfort. It's the same for your dog. As the days and weeks progress, he will be able to hold longer. You will have to be the judge of this. If you work at home, then you have the best of all worlds. You can take him out as many times as you want.

A Good Rule of Thumb

You can tell that your puppy might have to go to the bathroom if he is chewing nervously on his paws or toys or if he keeps flicking his tongue in and out while his mouth is closed. Sort of like the way a snake flicks his tongue. That is a very definite sign of a nervous dog, even as an adult. In this case, you can use this signal for housebreaking. Another signal that he has to go to the bathroom is the way he holds his tail. The tail isn't straight up and it isn't straight out. It's sort of like a sideways S. Don't worry, you will know, if not the first time then the next time.

After he knows where to go outside, or if you are paper-training him, you can start decreasing the number of times you have to take him out. You can start scheduling his playtimes and feeding times to fit in with your routine.

After dinner give your puppy a drink, take him to his area outside, the place where you will want him to go when he is an adult. Give him five minutes to go on his own; if he doesn't, match him. Don't clean all of it up. Leave something for him to be able to recognize his spot. If he has gone in the house prior to this, then take some of his accident down to his spot.

Before you go to bed, take him out. If he goes, great. If he doesn't, make him go by using the match trick. Then put him on his tether by your bed and go to sleep. If you want, you can reach down and touch him all night.

For those of you who can't use the match trick, confine your dog between his regular walks if he doesn't go when you take him out. You will have to take your dog out many times until he starts to get the idea to go outside and not in the house.

Once your dog is consistently doing the right thing and doesn't mess up at all in the house, he can be considered trustworthy and allowed free. But don't be too eager to let him run around your house. He might get into a habit of going where he is not supposed to and you will have to start teaching him all over again.

If your dog makes a mistake, correct him. Catching him in the act is the best way. Your dog will generally go to the bathroom when your attention is elsewhere or you aren't around. For example, you pick up the telephone, or you answer the doorbell, or you just bend down to put your shoes and socks on in the morning. Your dog watches you. He knows not to go while you are looking at him because you are always telling him how bad he is when you catch him. If you do catch him in the act, throw something at him or near him—it doesn't have to hit him—and tell him, "Stop it!" He will stop.

If you don't find him, just the mess, get a paper towel first, and then get your dog. Don't say anything, don't call him, don't say "No," just find him and drag him over to the mess by his collar, or carry him over to the mess, and not in a very nice way. Show him what he did by picking up the mess in the paper towel. Let him smell it, let him see it, then put the towel back down, give your dog a slap on the behind and let him go. You can tell him what he did wasn't nice, in your favorite choice of language, but don't yell at him and especially don't yell "No!" Also, it is not necessary to shove his nose into the mess; letting him see it is sufficient.

Even if you don't find the mess until well after the fact—that could even be days later—correct him anyway. There aren't any other dogs in the house, and you probably didn't do it, so he knows it's him. Just be sure he understands why he is being punished, and showing the mess to him will make sure he understands.

Stick to specifically scheduled walk times when your dog can go to the bathroom. First thing in the morning, last thing at night, and at least one and preferably two other times in between. Other walks can be added at the beginning if you want, but the core times should be held constant.

Remember, if you want to housebreak your dog to go outside, then don't start him off on papers in the house; otherwise, you're going to have to break him away from the papers, which you first praised him for, and that's confusing. And then you have to teach him a new behavior, breaking an old habit and restructuring a new one. This would be a puzzle even for a human being to figure out.

To put up gates across a kitchen or bathroom entrance doesn't teach your dog not to go to the toilet in your house; it only teaches him that it's all right to go in those designated rooms. What it also does is make your kitchen or bathroom not the most pleasant place for you to be because of the lingering smell and the obvious mess. Keeping all of that in mind, climbing over those gates could be a pain in the neck unless you're a Kareem Abdul-Jabbar or a Shaquille O'Neal. In that case you can just step over them. But you still risk stepping into . . . it.

Paper-Training

For paper-training follow the same steps as for housebreaking. Confine your dog using the tether, then take him to his papers at the specific times that he has to go. Have his papers in a part of your home that you will want him to use as his toilet. This should be well away from your dog's confinement spots and as far away as you can get from the places where he eats and sleeps. Remember, this should be in a place that you will want to keep as his permanent bathroom area. He should not have free access to the paper; you should take him to it at first. Then start guiding him to it until he gets the idea and goes there on his own.

If you don't guide him, then he will get his own ideas and use his own preferences, and they might be to go anywhere in the house he feels like. If this is the case, your paper will become a hit-or-miss proposition. Or it will become a game of dragging the paper around and tearing it up. We know he will do this because he watches you read the paper, fold the paper, pick the paper up, and put it down. As we explained earlier, your dog wants to imitate and learn from you, so he will use his mouth in the same way that you use your hands.

Tibby and her *New York Times*

When I would walk Tibby and Willy, Willy was never a problem. Being a little boy, he loved going outside. Tibby always took a long time, however, or many times she wouldn't want to go at all. I explained this to Paul. Without batting an eye he said, "She doesn't like to go to the bathroom in public."

I was amazed. Not just that my girl puppy was so sensitive, but how could he know that about her?

We made a Plexiglas underliner that curled up a half-inch on all four sides. It was the size of a fully opened *New York Times*. I put this plastic contraption in the spare bathroom and put a fresh section of the *Times* in it. Sometimes Arts and Leisure, sometimes Travel, or maybe the Business section to give her a little variety.

Now I walked the dogs and didn't worry about Tibby. She did like the sunshine, fresh air, and exercise. When we got home, Tibby would walk into her bathroom with her *New York Times*. I had to close the door because Willy always wanted to go in there with her and she needed to be left alone.

Willy and I waited. Willy is always very anxious when he is separated from Tibby, even for just a moment. They are very attached to one another, so he would always watch the door with great attention, ready for anything. Tibby would signal me by scratching on the door; Willy would jump up and down excitedly, and I would let her out. Needless to say, like the rest of the population, with the *New York Times*, the bathroom, and privacy, she was perfectly happy and well educated.

I was glad to find out about my sensitive little girl. But how did Paul know? I thought he must be psychic, that his Romanian Gypsy side was showing. He says, "Nonsense."

The Lockup

Mike is the proud owner of a Kerry blue terrier named Mazel, which means "good luck" in Yiddish. Mike couldn't figure out how to stop Mazel from drinking out of the toilet.

He asked other dog owners, he asked vets, he even asked his hairdresser. Everyone had an answer, but none of them worked for him. Even the simple answers like closing the bathroom door and keeping the lid of the toilet down didn't work. The door wouldn't stay closed. Mazel would simply push it open with her nose and nose her way under the lid of the toilet and have a nice cool refreshing drink.

Then one evening while watching television the idea came to Mike. A great idea, he thought, but a very bad one, he was to find out later. He hit his head with the palm of his hand and wondered aloud, "Why didn't I think of this before? It's perfect. It's so easy. I'll put a latch on the lid of the toilet and Crazy Glue it to the bowl itself, and lock it until I open it with a key. That should stop her cold. She's good but she's no Houdini." Mike hid the key anyway, just to make sure, in case there was some Houdini in her background.

A couple of nights later Mike ran into the bathroom with an uncontrollable attack of diarrhea. UH-OH, it was too late, the poor guy forgot the key-y-y-y.

What Mike should have done instead of locking up his toilet was to try to find out why Mazel was drinking so much. Eventually, he found out that the steroids his dog was getting for her skin problems made her drink lots and lots of water.

Mighty Victor

Now there was Mighty Victor, a five-month-old Great Pyrenees puppy. He weighed in at sixty-five pounds. That's a lot of puppy. His owners, Walter and Cheryl, swore that their growing-by-leaps-and-bounds puppy was putting on about ten pounds a day.

Mighty Victor was beautifully behaved and was housebroken quite fast, in just a couple of weeks. He slept in the bedroom with Walter and Cheryl, sometimes climbing into bed and sleeping with them. But lately he preferred the cool tiled bathroom floor. I guess with that wonderful warm, long, heavy white coat that was adorning his huge frame, the bed and the carpeted bedroom floor became too uncomfortably hot for him.

Mighty Vic suddenly developed a problem. Although he did

hold all night, he could never make it to the street in time to go. Actually, he couldn't get past the elevator without letting go. And a mighty dog like Vic made a mighty big puddle.

They tried everything. Stopped him from playing after eight o'clock in the evening, even took his water away before bedtime (ten-thirty), changed his food, gave him more food, gave him less food, nothing worked.

Then late one night, Cheryl woke up to a crunching sound in the living room and staring half-awake, she saw her Vic come lumbering back into the bedroom and without stopping go straight into the bathroom.

The slurping sound of water woke both of them up and startled them. "What was that?" they said. They jumped out of bed and ran into the bathroom, thinking a water pipe had burst. There they found half of the answer to Victor's morning leakage problem. He was inhaling water from his new favorite watering hole, the toilet bowl. Upon further investigation, in the living room they discovered the other half of the problem. It seems that Vic had found and been helping himself to all the pretzels in their new, big glass bowl sitting on the cocktail table.

After canning the pretzels, the problem was solved. Mighty Victor can now make it to the street with ease, no problem, the hall is dry. The salty pretzels made him guzzle lots of water. A bartender sells a lot more drinks in the same way.

When you're housebreaking your dog and everything is going great, then all of a sudden something goes wrong, don't immediately jump to conclusions and snap judgments that everything's falling apart. Because generally it isn't; your dog didn't forget what he learned. Something new has been added to the mix.

The stories above are some examples, but there are more. We've seen well-behaved dogs come back from the groomer's salon, or the veterinarian's office, or from a dog walk, or a kennel or whatever. And those well-behaved dogs have suddenly stopped behaving so well.

A black lab named Leonard was a perfect six-year-old gentleman. I had even used him in a commercial. One day, Leonard suddenly ripped down the kitchen door of his owner Louise's apartment. We later found out that a neighbor next door who didn't like dogs was teasing the dog by banging on the walls. It only happened once and Leonard has been the perfect gentleman ever since.

Even before the Good Samaritan neighbor explained what had occurred, Louise had called up her veterinarian and asked why her Leonard, after six years of being a perfect pal, had suddenly done this destruction. Her veterinarian said, "Your dog must have acute separation anxiety."

We hear this acute separation anxiety complex stuff whenever a dog does something wrong whenever he is left alone, like not being housebroken, being destructive, or barking. In fact, this is the excuse many trainers use when they are selling their training courses. This is the perfect excuse; it's easy to say and means nothing. There is always a good reason and a common sense answer as to why well-behaved dogs suddenly misbehave. If you think things through, you will come up with the answers.

Remember: Housebreaking is a very simple matter. And when we say overnight we mean exactly that. If you control the amount and kind of food you give your dog, and if you teach him a regular schedule of when and where to go to the bathroom, if you confine him with our tether when necessary, you'll find that he will be housebroken on the tether overnight, and within a week you can even leave him off his tether overnight. It's that fast. During the day, however, it will take a little longer because he is more active and he is left alone at times, which he has to get used to. But even then, within a few weeks he can be free, and the added benefit is that he will be bonded to you.

Compare our natural and quick form of housebreaking and bonding to training your dog in a crate or a cage, where it will take a minimum of months to years and maybe even forever. We've seen crates and cages become permanent fixtures in a dog's life, because these dogs have become crate-bonded dogs.

CHAPTER 6

The Basics—
Nothing to Them

**All made fast and easy:
Sit down, Lie down, Stay there, Go away,
Roll over, Bring it back, and He's in the bag**

Bunny

One couple I knew had to take a bunch of carrots to bed with them whenever they wanted to make love. They would throw these carrots on the floor as far away from the bed as they could. Their dog, who was appropriately named Bunny because she madly loved carrots, would jump off the bed, race over to get them, and eat them. The couple's lovemaking sessions were always quickies because Bunny was a very fast carrot eater.

Without a doubt, had Bunny been taught to go away or stay off the bed during these intimate times, the love life of Lee and Myrna would have lasted much longer. Of course the carrots were healthy for the dog, but that's another chapter.

Sit Down

The nucleus of most training programs is to teach the dog to "sit" and then to "stay." You are charged hundreds of dollars for your dog to learn these behaviors. Teaching your dog to sit is worth maybe about a nickel, and a wooden one at that, even if you taught your dog to sit down in both voice and hand commands and even adding different languages to the mix. Teaching this no-brainer to your dog should *only* take you a couple of minutes and with no endless practicing thereafter.

This behavior, so simple for your dog to learn and you to teach, has now evolved into a training industry, with volumes of books being written and published teaching the subject of "sit." You know, it's like writing a ten-thousand-page book on how to blow your nose.

Without the "sit" command the industry would probably lose 99 percent of all trainers and training schools. That's not to say there aren't any good trainers. There are, but they are getting harder and harder to find.

Your dog, whether you teach him yourself, take him to school, or bring a trainer into your home, will learn very quickly how to sit down and stay for you. That's a great feeling of accomplishment. But he can also learn very quickly that he only has to listen to you at practice times.

If you don't practice you might find him responding less and less to you, and you will also find that you're needing more and more practice time, until there is not enough time in the day or until you just give up trying. Your dog didn't forget how to sit down and stay there; what he did learn was he didn't have to because he knew you would eventually give up. Trainers are quick to jump on you and blame you for not practicing enough, then show you how their techniques work for them.

These techniques work for the trainers because they don't have to live with your dog and your dog doesn't have the time to find the trainer's weak points. If he did, your trainer would have the same problems you do. Your dog has to be taught to fit into your lifestyle and taught your way, by you.

For sure, you will start blaming yourself for not training correctly, and for sure, your trainer will put the blame on you. Many dog owners even shift the blame and their problems onto the dog, saying it's his lack of intelligence and referring to a dog breed intelligence list to prove their point. Don't show this list to your dog; he might eat it and then give it back to you a couple of days later rewritten in its proper form.

Civilized Setter

It was cold, the dead of winter. Snow covered the avenue. Ahead of me I could see a woman chitchatting with three friends, mostly guys. With her was her English setter, restless and edgy. As I approached I could hear it. "Sit, sit, sit," she said impatiently. As I got nearer I heard it. "Sit, sit, sit." And as I passed her I heard it. "Sit, sit, sit." "I sure am glad," I thought as I walked on, "that I don't have to sit, sit, sit, in the cold wet snow, especially with no pants on."

Two things we must point out. Number one. The dog was smarter than his owner was, because why should he sit in the wet snow? And secondly, why did this person want her dog to sit down in the first place? If it was because the dog was being a pain, then she should have stopped whatever the pain was. If the dog was jumping up on people, instead of commanding her dog to "sit" she should have asked him to stop jumping and made the dog stop jumping. If the dog was putting his nose into everybody's business, which is where a dog of this size could easily put his nose and does, she should have stopped that.

But this dog owner shouldn't have used "sit" as a cure-all for whatever her dog was doing that she didn't want. The reality was, this English setter was cold and just wanted to go home.

What we think this English setter's owner should have done was to get her cold and uncomfortable dog home and make him a nice bowl of warm chicken soup, and one for herself. You know, "It can't hoit."

English setters can be very civilized dogs. Or is it English people? We forget now.

Overrated and Overused

"Sit" is probably the most overused and overrated command in the dog's lexicon. Think about this. When would you want your dog to sit, and why? Would you want him to sit if he's jumping? No. You would want to stop him from jumping. Would you want him to sit if he's barking? I don't think so. You would want to stop him from barking.

"Sit" has also become a cure-all command when the word "no" is added to it. It then becomes the solution for confronting all your problems. Your dog pees on your rug, you run over to reprimand him. You yell at him, "No! sit! no!" If your dog is barking, jumping, pulling you, chewing your house down, or whatever, all you hear is "no, sit, no, sit, no, sit." It's enough to drive a dog to therapy.

Although this sounds ridiculous, I know from teaching for over forty years that owners do this all the time. Your dog becomes totally confused. He will start believing that "Sit!" is a punishment, and that when he hears it, he's done something bad. Don't use "sit" and "stay" as part of a reprimand. Ever!

When You Might Want Your Dog to Sit Down

In an elevator, where standing takes up too much room. In a car, where standing takes up too much room, but then he can lie down if he wants. At an obedience trial, if you are asked to sit your dog. If you want to check out one of his front paws for any reason. If you want him to shake hands, or as some people say, "Give me five or give me your paw." I'm sure there are a few other reasons, but just a few.

To be honest, it's not really a very important behavior to teach your dog, and it is something he probably doesn't enjoy doing. Oh, yes, we almost forgot, when your dog is tired, he'll sit down, just before he lies down.

In any event we will teach sit down, because after all, this is a training book, and what would a training book be without sit down?

Before Starting

You must teach your dog to come to you, first and foremost, and pay attention to you, before you teach him anything else. If you don't, then all other lessons will become only temporary ones. Eventually your dog will listen to you only when he feels like it. And we wouldn't blame him at all.

Once you have taught your dog to come to you, as you learned in the earlier chapter using our throwing technique, then sit down, lie down, stay there, and go away are taught without any practice and taught in a matter of minutes, even while blindfolded and with one hand tied behind your back. Notice that we don't use "sit"; we ask our dogs to "sit down."

Remember: Do not use one-word commands or the word "no" when working with your dog. Use a sentence. For example, "Rover, sit down." You'll notice just like every other lesson taught in this book, don't repeat yourself, be yourself, give your dog six to ten seconds to think things over, and tell him he's great after he does what you want him to do.

How to Get Your Dog to Sit Down

First, you sit down and make yourself comfortable. Call your dog over to you and ask him to "sit down." Wait ten seconds. You will find that it takes between six and ten seconds for your dog to sit down. If he does, praise him; if he doesn't, take hold of your dog's collar, push his butt down gently but firmly, tell him to "sit down," and he will.

If you're right-handed, hold the collar with your left hand. If you're left-handed hold it with your right hand. Your dog is the expert on body language, and he knows your stronger hand. This teaches him what "sit down" means.

Once he learns to sit down, then you might want to point in front of him. Don't point to his tail, there aren't any eyes back there. Just point down in the direction you want your dog to go and tell him to "sit down." Hesitate for ten seconds. If he doesn't sit down, push him down to the sitting position. He will learn very quickly that when you point down, you want him to sit down.

Give him a hug or a kiss, a treat, or all three if you want. Lesson is over. If you do this a few times, you'll be very surprised to find that your dog is sitting for you on his own.

When he sits down, either on his own or with your help, lesson is over. Do not keep doing it. It is boring for both of you. Once your dog's got it, he's got it. And if you keep practicing over and over again, he might start not liking to do this for you. Ask him to sit down only when you want him to. And don't make a big deal out of it. If he does it, fine, if he doesn't, push him down.

When you are standing and he is at your side, tell him to "sit down," point down in front of him, and give him ten seconds to think it through. If he doesn't sit down, help him by pushing his butt down. You'll see how quickly he'll follow through on this.

Transference: Different Ways to Teach the Same Thing

Once your dog learns to sit down, then you can transfer your techniques of teaching this command. Snapping your lead is another way to get your dog to sit down. For example, tell him to sit down and snap the lead back at the same time. He will sit down. Then you can just snap the lead if you want to, without saying anything, and he will sit down. Or, you can even use dif-

ferent languages—Yiddish, French, Italian, or whatever—
while you point or snap the lead, and your dog will sit down.
That way your dog will become multilingual.

This exercise we call transference. It is using a different signal to perform an already learned behavior. Transferring an already learned signal to another one that you might want to use
instead is not difficult for either you to teach or your dog to
learn.

You and your dog do not have to be stuck with only one way
to do something. If you find certain ways you have taught your
dog to be not to your liking, or limiting, then this is the way you
change them.

The old methods were to teach your dog a certain way, and
then lock his thinking into only that way. Dogs are very smart
and are capable of learning more than a hundred behaviors in
their lifetime, and are able to learn them in different ways.
This is very important. If you decide you want to teach more
complex behaviors, your dog is now ready to learn to link these
behaviors.

For example, if you want your dog to come to you, and then
you want him to come around to your left side and sit down,
you just link the behaviors. Come here, first, then you point to
the side of you, exactly where you will want him to sit down,
and he will come and do it.

At the Curb

If you want your dog to stop and sit down at a street corner,
or in an elevator, or while waiting for an elevator, and you want
him to do this automatically and without your telling him,
then don't tell him to sit down. Quietly push him to a sitting
position and then praise him when he gets there. He will learn
very quickly that that is what you want. You will be surprised. If
you tell him to sit down, he will usually only sit down when
you tell him and you will always have to tell him.

As a matter of fact, by teaching him to sit down this way, without verbalizing, you will find that you'll be making the mistakes, not him. You'll be stepping off the curb and feeling foolish because your dog will be staying at the curb. You might even have to turn around and ask him to teach you how not to step off the curb until the light changes.

But given all of this, we can understand your wanting your dog to sit down in an elevator, because he will take up less room that way. But why would he have to sit at a street corner if there is snow or ice on the ground? He could easily catch his death of cold, or at least a cold behind.

To Lie Down

Generally people teaching their dogs to lie down will first ask them to sit down. The wisdom being that teaching your dog to lie down is just an extension of sitting down, and it is an easy next move. Your dog will think otherwise. What happens is that he will anticipate your thoughts and will lie down when you ask him to sit down. Dogs are sharp cookies; they know what comes next, and jump right to the conclusion.

The way to avoid this very common problem is to teach your dog to lie down by quietly pushing him into a sitting position first, without verbalizing. Then you can teach him to lie down.

How to Teach Your Dog to Lie Down

Hold your dog by his collar, and with your other hand push him gently but firmly to a sitting position without saying anything. Gradually pull him toward the floor by his collar, exerting pressure as you need. Tell him to "lie down." Count to yourself six to ten seconds. Give him time to think over what you are asking him to do. If he starts to lie down on his own, release the pressure and praise him when he gets there.

If you find that your dog is too strong for you and you can't pull him down by his collar, then let go of his collar and pull his front legs out and push down on his shoulders so he goes to a lie-down position. Again, tell him to lie down. Praise him after he does. Remember, don't praise him until he is down. The best way is to praise him after he goes down on his own.

But if you're tired or the phone rings, push him down, hold him down, and tell him he's a "good boy." Then let him go and answer the phone or the bell or take a nap.

Standing

Another way to teach your dog to lie down is while you are standing up. Don't use this technique until your dog has learned the basic ones above.

Put your dog's six-foot training lead on him and put him by your side. Holding the end of the leash in one hand, step down approximately in the middle of it. The lead should be between the sole and the heel of your shoe, actually the arch, where you can pull it through. Push your dog to a sitting position, without saying anything, then point down in front of your dog and tell him to lie down. Give him the old six to ten seconds, and if he doesn't lie down, start pulling up on the leash, exerting steady pressure.

What should happen is that the lead will be coming down from his collar, to your shoe, underneath it, and up where you are pulling, causing him to be pulled towards the floor. This should be gradual pressure until your dog starts to lie down; in that case release the pressure, because we want him to go down on his own. But don't drop the leash. If he doesn't lie down and he fights you, keep exerting the pressure until your dog does lie down. If you find you can't get him down this way, then push down on his shoulders until he lies down.

By hook or by crook, he must lie down for you before you praise him. Whatever you do, complete the lesson before stopping. If you don't and he learns that to fight you means to beat you, you'll never be able to get him to completely listen to you. Anytime that you're teaching your dog anything, finish what you start and don't give up, because he won't; he is very determined.

Remember, even making him physically lie down or sit down is a success. After it's done, stop. Don't get angry or frustrated. If you do, then leave your dog alone and walk away.

All you want your dog to know is that he hasn't any choice when you ask him to do something for you. And then when he does what you want, every time you want, you will give him everything that he wants. Within reason, that is.

Some dogs have weak or injured legs. If your dog is one of those, then be careful when pushing him down. You can still push but just be careful and don't hurt him. It isn't necessary.

Once your dog has learned sit down and lie down as separate but equal behaviors, then you can combine them. You now can ask him to sit down and then lie down for you. You can even ask him to lie down and then to sit up, if that is what you want, because you have by this time taught him to follow your hand movements, your body language, and your voice instruction.

Just remember that the hand movement for sit down is halfway to the floor, lie down is pointing all the way down to the floor.

Teaching Your Dog to Stay Where You Want Him to Stay

This lesson can be learned at the same time sit down is learned. You just add "stay there" to "sit down." To first teach this behavior it's best to use a corner of a room. That way, you have more control of your dog. He won't be able to run away as easily, and the corner gives both of you a point of recognition. Place your dog in the corner. Tell him to sit down, or point down in front of him, or both. Remember, as we said before, do not point at his rear end; there are no eyes back there.

Once he is sitting tell him how good he is. Hold the palm of your hand straight out to him as if you were a policeman stopping traffic and, tell him to "stay there." Turn around and walk away a few feet, but keep the palm of your hand facing him, even when your arm is at your side. Turn back to him again, hold your palm out toward him, and tell him, "Good boy, stay there." Do not say, "Stay there, good boy." Your dog might think the lesson is over and leave.

You might ask, "What's the difference?" The difference might seem minuscule to you, but to your dog it can be the difference between staying where you want him and not staying there. Your dog might think "Good boy" means he doesn't have to stay where he is. And this happens quite frequently.

The reason this happens frequently is this: Generally when people teach their dogs to do something and the dog does it, the owner gets so excited with the accomplishment that he happily praises his dog, "Gooood boooy!" The dog is so happy and excited to see his owner so happy and excited that he stops doing what he is supposed to do. So tell him "Good boy!" first, then tell him, "Stay there," because the "stay there" command is still in play and he must stay there until he is released. Walk over to him, touch him, praise him, and then if you want, you can release him. Use whatever release word you like. We like the words, "Okay, good-bye, so long."

When you turn around to come back to your dog, and he's gone, or if he just isn't staying where you put him, go and get him quietly, not a word, and bring him back to the designated corner. Start over again.

A lesson is over and *successful* even if you had to hold your dog in position and then release him. If the phone rings or the bell rings or you're just tired or there is some other distraction that you have to deal with while in the middle of a lesson, hold him in his staying position, tell him how good he is, and then release him. You must finish what you start when working with your dog or he will learn very quickly not to listen to you!

You can now give your dog his treat, praise, or both. I like to give my dog some ice cream, or any good people food. Something that you'll like, I'm sure he'll like.

Don't turn to your dog as you're leaving your house and tell him to "stay there." He might just do that and stay for an hour after you're gone and then he will walk away. So the next time you want him to stay somewhere he will remember that you don't really mean what you're saying.

Getting Him to Go Away, Get Out, or Just Leave

All the behaviors up until now have been ones that would enhance your dog's security and his bonding with you. Coming to you, staying with you, following you, walking with you, sitting with you, all of these.

When you asked him to "stay there" and you walked away, that was the first time your dog had to stay someplace without you and trust that he would be secure by himself.

This wasn't difficult because when he stayed on the tether, he learned this. But now, you are teaching him to go away, which is diametrically opposed to everything he has learned so far. To put it a simpler way, you are asking him to leave while you stay put.

This is a very important behavior for your dog to learn because if you ever want to teach him to retrieve something, then you will have to point in a direction and he's going to have to go out to find it. Chasing a Frisbee, following a scent, or if you want to teach him to jump certain objects such as a bench or obstacles at obedience trials, he has to be directed away from you.

Some of our client's dogs retrieve magazines, not just any magazines, but the ones of their owner's choice. If a *Time* and a *Newsweek* are lying around and you want one of them, your dog will get the one that he was asked to get. This will be done by either voice or hand point. This is the way we trained you in this book. Some of our clients' dogs will even distinguish a twenty-dollar bill from a one-dollar bill. Just ask our editor, he saw it happen.

Getting Him to Move Away from You and Go in Another Direction

Stand up and face your dog. Point in the direction you want him to go. It's a good idea to start off in one room and make him leave using the open doorframe as the boundary. So when he crosses that doorway, he can then be praised for successfully doing what he was asked.

Slowly walk into your dog, not to hurt him but just to make him move away from you and in the direction you want him to go. Always keep pointing. If your dog starts to move in the direction you want him to go, then you stop. Remember, you want him to eventually do this on his own, when you point or ask him to go. You could get lucky and he might go all the way out across the doorway. If he does, hold your hand up as if stopping traffic, as if you were telling him to stay, and quickly say, "Good boy! Stay there." Then go to him, touch him, and tell him how good he is, tell him okay, lesson is over. But then again, that's if you're lucky. Real lucky.

If he stops you move into him. Even if you have to push him all-l-l the way out of the room, the minute he crosses the door threshold, tell him how good he is, praise him, and stop. It's the same as telling him to stay anywhere.

If when you are pushing him out of the room he tries to go around you, don't let him succeed. If you have to reach down and pull him by the collar and push him out of the room, then do that. The end result has to be you asking him to leave, and him leaving.

Don't keep working your dog until it gets boring for him, or for you. You want it to be fun. Work it once or twice, even if you have to take him out of the room by hand in order to end the lesson.

At first, don't ask your dog to leave a room where he has to move a great distance. The beginning should be simple and direct. Don't send him more than five or ten feet. Teach him inside, of course, under controlled conditions, until your dog gets the idea. When you have control, you can take him outside. But you must have control; otherwise, if you tell him to go, he might go and come back a few hours later.

Remember, we've said this before and we will keep on saying it: None of these lessons should be taught until your dog has learned to come to you.

Getting Your Dog to Bring Something to You

Once your dog has learned to sit down, lie down, and go away when you tell him to, you can link all of these behaviors together and form more complex ones. From the four simple behaviors that your dog learned very quickly, you are now able to control him at distances.

Ask your dog to go out a certain distance by pointing, and he will continue going away until you ask him to stop, stay there, and then maybe sit down or lie down, depending on what you want. And when he's out there, you can ask him to bring back an object.

At first your dog may be a perfect retriever, even if he is just a mutt. You throw something and he brings it back. But have you ever noticed that after you throw a ball, a Frisbee, or a stick a few times, your dog gets you to bring these things back for him? He does this by bringing back the ball or stick but dropping it further and further away from you, making you chase after him and the stick or the ball.

That is why we asked you to teach your dog to come all the way to you at the very beginning of our program. Not just near you. Making sure you touch him or his collar before you tell him he is a good boy prevents your dog from teaching you his way. The key is to first get your dog to come to you. This unlocks the door to teaching your dog many more behaviors and some very complex ones.

Another way your dog will make you play his retrieving game is to drop his ball or his stick on you when you're sleeping, reading a newspaper, or just not paying attention to him. In effect, he will annoy you until he gets his way. That is, if you let him. This is the way your dog learns to teach you. This is basic reasoning, contrary to some experts who say that dogs cannot reason.

By teaching him the basics the way you've learned them in this book, your dog knows that when you ask him to do something, he must do it for you. And he will. If he gets too ambitious, as we've explained above, you have also now learned how to stop him and make him wait until you are ready to play with him. We're not saying you have to stop him altogether from his suggestions of "Come on, let's play right now." We are just asking you to teach him to be patient and sensitive to your world.

Complex Combinations Made Easy

The only thing missing in bringing back an object is getting your dog to hold something. There are two ways to do this. The first way is to throw something for him to get. He should naturally, with excited enthusiasm, bring it back for you. Take the object in your hand and ask him to drop it. If he doesn't, just open his mouth, take it out, and tell him "Good boy." It's that simple.

The second way is to sit him down and put the stick or the ball in his mouth and make him hold it. He might hold the object the first time; that's good, praise him. If he doesn't, keep putting the object back in his mouth, time after time, until he does hold it. He has to know that he must listen to you. We like to ask our dogs to hold an object they like and are familiar with, their favorite toy or ball, but not food, please. By asking him to hold food, he might hold it for you, yes, but in his stomach. Once your dog holds an object for you, then this behavior is complete.

Getting Your Dog to Roll Over

Using the lie-down command, you then can teach your dog to roll over. Point down. When your dog lies down, move your hand down further and touch the floor in front of him. He will roll on his side. Take his favorite treat (chopped chicken liver works well; strawberry shortcake works well also, but it could become messy) and move it across his nose. Let his nose follow the food. His body should follow his nose and he will roll over to his other side.

You might want to hold him down with your other hand just in case he decides to get up rather than roll over. When he rolls to the other side, pull your hand back a little so that he has to get up to come after the treat. Give it to him and tell him how good he is. What you have done was make a circle with your hand, and that becomes the hand signal for roll over.

Linking All the Behaviors

Now, your dog will hold something for you if you ask him to. He will drop it or give it to you when you ask him to. If you throw something and then ask him to get it for you and bring it back, he will. You can vary the order of all of these behaviors. Make him sit down first and then go get an object; you can have him run out and sit down or lie down next to the object. You can get him to roll over next to the object because he's learned to do that too. Or you can even get your dog to distinguish and pick up different objects by pointing at them.

And now all of this can be taught very quickly because you are becoming a dog-smart person. At this point what you can teach your dog is limited only by your own creative abilities.

The Un-Retriever

Tony taught Sonny, his chocolate Lab, how to retrieve a ball when he was a very young puppy. Both Tony and Sonny were very proud of their successful ballplaying talents. As it happened, whenever Tony or Caroline, his wife, would step outside of their house, Sonny would bring his ball, stick, toy, or anything that he could find and put it in their hands. If they wouldn't play with him, he would jump up on them and drop the object on them. And then, if that didn't work, Sonny would assume his best "hangdog" expression look. Sonny was determined to play ball and he always got his way in the end.

Caroline, without realizing what she was doing, managed to untrain Sonny from this retrieving game. She was able to accomplish this incredible feat by kicking or throwing Sonny's ball as far away as she could and when Sonny happily bounded after it to bring it back, so she could throw it again for him, Caroline would run into the house and shut Sonny outside. Caroline said that she didn't want to get herself all messed up and dirty from that filthy, muddy, disgusting ball.

Sonny figured out that when Caroline kicked or threw his ball for him, it really meant that she was going to run into the house and lock him out. So now, when Caroline throws the ball or kicks something for Sonny, he runs right into the house and waits for Caroline to come in. To this very day Tony still can't understand why Sonny, all of a sudden and for no apparent reason, stopped retrieving and runs into the house whenever Tony throws a ball for him. Caroline won't tell him, and neither will Sonny.

The Avid Runner

Michael was a designer of women's sportswear. Harley was his harlequin Great Dane, who looked ferocious but was a big softy. They loved to go running in Central Park.

One day, while the two of them were racing up past the Ninetieth Street exit on the east side of the park, they were accosted. Suddenly, out of nowhere, a man wielding a large knife jumped out in front of them.

Michael, startled, stopped short, and stepped back, pulling Harley with him. He screamed at the man, "What's going on here? What, are you crazy!" Harley didn't know what the hell was going on and his confusion showed. He was frightened. This 140-pound lover was shaking from head to paw.

"Hey, that's a nice watch you're wearing, looks like a Rolex. Better let me have it, or else I'll cut you up but good." No surprise, the man turned out to be a mugger. Michael, with years of experience in the fashion industry, quickly sized up the man. He was an extra large–size mugger.

Recovering from his initial shock, Michael gathered up all of his five-foot three-inch frame, then yelled out as loud as he could and with as deep a voice as he could muster, "Be careful, you bastard, I'm a black belt in karate, and my dog is attack-trained, and that makes it two to one!" With that, Michael jumped back into his fighting stance with the confidence of a wild tiger. Maybe.

Harley, now thinking it's playtime, was looking for some way to get a signal from Michael that everything was copacetic. Apparently when Michael played with Harley, this is the way their game went. Harley, tail wagging, wheeled around and

SMARTER THAN YOU THINK

jumped up on Michael, knocking him to the ground. Michael, shocked, screamed at Harley, "Harley! Sit! Stay! No!" Harley did just that. He sat right on top of Michael, stayed there and licked Michael's face as he always did when the two of them played together. The XL mugger, amused by all of this, smiled, took Michael's Rolex, thanked Harley for being an able mugging assistant, and left.

Remember: When teaching your dog any behaviors, especially when you're linking them together to form more complex ones, think them through and use your common sense. Make sure that you communicate the right signals as clearly as possible so that your dog can understand exactly what you want from him. That way he won't make any wrong reads as to what you want and you won't be disappointed or discouraged. And for sure you won't end up being a Michael, a Tony, or a Caroline.

CHAPTER 7

Not So Civil Disobedience

Aggression, Barking, Biting,
Running out the door, Jumping, and more . . .
Why they occur and how to solve them

More Than a Handful

A client called us because he was having problems with his four dogs. He had two Dobermans, a boy and a girl, and two boy poodles. He wanted the two Dobermans to protect his house and family, thinking that the Dobermans would do that naturally. But they weren't protecting the family or their large house. Not only were they not protecting everybody, they were attacking the smaller poodles and starting to stalk the family children as fair game also. You could say they were working their way up the ladder of success. This client called us when the girl Doberman took his son's head in her mouth.

First of all, no dogs are born vicious or aggressive, nor will they be natural "protectors" of people and property. Dogs need to be taught these behaviors. Unless dogs are taught how to fight, they probably won't fight. They might bark and growl and protect you in that way, but they have to be taught to attack.

Dogs might also learn to bite you if and when they can get away with it, or if it is to their advantage to do so. If dogs learn that they can be just as successful by faking a fight or a bite and making a lot of noise, then that's what they'll do, and that's all they will do because they don't have to go any further. Why should they waste their energy? Dogs are just like some politicians. They will let the other guy do all the fighting and then they will take all the credit. They will only do what they have to do to get all they want and need.

Secondly, no one particular breed is better equipped in this area. There is no most dangerous dog. A vicious dog is a vicious dog. You can't say that an Akita, a German shepherd, or a Great Dane will be more or less aggressive automatically than a Chihuahua, a poodle, or a Jack Russell terrier. If any or all of these dogs are taught or learn to be aggressive or vicious, then they will be. Of all the thousands of dogs I've worked with over the years, the worst bite I ever received was from a nine-pound dog who was totally committed to what he was doing, and did it very successfully.

With this family, no one had taught the two Dobermans the rules of the house. In essence, they had no direction whatsoever. However, once we taught our basics, with the throwing technique, all the dogs started listening. When one of the Dobermans tried to grab one of the small poodles, he got a slap for his efforts and he stopped immediately. At the end of the three hours, the relationships in the house had totally changed.

These two dogs now looked on their owners and their children with the respect that "children" should have for their parents. This was the first step. Now that the family had become important to the dogs, and the owners were now parent figures to the dogs, the dogs could be taught complex behaviors. Protection was one of them, and not biting the children or the smaller poodles was another.

Teach your dog to listen to you and stay with you, and not to go to other people unless you say he can. Make him a family dog; then your dog will naturally want to protect you and your family with an uncompromising loyalty. Just as they will naturally want to protect what's theirs. This way you will have complete control of your dog and you will know him from his nose to his tail; you will know him better than we would, and better than any expert.

All-Too-Common Headlines

Aggressive dog gets loose and attacks the mailman, a child at play, another person walking their dog, or even kills a dog or a person. You see this in the news every day. No laughing matter. These are all terrifying incidents. Ones that will remain with the person or persons or dogs that were attacked forever.

And as for the owner of the aggressive or vicious dog who did this, his dog could be taken away from him and killed. He, the owner, could go to jail and lose everything he owns. And deservedly so. These violent and aggressive behaviors should never have been allowed. They should have been stopped when the dog showed the first signs of aggression. And as for people who purposely encourage their dogs' aggressive behavior, they should be in jail.

The aggressive dog wasn't born this way. He was taught to be this way, either on purpose or because the owner didn't know how to control his dog's aggressive behavior at the beginning. Owning a vicious dog is like owning a loaded gun. Actually much worse. You can put a loaded gun in a drawer. A dog, you can't. With a loaded gun, you can put its safety on, or take the bullets out. With a dog, you can't.

There was nothing in the dog's genes that said, "Hey, dog. When you come out of your mother, you are going to be ferocious and vicious." Not even the specific breeds that are used for violent confrontations are born that way. They just have the genetic abilities—the thousand-pound bite per square inch, the small compact fighting body, or the large fighting body, the ominous looks, the speed, the agility, even the reputation, which is many times a bum rap. You can breed the shape that you want but you can't breed the working machinery that you want them to become. That you have to teach.

Dogs are fast learners and very loyal companions. They want to please you no matter what your pleasures are and they all have plenty of heart. So it's up to you to know the right things to teach them.

The bad habits that your dog has picked up are his all right, but learning them was not necessarily all his fault. Your dog didn't just start behaving badly out of the blue. All of his habit patterns are learned behaviors. Yup, and he learned them by trial and error, by success and failure, but primarily by your encouragement or your neglecting to stop them. The lack of proper and constructive supervision on your part is the major culprit.

That means either you didn't know what to do, you just didn't care to control him, or you were too ready with all of the excuses. A vicious problem doesn't always look like a vicious problem at first. Sometimes it starts off looking like a cute game. For example, your dog takes one of your very expensive shoes. He walks around with it, and even brings it near you but growls when you try to take it from him. But you still can take the shoe from him. You are so glad to get it back in one piece that you didn't bother to reprimand him. Instead, you told him how good he was for giving you back your expensive shoe.

Then one day he brings that expensive shoe to you, and it has been altered by his newly acquired and successful tooth sculpture. He probably was very happy with the taste and the changes that he made in your shoe, but I don't think you were. You probably were angry and yelled at him, and he growled back at you. That's how it starts.

Your dog doesn't care that by jumping up on you for a kiss his muddy paws might change the design on your beautiful white suit. All he cares about is the kiss. He knows that by showing his affection he might get a nice treat. How can you get angry at him? Well, you can, and you should. But more than that he should have been taught right from wrong, right from the beginning. And that was not to mess up your good suit, or any suit for that matter. You can still love him and kiss him and hug him, and even give him an allowance if that is what you want. But only after he does the things for you that you like.

By being destructive at first and getting away with it, then by learning to growl, then bite playfully, and still getting away with it, your dog can very well become a bully. And it can go on to what you see in the newspapers. Not always; those are extreme cases. In any case, dogs do learn bad habits because in their minds, they are not bad habits, they are successful ones. Your dog will always look for and many times succeed in finding ways to have things his way. Like the song says, "I'll do it my way." And he will if you don't teach him your way.

In the wild, dogs learn to hunt down their food, kill it, and eat it. And that isn't a bad habit. That's survival. Since your dog is coming into your way of life he should, from the very beginning, learn your rules for his survival. He doesn't have to kill for food. He doesn't have to kill or hurt another dog to protect his territory. So he should learn to be civilized. If you can't control your dog, you always have the option of getting rid of him. What option does he have? So for his sake and existence, teach him the right way. Even if at times you have to be stronger or tougher than you want to be.

You get upset and annoyed when your dog does something you don't like. That's only natural, you're allowed. But more than that, you should do something about the problem instead of making excuses for your dog. Understand that you caused these problems by not teaching him better manners when he was a puppy, if he was a puppy when you got him. If he was an adult dog when you got him, and he already had some bad habits, then those should have been broken and restructured right away and in the right way.

Excuses and Denial

You have to be able to admit that you are having a problem with your dog before you can solve it. A major problem plaguing dog owners, and the most common one, is denial.

Many dog owners, for example, will not admit that their dog bites. What they will say is that he nips. To us a nip is a drink. When a dog puts his teeth into you, it is a bite. Nipping may be a more endearing and accepted term than biting. However, if a dog *nips* you and leaves tooth marks or holes or *bites* you and leaves tooth marks or holes, it's the same thing. A hole is a hole, a tooth mark is a tooth mark, and a rose by any other name is still a rose.

Of course it's always easier to give away a "nipping" dog than a "biting" dog. But no matter how you try to say it, your dog is learning to bite. It works this way. The first nip or bite might happen because your dog is frightened or it could happen accidentally while playing with him. But whichever way it happened, your dog learned that by nipping or biting he gets his way.

Another excuse is, my dog tore up the house and peed and pooped everywhere and wouldn't stop barking because he was suffering from (a) an acute separation anxiety complex, or (b) he was angry at me because I left him alone. And this was his way of getting even.

Still another is, my dog is only aggressive with girl dogs, boy dogs, small dogs, big dogs, or just any dog that looks at him wrong. He's only aggressive with house guests, strangers, children, the mailman, men, or women. The rest of the time he's never aggressive. So he has no problem. All I have to do is keep the whole world away from him. And then he's fine.

If dog owners do admit that there is a problem, then they might use the abuse excuse. That is, that because the dog was abused, that's why he bites, that's why he's destructive, and that's why he has all of these antisocial behaviors. Professor Alan Dershowitz of Harvard University wrote a book called *The Abuse Excuse* about people who commit crimes and use the excuse that they did it because they were abused.

So because their dog was abused he can't be disciplined or trained properly. We hear it all the time. "My dog, or my cat, or my bird, has been abused. That's why he behaves this way." You don't know if this is true or not. This is just what you're told when you adopt or are given a dog. Or this is what some people surmise when their dogs misbehave. This is a great big excuse. Yes, it is true dogs can be abused. Just as it's true people can be abused. Don't use the abuse excuse to justify having a dog that's out of control. This excuse will only work if your dog can afford a good lawyer.

All of these excuses lead to major problems. The one problem that bothers us the most is that the dogs are many times given away. And unlike people, they can't even tell us what really happened and these "giveaway" dogs might become dead dogs.

Aggression: Three Types, and Both Sexes Are Good at It

Dogs aren't born aggressive; they learn this behavior. People aren't born aggressive; they learn. But dogs and people both learn very early on what behavior will suit them. Think of a child who throws a temper tantrum everytime he wants to get his way. And if he gets his way, he's learned a successful working formula that he will use as long as he can get away with it.

Fighting is the most direct and final aggression. A dog will aggressively attack another dog or even a person to establish dominance. If he wins, it's over. Mounting another dog of the same sex or even a person is another form of aggression and intimidation. The third way a dog asserts his dominance is by urinating.

This is also the way a dog will claim and mark off a territory, and it is the most common of the three because it takes little effort on the dog's part and he can intimidate and claim as much territory as his bladder allows. And he can do this one with a smile. In this form your dog can even claim you as his without your realizing it until much later. But for him it's a safe bet, because he doesn't have to worry about getting hurt. The only drawback here is that it's the least permanent of the three ways, and can be washed away by a very strong soap.

We had a client who owned a ranch and a wine vineyard in California. He hired us because his dog was killing the local wildlife, including his cattle. Not just calves but adult cattle. It seemed his four-year-old female German shepherd had put a gang of local dogs together and led them on hunting parties. We don't know where she learned how to kill; it must have been by trial and error. Her learning process must have been terrible for the animals that were being killed in her practice sessions. In this case we solved the problem in three ways.

One was employing the throwing technique, teaching her to come back and stay with her owner. If she did show an interest in any animal, something would be thrown at her until she left that animal alone. Second, she was not allowed outdoors on her own anymore. And third, we changed her diet to people food. We figured that a nice home-cooked meal would taste much better than her former meal on the hoof. This new food source was much easier for her to get. She loved her new food. It's now been three years, and there haven't been any more killing problems.

Biting the Hand That Feeds Him

Why not? If he can get away with it.

Believe it or not, some experts actually say that if your dog bites you, you should bite him back. That's poppycock. Some experts believe that if your dog bites you, you should yell "No!" as loudly and as strongly as you can. That's poppycock. If your dog bites you, you should give him a good slap and tell him not to do it again. Ever. He'll stop.

The first time that your dog nips or bites could occur when you are playing. Your dog uses his mouth in the same way you use your hands, so when your dog chews on your hand, he isn't teething, mouthing, or nipping. Even if it's in a playful way and there is not much pressure. You'll find as your dog plays with you this way, and if you allow it to continue, the pressure will get to be more and more and more. He's testing the waters to see what it would take to get you to back off, which means to control you. It's the same way a dog would attempt to dominate or intimidate another dog.

When puppies play with other puppies, or when dogs play with other dogs, they play fight. They don't play Monopoly or cards, they play fight. They push, jump on, or bite as hard as they have to to establish their dominance. If they win, they are the top dog; if they lose, they are just one of the gang to be intimidated and controlled by the tougher dogs.

If you stop this habit pattern at the beginning, it will be much easier for both you and your dog. If you let this "game" go on, and you do not take it seriously, you might regret it later. As your dog bites harder, and he will, and he sees that he can get more control over you, you could have a biter on your hands. When he becomes a biting dog, two things will happen. The first one is that you will give him away because you are frightened of him. Frightened for yourself or for your family. The other one is you might keep him but not live a too comfortable life with your loaded gun running around for fifteen years. There is another option, which is what we would do, and that is to stop him from biting. Period.

If your dog is mouthing, or playing with your hand, you can allow this to go as far as you want, and stop it when you feel it's gone far enough. This way you can also have the luxury of having your dog hold your hand without biting it. The same way a mother dog would hold her babies. She knows how much pressure she can apply. And your dog will learn how much pressure he can apply to your hands without upsetting you.

How to Teach Your Dog Pressure Control

Your dog has your hand in his mouth. You feel he's putting a little too much pressure on his play bite. Leave that hand where it is; don't pull it out, for you could get bit. With your other hand slap the side of his mouth, and tell him to stop it, or that's enough, or whatever else you feel comfortable saying. A good rule of thumb is not to slap him on top of his mouth or underneath it because you could be pushing his teeth into your hand. Your dog must release your hand. If he does, tell him how good he is. If he doesn't, slap him again, until he does stop. If you have to do it harder, then do it harder. But he must back away from your hand. After you physically tell him to stop biting your hand, hesitate, let him think it through. It does take a few seconds for him to make up his mind and understand what you are trying to tell him.

This is the way he learns to be gentle in his bite. Once he's released your hand, offer it to him again. He might hold it gently, he might kiss it, or he might just look at it. But whatever he does, his decision should be an acceptable one to you. Tell him how good he is. Remember your dog shouldn't bite you. If he bites you again, stop him again.

This works very quickly. It's more humane than making excuses for your dog, giving him away, making him wear a muzzle for the rest of his life, or for you and your family to be living with your dog in an uncertain environment.

Muzzling your dog will only stop your dog from biting when the muzzle is on him. When it's not on him, he'll bite. We're human, so we might forget sometimes to put on his muzzle and he'll bite. More important than that, your dog for sure will learn to prevent you from muzzling him, because he doesn't like it. He might use his only weapon, a nice bite, to stop you. When you are afraid to put the muzzle on him, what do you do next?

When people come to visit and your dog is wearing a muzzle, your company might be uncomfortable, especially if they see your dog trying to get his muzzle off, and he can work his way out of a muzzle. Last but not least, let's talk about inhumane. It's very inhumane to keep a muzzle on your dog. It's like you having to walk around with handcuffs or your hands tied behind your back, because their mouth is as important to them as your hands are to you. A muzzle will make your dog feel insecure and defenseless.

But by far the most cruel way, which seems to be the way many experts and trainers employ to deal with an aggressive dog, is a choke hanging. This technique is to keep a leash on your dog and when he goes to bite you or anyone else, you quickly pick the leash up in the air and hang him until he stops. It is a horrible way to try to break this habit, and you could be teaching your dog to bite whenever you try to put a leash on him.

We can see holding the leash so the dog doesn't bite you, but that's it. Not choking him. And even this will only stop the problem when you are hanging him. The dog has to stop biting, period—with or without a leash.

If your dog tries to bite or becomes aggressive with other people, you can throw a magazine or a sneaker at him. When it hits, he will stop. Then you can tell him how good he is for not being aggressive. Our throwing technique will give you full control of your dog from the very beginning, and he can never test you and win.

The worst thing to do is to do nothing. If you do nothing then you don't solve the problem. It will only get worse because the dog will continue to get better at what he's doing. He's not doing nothing, he's doing something.

The second worse thing to do is to make excuses, like my dog bit me but it was my fault. Whether it's your fault or not it really doesn't matter, he shouldn't bite. There's no excuse for people being violent, or for dogs being violent. In the dog's case a good slap on the behind isn't violent. It solves the problem.

This might seem to be very harsh, hitting or slapping. But so is biting, and the consequences of biting can be far worse. This is truly the area where you physically and strongly must teach your dog the limits. Of course, it all will depend on what stage of development your dog's aggression has reached. For example, with a little puppy you can just tap him with your finger and he will listen to you. But you can't use your finger to tap a two-hundred-pound Great Dane that is looking to get a piece of you. And we don't mean on a contract.

As for your finger, once you have a partition between you and the Great Dane, and bulletproof glass, then by holding your index finger straight up in the air you can show him who you really are.

Another Way a Dog Learns to Bite

"Uh, oh! Here comes that tail-pulling, ear-biting family visiting us again. I guess this time I'm going to be called Jaws when they leave." That's Fido talking.

It's not a good idea to allow your dog to be everyone's play toy, especially if they play rough and wild with him. This type of atmosphere could harm your dog or even teach him how to bite at first in self-defense, and then when he sees how successful he is, well, then you draw your own conclusions.

Children who play rough and wildly with dogs, or parents who allow their children to play rough and unsupervised with them, can be inviting trouble and injury to the dog, the child, or both of them. It's a good idea, just as you would stop a dog from biting and hurting a person, that you stop your child, or anyone for that matter, from hurting your dog. Because it's not just dogs who are aggressive. Your dog is a living, breathing creature and your responsibility to take care of. He is not just everyone's play toy.

A Dog Who Bites Out of Fear

The fear biter starts out as a dog that will bite only if he is cornered, frightened, or hasn't any other way of communicating his feelings. But as soon as this dog sees that by biting he will get his way, then the words "fear biter" become just words. Now, this dog is a biting dog.

For a dog that initially starts biting out of fear, you don't solve the problem by just fighting back. You have to also get him to trust you. Our throwing technique is custom made for this particular type of problem. Step back and throw something. Don't get in there with your hands. Chances are you will get bit, for he is faster than you are.

Remember, *do not corner this dog, or any dog, for that matter*. Give him a chance to go away or to come to you. Let him know that first of all he is not allowed to bite you, and that you can and will defend yourself. The throwing technique will take care of that without anybody being bit or hurt, including the dog.

Secondly, once you throw and the confrontation is broken, then two things will happen. Either he will walk away or he will come to you. If he comes to you, give him a treat or praise him. Make the treat something really good. Not dog food.

If your dog walks away, you can also give him a treat. You can toss it to him, walk over and give it to him, or you can just drop it in front of him or near him. Don't call him to you, don't walk up behind him, and don't corner him. Leave him alone, and let him think things through.

If you throw something to stop a dog from biting, don't call him. You want to stop the biting habit; you're not interested in whether he comes to you or goes off to sulk somewhere. You must wait about five or ten minutes before you ask him to do something constructive for you. You might feel bad for what you've just done. I know we would; nobody likes to have a major confrontation. But you must wait for five or ten minutes before offering your dog a treat or praise.

The reason you wait five to ten minutes before offering your dog his treat or other reward is that you don't want to confuse him; you don't want him to think that he's being rewarded for being bad or punished. The time span gives you both a chance to think things over and cool down. This is most important.

Trust comes over time. Be consistent. Let your dog learn that you are really his friend. And hopefully the best friend he'll ever have. If you know for certain that your dog has been abused and that's why he's biting, then the trust takes even more time. Be patient. But you can't let him take advantage of you no matter what.

The Dog You Don't Know

Just because a dog looks cute and cuddly and wags his tail at you doesn't mean you should walk right over to play with him. You should ask the owner's permission first, out of respect. You wouldn't walk over to a baby in a baby carriage and pick him up or touch him unless you were given the okay.

Secondly, the dog could be wagging his tail and smiling at

you just to get you to come close enough to him so that he can get a real good well-placed bite out of you, with as little effort as possible on his part. We've seen animals that have killed other animals and were wagging their tails and smiling as they did so.

Getting Rid of the Competition: Dogs Fighting Dogs

The Scullys have three cavalier King Charles spaniels. Henry, the oldest of the two boy dogs, is two years old, and quite a bully. Then there's Red, the younger one, almost a year old and a good-natured little guy. Last but not least, the undisputed leader of the pack and the smartest is Georgia, the three-year-old girl dog.

Henry was attacking little Red, and the fights were starting to get very nasty. It wasn't always this way; as a matter of fact, they all used to get along quite well and played together beautifully. The three of them used to be a pleasure to behold. They looked like a single wave, running side by side, as if they were attached to each other.

But now it's teeth-snapping and hair-flying time between Henry and Red. Karen Scully called me and asked how to stop the dogs from fighting. If nothing could be done, then one of them would have to go—she couldn't take it anymore. Karen started to get emotional at the dismal prospect of having to give up one of her dogs.

I had worked with these little dogs. They were good dogs. I had to see this for myself. There wasn't any reason for them to start fighting at this stage of the game.

The Scullys' son Norman had recently come home from college for spring break. He liked his dogs and enjoyed playing games with them, especially in the mornings, when they ran into his room to wake him up.

However, this time home, Norman had devised a new game for the dogs to play. It was a retrieving game. He would throw a ball across his room for the dogs to chase and then bring back to him, and reward the winner with a piece of his buttered bagel. Norman, a fair man, then gave some of his bagel to the other two dogs. Georgia learned very quickly that she would get a piece of buttered bagel even if she didn't chase the dumb ball, so she didn't bother.

But for the boys it was a different story. The competition was fierce. They would try and beat each other to the ball and win Norman's favor. And I guess also to get the first bite of the bagel.

Red, the little guy, was faster. He would always get to it first. Henry, older and stronger, couldn't beat Red to the ball, so he decided to beat Red up and intimidate him instead. He would then grab the ball from Red and give it to Norman.

It worked. Red put up a valiant fight, but it was to no avail. He would lose. The fights got worse. It might have started as a simple game, but Red was in danger of being hurt very badly. This escalated, and now they fought over everything. Even a stare turned into a fight. The dogs had to be separated and kept apart in different rooms. Norman didn't realize what he had done.

Norman felt that if one of the dogs had to go, it should be Red, because Henry had been there first. Frank, Karen's husband, wouldn't accept that. He liked Red, he liked Red a lot.

I explained that the fighting problem between the two dogs was caused by the competitive game, which was not just a game to them. I also reminded Norman that he was the younger of two brothers, and when they got into bad fights, did his parents entertain the thought of giving him away?

He looked at me and laughed. He said, "That's why you came here? Just to tell me that?" I said, "No, I'm here to stop the dogs from fighting." I did. The throwing technique worked real fast.

You can have as many dogs as you want, as many dogs of the

same sex as you want, you can play competitive games with them if you want, but when one of your dogs decides to hurt or bully another one, you must step in and physically and immediately stop the aggressor. Norman had not done this. So, he had unwittingly encouraged the fighting between the two dogs to continue, to get worse, to get out of hand, and finally, to be downright dangerous.

Generally, a good slap on the behind will stop a fight. If the dogs are fighting at a distance from you, then throwing a magazine or your sneaker will stop the fight. Make sure, though, that you stop it. Not by just taking the aggressor and walking away, or picking the other dog up and putting him in a cage, but make sure you stop the fight. These dogs have to learn that they can't just tear each other up. Some people feel that the dogs should work out their own problems. We don't think a missing ear or plenty of stitches is the answer to working out a problem.

If you own other pets, a cat or a parrot, for example, and your dog is annoying or intimidating them, or vice versa, you treat the problem in the same way. Whoever is being the aggressor gets it. Then all of your pets can relax and rely on you to handle all security and social problems.

I have a friend who owns a farm with all kinds of animals: dogs, peacocks, cats, deer, chickens, geese, horses, and a donkey. All the animals get along just fine without fighting or hurting each other because my friend Susan rules the roost. And, p.s., they all adore her.

The Doctor's Patience

Dr. Ann Lynn, a psychologist, lives and works in her three-bedroom apartment on the top floor of a prewar building on the West Side of Manhattan. Her office consists of a pleasant waiting room and a separate area where she sees patients. The apartment is sunny with skylights throughout and a comfortable terrace. Dr. Lynn takes advantage of this sunlight with an exotic flora and fauna collection. Sharing the apartment with Dr. Lynn is Patience, her beautiful, black-spotted, slim-waisted Dalmatian.

What's wrong with this picture? Well, Patience is beautiful, yes, but also obnoxious, self-centered, domineering, and to put it bluntly, spoiled rotten. She is totally out of control in spite of all Dr. Lynn's therapy. But on the other hand, Patience is a very happy Dalmatian because of the way she has successfully trained her doctor.

Dr. Lynn was at wit's end. Patience was stopping her from working. Whenever the doorbell rang, she barked incessantly, and when the doctor's patients came through the door, Patience attacked them. Lynn explained that she couldn't shut the dog in any of the rooms because Patience destroyed everything. And when she was allowed in the office, she ran up over the backs of the couch and chairs, jumping in Lynn's lap, jumping in the laps of the patients, sometimes biting them and other times peeing on them, depending on her mood.

As if that were not enough, "What about my love life!" Lynn screamed. "Patience will not leave my boyfriend alone when I'm in bed with him. She'll pull the covers off us, then jump in between us, growling at me, then cuddling with him, hugging and kissing him." Lynn confessed reluctantly, "I really think my boyfriend likes it this way. And when I try to keep Patience out of my bedroom or my office, she makes such a racket that the neighbors think I'm killing my dog when in fact my dog is killing me."

Barking at the Bell or Any Incessant or Annoying Barking

We get many calls from dog owners who are having problems with their landlords, with other tenants, and in some cases even facing eviction from their apartments because their dogs are always barking. Either they are barking when no one is home, when the doorbell rings, or just incessantly, for no apparent reason.

Barking can be solved very quickly with the throwing technique. If your dog barks when the bell rings, when somebody is knocking at the door, or when the phone rings, all you have to do is take a magazine, toss it at him or in his direction, and tell him to stop. He will. Because he was trained with our throwing technique. The only difference here is, we are not throwing to get him to come to us, we are throwing to stop a problem, the barking. So make sure you don't call him. Let him figure out what he wants to do other than bark. When he does, praise him. If he barks again, repeat the procedure. You will be surprised at how fast he stops his barking. We would say it should happen within a couple of minutes.

When Barking Might Be Good, and How to Make Your Dog Bark As Many Times As You Want

Sometimes dogs will bark to alert or warn you of something. That's good barking and should be encouraged. But you also have to teach him when to stop when enough is enough. If you teach your dog not to bark at all, you might be stopping something that's beneficial to both of you. Something that you might later regret.

You can teach your dog to bark three or four times or as many times as you want him to, and then you can stop him. It isn't confusing at all. This is done by letting your dog bark the specified number of times that you want him to, then tell him how good he is for barking. Then stop him by saying "That's enough" or whatever you like to say as a stopping signal. If he stops barking, tell him how good he is; if he doesn't stop, throw something. He will smell what you threw and know that the flying object came from you. He will stop barking. Tell him how good he is. He now has two new choices. He will either come to you or he won't. This shouldn't make any difference to you. But he will stop barking. If it was the pizza delivery man that he was barking at, when he stops barking, then you can give him some of your fresh, hot pizza.

If your dog barks when you leave your apartment, take a magazine with you when you go out and close the door behind you. You'll hear the barking. Open the door, throw the magazine at him, and tell him to be quiet, and then leave. You'll be surprised at how quickly this works. If he barks again, go back and repeat it until he stops. Some dog owners find that their dog waits until he hears the elevator coming or leaving before he starts his barking. So even if you don't hear your dog barking when you leave, ring for your elevator, but don't get on it. If your dog starts barking, then go back and repeat the process.

Remember, this will only work if you teach your dog about the throwing technique, and that is, to come to you first, before you use this for breaking any bad habits. Otherwise, if you don't teach your dog about the throwing technique and to come to you, it still might work anyway, but it would only be a temporary solution, and to us that is no solution at all.

You don't have to leave music or the television on for him. You probably won't know his taste in these different media until you have him around for a while. An afterthought: If you find that your dog does like particular television shows or particular selections of music, there is nothing wrong with that and it isn't rare. I know a dog that will sit by the television set even if it isn't on, on a Sunday evening close to eight o'clock, expecting his owner to put on the *Nature* series.

Leaving a television set playing to keep your dog company could work against you. What if your dog doesn't like the program you choose for him? These programs are designed for your entertainment, not his. So the sounds could be annoying to him, and he will complain in the only ways he knows how, by barking, howling, and scratching.

Some people try to stop a barking problem by using a collar with a high-pitched noise, thinking that it won't hurt their dog and that it is humane. This isn't exactly true. The hurt comes to his sense of hearing, which is very sensitive. It does hurt.

Another method is the electric shock collar. This hurts. Put your finger in an electric socket and you will see what we mean. Or put the collar on yourself, bark, and you'll get the idea. Then, some people even go to the extreme bark stopper: They have their dog's vocal chords removed to stop a barking problem. It stops the barking problem all right, but at what price to your dog? And we don't mean money. This is the ultimate in cruel and inhumane punishment. And guess who performs the operation?

Compare all of these above solutions with just tossing a magazine at your dog. We'll let you be the judge.

The Noise Heard Around the World

Have you ever walked your dog and he barked, or another dog barked and almost at the same time an automobile alarm went off? Your probably didn't put the two together, and why should you? I didn't realize that there might be a connection either until one day I was walking with Willy.

I met a friend who was also walking her dog. We stopped to chat for a while and the dogs got into a barking match. Almost immediately, car alarms started to scream away. We decided to walk away because the alarms were so deafening, we couldn't hear ourselves think, much less talk. We walked to what we thought was a safe distance and continued our conversation.

But when the dogs again got into their conversation, more alarms started to go off. Now I was curious. I walked away, away from the deafening car alarms. Willy is a little guy who likes to talk. He always tries very hard to communicate this way, and he did start barking again. Lo and behold, more car alarms went off. Well, it was Willy's high-pitched barking that could and did set off car alarms. We never told this story until now because we thought if it did get out it could become the noise heard around the world.

Running Out the Door and Beyond

Whenever we meet a client for the first time, they are usually hanging on to their dog's collar with one hand and opening the door with the other. Or they've got their foot across the door, or someone's holding their dog, or the dog is already jumping on us or running out the door, and sometimes the dog is already long gone. With the throwing technique these problems are solved instantly.

This is the way it should be. The doorbell rings. Your dog barks once or twice, you tell him how good he is, and he stops. Then you go to answer the door. Your dog comes with you but stays a little behind you. You open the door to see who it is; your dog is still with you and still a little bit behind you. You ask whoever it is to come in, if you want them in. Your dog is still next to you, and still a little behind you. You close the door, everything is fine. That's the way it should be.

How to get it this way. The door bell rings. If your dog barks and runs to the door, you throw something at him. You walk up to the door; he should be behind you or at your side. If he isn't, and he is in front of you, throw something at him. Pick up the object and continue to the door. When you get to the door your dog should be at your side or behind you. If he is in front of you, drop the object, the magazine or whatever, down in front of him, or on him. He should then back up. If he does, tell him how good he is.

If he doesn't back up, push him out of the way or repeat the process until he does back away from the door. He will. Pick up the magazine, put it under your arm, and answer the door. Greet your company. If your dog then decides to run out the door, throw the magazine in front of him. If you throw it behind him, you will push him out the door.

If you want to, you can ask someone you know to ring your doorbell so that you can solve the problem before company comes. Once you do this, you'll be ready and experienced, and your dog will know his place. The problem is solved within fifteen minutes. Don't tell your dog that he's bad, ever. Stop the problem physically and then tell him he's good when he's good. That's called positive reinforcement.

Jumping on You or Other People

Whenever you greet or meet somebody, or if you answer your door, or even when you come into your house, your dog very happily enjoys jumping up on you or others. We guess being brought into a society of two-legged beings, he wants to be one also. So he's up on his two legs, greeting you by shaking hands, shaking your belt, or shaking your good clothes with his front paws. He should learn not to do this even though he might think he's shaking hands. We all know he isn't.

When a dog jumps up on someone, the person tries to push the dog down with their hands and looks to the dog's owner for help. The dog's owner generally says to the dog, "That's not nice" or "No!" or "Get down!" or "Bad dog." Then the dog owner apologizes to the person the dog jumped on, but meanwhile the clothing is ripped, stained, or marked for the cleaners. If you don't stop your dog from jumping, he will jump on you until he's around fourteen or fifteen years old and then Mother Nature will stop him. He'll be too tired to jump.

One of the remedies that experts recommend is for a person to pick up their knee when a dog jumps up on them. The person picking up his or her knee either does it from a stationary position or backs up, not wanting to hurt the dog. The dog sees this as a sign of weakness, something that he can take advantage of, because the person either backed up or didn't move. This confrontation comes out in the dog's favor. At this point, the dog presses the jumping aggression further. He now starts to jump up from the side, or uses the knee that's being offered as a platform to jump even higher or to get a better grip. Or he continues to jump up on the person because the knee isn't telling the dog to stop.

The way we do it is if your dog, or any dog, jumps up on you, you should pick your knee up, but when you do, you must take a step forward and into the dog, pushing him off balance. And continue walking into him, picking your knee up, as if you were walking up steps, until he stops jumping. If he decides to jump up on the side of you, then quickly turn into him. Whatever he does, you counter it by turning into him. Even if you have to turn completely around to stop him from jumping up behind you.

Continue to do this until he stops. Then you can tell him how good he is for not jumping on you. Don't say anything to him until he stops. Don't use the word "No." By just walking into him quietly, he will stop his jumping very quickly.

If the dog jumping up on you is a small dog that does not reach your knee even in his greatest jumps, then just keep walking into him the same way you would for the large dog. We call this nudging. Remember, don't just stand there and let the dog jump all over you. Always walk into him and continue nudging him until he stops jumping. Then tell him he's great. You must continue this until he stops. Do not use your hands in any way.

Nudging and walking into your dog doesn't in any way hurt him. It shouldn't hurt him and you shouldn't look to hurt him.

What the nudging does is take away something that he values greatly, his incredible balance.

Nudging is also a good way to get your dog's attention. When we are working with groups of dogs or other animals, the nudging technique works very well. We will nudge or push gently (it's the same thing) some of them out of the way to allow us to work and control the rest of the group while concentrating on certain individuals. When dogs are at play, you will notice them pushing each other around. Whether it's in a very subtle and gentle way or in a more aggressive way, they will still push or nudge each other.

If you want your dog to jump up, then encourage it and use a trigger word. Some people slap their thighs and say, "Up, come on up!" Some people enjoy their dogs being jumping jacks, jumping on them and on other people. When else can you get so much friendly attention with so little effort on your part? Your dog will greet you as if you were a long-lost friend, whether you are long lost, or have just been lost for a few minutes. So, if that is the case, then don't bother to stop him.

Asking the Same Question in Every Which Way

No matter how or what you teach your dog, no matter how simple or direct or complete your lessons are, some people just will not get it.

Betsy, a good friend of ours and a client for the last twenty-five years, not with the same dog we might add, is one of these people. She is a very successful and a very intelligent person, except when it comes to her dog. Even though Rose, her small Yorkie, is beautifully trained, Betsy cannot understand how she got that way.

For example, in the last six years, Betsy has asked me the same question about the same behavioral problem. "What do I do when my dog jumps up on me?" I told her what to do, and it worked. Two months later she asked me, "What do I do when my dog jumps up on me when I'm sitting down?" "The same thing you do when your dog jumps up on you when you're standing," I told her. Six months after that, the same question, only this time it was when Betsy was lying down. When it comes to understanding her dog, Betsy seems to have a block. Don't be a Betsy. Think things through and use your common sense.

Jumping on Furniture and Knocking Things Over

We believe that a dog—or any pet for that matter, even a pet horse—shouldn't come up on your couch, your chair, your bed, or even the kitchen table without an invitation. Some people don't mind, and that's okay with us also.

If you do mind, when your dog jumps up on the couch, take him by his collar, give him a pop on the behind, and make him get off the couch. Tell him how good he is when he gets off the couch, even if he got off it with your help. If he stays off, that's great. If he comes back up on the couch, repeat the process. Let him know that he cannot come up until he's invited. After he stays off, you then can call him back up on it. You might think this is very confusing to your dog, but it really isn't. It's quite direct, and your dog will learn very quickly what he can do and what he cannot do.

The other way to get your dog off your couch is to keep telling him to get off, begging him to get off, bribing him to get off, yelling at him to get off, shaking cans at him to get off, and pushing him off. Maybe, after a hundred or two hundred times, it might work. We doubt it.

If your dog is like a bull in a china shop, knocking over and breaking furniture, this is a very easy habit to break. All you have to do is take a chair and gently move it in his direction and nudge him with it. The idea here is to get him to get out of the way of your furniture. Same thing for the dog that continually wants to lie down, sit down, or walk in front of you when you want to walk from room to room in your house. Walk into him, gently pushing or nudging him out of the way, drop a magazine on him gently, and continue moving into your dog and nudging him out of the way. He will learn very quickly to stay out of your way.

If you get out of his way all the time, then he will always expect you to get out of his way. Sometimes, he might make a game out of it and purposely walk in front of you, sit down in front of you, or lie down in front of you, just to see how many times he can make you get out of his way. The choice is yours or the choice will be his, and his choice will not be to your liking.

For example, you are walking from point A to point B, say, from your living room to your kitchen. Your dog decides to get in your way. If you tell him to get out of the way, he might and he might not. If he does, he'll be in your way the next time and he will always be there waiting for you to tell him to get out of your way. So sometime when you're walking and the lights are out, you might not see him and you will not be able to tell him to get out of the way. Then you will trip on him, guaranteed.

Another side benefit of nudging or bumping into your dog is that it will also teach him to walk at your side when you are walking with him and not way out in front of you or across you. It certainly gets his attention.

Chewing

This habit is mostly tied in with diet, toilet-training habits, and nerves. But if your dog chews things, then take him by the collar over to what he has chewed or destroyed, show it to him, show him that you are not happy, and let him go. Do not call him to punish him. Go and get him without saying anything.

Mounting: It's Still Aggression

If your dog mounts you, he still loves you but he also loves to mount you. He wants to show you you're his property. Mounting is still aggression. If your dog mounts you, give him a slap and push him off. If you just push him off he will probably come back on and continue securing his property until it is fully secured. If he mounts anyone else in your house, company, or even another dog, stop him. Throwing also works very well. This is not a nice habit, so stop him.

The Aggressive Pee-er

This form of aggression, even though it's the least threatening, still shouldn't be tolerated. This kind of peeing isn't an accident; it's being done on purpose. So stop it. It generally occurs when a dog marks off his turf, but we don't think your home should be part of this turf. Remember, if you have a boy dog he will compete with all the other boys in your household. That includes cats, people, and even parrots. And all the girls in the household will be considered the prize. That includes the girl parrot also, if you have one. It's vice versa if you own a girl dog. Then all the boys in the household become the prize, including the parrot.

It happens this way. At first your dog will pee in out-of-the-way places. As he builds up confidence in his markings, he will move on to the areas that you frequent most: the bedroom, all around the bed, the living room, all around the couches, and so forth and so on.

This form of aggression is very easy to stop if you catch it in the beginning. But if you let it build up—we mean the act itself, not the amount of the marker—it then becomes a little more difficult. But still it can be stopped. It doesn't matter when you find his signature. But when you do find the markings, don't call your dog over to what he did. Go and get him, don't say anything to him, quietly take him by his collar, and drag him over to what he has left for you and wipe it up with a paper towel.

Let him see you wiping it up, then put the paper to his nose to give him a closer look and smell of what he has done. Give him a slap on the behind and let him go. At this point, you can use any choice words you want to as long as you use a complete sentence.

This process can be used even if you find his markings two weeks later, because the markings are an acid, uric acid to be exact, and acid if not cleaned up will become his permanent marker. Just the way you sign things with pen and ink, it's permanent. So, even if you find the mess a year later, you can still punish him; he knows that it is his. As a matter of fact, he will smell what he did from time to time and remember the lesson you taught him: not to do that again.

If you see your dog urinating in front of you or you just happen to glance over and see him in the act, then throw something at him. He'll stop. But then go through the process as if you didn't catch him in the act.

He's like a Child

When you do scold your dog, whether physically or vocally, don't allow him to go over to someone else for any reason at all. If he does, then go and get him and take him away from that person. He must listen to you, and only you. Especially when he's being taught what to do or what not to do.

Once he has learned whatever you want to teach him, then he can go to whomever, as long as you tell him that it is okay.

But he shouldn't go to anyone until you do give him the okay. This is not difficult to achieve as long as you start out by not allowing him to go to anybody while you are bonding with him and teaching him the rules.

When we were kids, and one of our parents would scold us or discipline us for any reason, the other parent wouldn't interfere. We all know that people will play people against people, children will play their parents against one another, siblings will play siblings against one another, even friends will play friends against one another. We want to avoid your dog going to someone else and playing them against you.

The Submissive or Happy Pee-er

When you open your door and say "Hi!" to your dog and he squats and pees, he's a happy pee-er. Some call it submissive, we call it happy. Your friends come over to visit, they smile and touch him, he squats and pees, he's a happy pee-er. Some call it submissive. We call him a happy pee-er. Whenever someone looks at him and he looks back, or somebody offers him a treat and he smiles, no matter what happens, whenever he's touched or looked at he squats and pees. Or rolls over and pees. No question about it, he's a happy pee-er.

It's easy to stop this. Whenever your happy pee-er pees, quietly take him by the collar, give him a little pop or tap on his behind to let him know you're not happy with his happiness. But don't be too firm with him. This isn't an aggressive act. Then let him go, get yourself a paper towel, and take the towel and your dog back to the spot where the happy pee is. Don't say anything to him, just let him see you wiping it up while you hold him by his collar, show it to him, give him another pop or tap, and let him run away.

If you feel uncomfortable or bad because of what you did, about five minutes later go get him, pick him up, and hug him and kiss him, but if he pees happily, repeat the entire process. In a few days your happy pee-er will happily pee no more.

If you think your happy pee-er is really a nervous pee-er, trust your instincts, you could be right. In any case treat it in the same way by using the happy pee-er technique.

Caution: If you are teaching your happy pee-er to come to you, or any other lessons, and he happily pees while you are doing this, ignore it, finish what you are teaching him, then let him go. Go get him ten or fifteen minutes later and correct the happy pee problem. He will still remember because he remembers what's his.

Someone Else's Dog Isn't All That He Should Be

You have a perfect dog. He listens to you, stays with you, walks without a leash, has been taught to respect and leave other dogs and other people alone. Is this the end of your problems? Unfortunately not.

What do you do when you and your perfect dog are suddenly confronted by a surprise attack from someone else's not-so-perfect dog? This attack can be anything from another dog just growling at your dog, trying to get him to play or annoying him, to an actual all-out assault. Now it will be up to you to control the situation and protect the both of you. Your dog and yourself.

Keep in mind that even a man-eating shark doesn't go directly into an attack. They test their adversaries first. That's why a shark might bump or nudge you first, and then either leave you alone or attack. Most predators want to be totally sure of their own safety. They want to make sure before they attack their prey that whatever they are going after cannot turn the tables on them. They're smart.

And so it is with a dog bothering you. First, he will try to come between you and your dog and try to push your dog away from you so that he can get at him better. Either to fight with him, play with him, or get him to run away as a buddy for himself.

You want to keep your dog close. Step forward, facing the strange dog, and then either throw something at him, your leash for instance, or smack him. If the irate owner of this problematic dog clobbers you back or screams at you, we have no good advice for you. Handle it the best way you can. To us, your safety and your dog's safety always comes first.

Jeannette, a friend and client for many years, took her small Italian greyhound, Juniper, for a walk in the country. There they encountered a person with a large golden retriever. When the golden saw Jeannette and Juniper, he started to bound over. Juniper saw the other dog coming and jumped up into Jeannette's arms. Jeannette held Juniper as the golden started to jump up on her to get at her dog.

Jeannette did what she was supposed to do: walked into the golden and kneed him to stop him from jumping. At this point, the owner of the golden caught up to the action and told Jeannette not to do that to her dog. That her dog was very gentle and playful and wouldn't hurt her little dog. The owner of the golden also identified herself as an "expert," a dog trainer.

Jeannette reluctantly put her dog down, and the golden promptly attacked Juniper and put four holes in his back and killed him. It was that fast and that simple. And that's why we say to you, yes, you can control your dog, but you can't allow somebody with an uncontrolled dog or for that matter his owner to dictate the situation and to tell you what is and what is not a problem.

If your dog doesn't want to play with another dog or to be held or even touched by another person, even a playful child, then respect your dog and his feelings.

Juniper had known something was wrong. If a dog is coming

over to your dog, and your dog doesn't want to play with the other dog, then stop it. Either chase the other dog or pick up your dog. Throw your leash or whatever you have at the other dog; he will go away. If you won't throw something, whatever you do do, make sure that you listen to your dog. Because he's telling you something.

This was a major emotional trauma for Jeannette, as it would be for anyone who sees a loved one killed right in front of their eyes. Especially in Jeannette's case, where her dog even tried to tell her something was wrong, but a pseudo-authority "expert" figure neutralized her instincts. Initially, Jeannette pursued this matter in court. But realizing that this would become a long, drawn-out costly legal battle (especially since the judge and the "expert" kept insisting that this had been an accidental "fluke" occurrence), and because she wanted to put the incident behind her, Jeannette reluctantly abandoned her action. The biggest lesson she said she learned, and unfortunately learned the hard way, was to listen to herself, trust her instincts, and make her own choices and decisions. And not to listen to anyone's advice and opinions unless they made perfect sense to her. After all, nobody knows your dog better than you do. Whatever decisions you make, right or wrong, you are the one who will have to live with them. And that includes the so-called accidental "fluke" occurrences.

Problems You Can Solve by Looking in a Mirror or Talking to a Psychiatrist or a Judge

Not all problems are your dog's fault. Many people will use their dogs as a key to control each other. If you are having a fight or an argument with a spouse, or one of your children, or someone close to you, you shouldn't use your dog as a bargaining chip or a wedge. He shouldn't be part of the argument at all.

Control isn't just dog over dog or person over dog; it can also be a person using a dog to control another person. Or using the dog to get even in a squabble. Your dog is part of your family. And if any members in the family get into an argument or a fight, don't expect the dog to take sides, and don't get angry if he doesn't. He will only take sides if he belongs solely to one person in that family. And if he likes that person best.

A New York Divorce Case

The following case was a high-profile divorce case between two professionals, a psychiatrist and an attorney.

My client was the psychiatrist. She had hired me to train her German shepherd puppy for her and her son. I did. She was happy. However, she was in the middle of a nasty divorce, and her husband, attacking her in every way that he could, centered on using the puppy to get at her. Getting the puppy for their son, after all, had been her idea. So he figured he could still control and punish his soon-to-be ex-wife by dragging her and the puppy into court and persuading the judge to make her get rid of the puppy. Luckily, in this case, he didn't succeed. I was brought in as a professional witness for the woman, the dog, and her son.

He, the husband, told the judge, "The dog must go! It's dirty, dangerous, and disgusting." She, the wife, told the judge, "He is not! He's a very smart little puppy, and I had him trained for my son so there would be no problems between the two of them. And there aren't. The two, they're inseparable." I told the judge, "He's a good dog, he's a smart dog, and it only took me three hours to make him into a great little dog." The husband's lawyer said, "Impossible, no one can train a dog in three hours." The wife's lawyer said, "This dog is perfect, I've seen him with my own eyes." The little boy just said, "I want my dog, I want my dog, please." The judge said, "I'll decide."

200

The judge came out from behind his bench, knelt down, and called the little puppy. The puppy trotted over to the judge, as puppies do, and kissed him right on the nose. So much for this vicious dog. The judge, giving the husband a dirty look said, "The dog stays with the little boy. Now, let's get on with the financial settlements and the rest of this blank, blank, blank, divorce."

Carol was the owner of a rather large German shepherd, a boy dog named Ruffy. Ruffy, it seemed, would refuse to let her husband, Bill, into bed at night. Quite a problem. I told them that their problem was threefold.

First, the natural one, where the dog, a boy, competes with Bill, another boy, for the prize, Carol, a girl. That was easy. Second, when the dog would growl at Bill, Carol wouldn't stop him. As a matter of fact, she encouraged Ruffy, telling him how good he was for growling. So in effect, without realizing it, or maybe she did, Carol was telling Ruffy that it was all right to growl at Bill. The dog was Carol's dog. The way things were going, this dog would most definitely bite Bill, and soon. Third, Bill was genuinely frightened of the dog, and Ruffy knew it. In fact, Bill was frightened of dogs, period. When I showed Bill how to stop the dog from intimidating him, he told me he would let Carol deal with it and that he couldn't be bothered.

Bill and Carol didn't need me for their dog, they needed professional help for themselves. And if they ever got that straightened out, then maybe I could help them with Ruffy.

Aggressive behavior runs the gamut from dangerous and frightening experiences with a biting dog to just annoying habits like peeing or mounting. With the biting dog you have two choices. One is throwing, and the bigger and more aggressive the dog, the bigger the object should be. The other option is a well-placed slap, done not out of anger but to teach him not to bite or commit any of these aggressive acts.

We don't like to slap a dog; we don't enjoy it and wouldn't

do it if it wasn't necessary. But we do want to have this option in case it is necessary. For example, if your dog runs across a street into traffic, if you get that dog back alive, a well-placed slap, not in anger but with a purpose, will tell your dog that he shouldn't do it again. Ever.

There are dog owners who will use the excuse that it is cruel to slap a dog. Only they don't use the word *slap*; they make it sound cruel by saying "hit" or "beat" or "abuse." It's not hitting or beating or abusing, it's one well-placed slap without anger, but with a purpose.

Some dog owners send their dogs away to training schools and trust that when they get their dog back he was trained with kisses and hugs. That's like putting your head in the sand. We call this ostrich-type training. And then there's the last resort of a "failed dog," and we don't mean an incredible vacation resort. We mean that last resort chain, the animal shelters. The dog owner gives their dog away and rationalizes a very good reason for doing so.

To confront aggressive behavior, some experts say to use a newspaper or shake a can of pennies or bust balloons or yell loudly or even choke him. These so-called solutions don't solve problems, they will only confuse the dog, and in his confusion you might get bit.

Put yourself in your dog's place and watch yourself shaking, breaking, and yelling. You would probably think that there is no way you could learn anything constructive from this teacher, or his tricks. They don't do the one thing that has to be done, and that is to get your dog to respect you for who you are and learn from you, not from any of these aids or tricks or quick fixes that don't fix.

We believe that our way is the best and the fastest way to get your dog to listen to you so that you can give him more freedom and more love. These techniques have been tried and true with over twenty-five thousand dogs and their owners.

They have been honed and refined for over forty years, and the changes have evolved into this very effective and no-nonsense form of communication and teaching.

If you must categorize, then call it tough love. We don't think it's tough love, we think it's true love.

CHAPTER 8

Problems, Puzzles, and Mysteries

Getting By Successfully in a No-Dogs-Allowed World

Ovario Hysterectomies and Castration: Not Spaying, Neutering, Fixing, or Altering

I overheard these two dogs discussing one of their owners the other day. "I was castrated, you had an ovario hysterectomy, and we were both sent home the next day. I wonder why your owner is making such a big deal about getting his teeth cleaned?"

Denise, a very pregnant Dandie Dinmont, waddled by. Looking very surprised, Splash, a Portuguese water dog, asked Gigi, the chicly coiffed French poodle, "How come? I thought Denise had an ovario hysterectomy?" Gigi looked quizzically back at Splash. "What is this O. H.?" Always the philosopher, Splash replied, "If you want to hide from reality you call it spaying, or fixing, or altering, or even neutering. But when you say to fix or to alter, I would think you're talking about a table or even a pair of pants, but not about a dog. A dog is a dog, a table is a table, and a pair of pants is a pair of pants. They are three different things. What it is, is an ovario hysterectomy, and by the way, with a boy dog it's castration. Not fixing, not altering." Gigi concluded, "Well, whatever it is, I guess Denise didn't get it."

Sleepy Joe, My Son

I had many dogs in my life. One of them was a little gem named Sleepy Joe. He was a cute little guy, a Maltese, weighing in at four pounds. He was very good-looking. So much so that I felt he should become a father and pass some of those good-looking genes on to the rest of the world. What woman could say no to him? Why, any girl Maltese would give anything to be the mother of his children. I hoped. You know how parents are.

I introduced Sleepy to a beautiful Maltese girl named Effie. By the look in her eye and the way she went after him, it looked like love at first sight. but Sleepy looked at Effie and took off. He ran right under the couch. Maybe it was Effie's aggressive attitude, or Sleepy just wasn't in the mood for love.

Effie was beautiful, smart, and an exciting free-spirited girl. She knew what she wanted and she went after him. But still, it didn't work out. Sleepy hid under the couch and stayed there for hours after Effie left.

Maybe Sleepy was too young, or Effie wasn't the type. I didn't know and decided to try again. But whenever this reluctant Romeo was introduced to a potential new Juliet, he would disappear under a couch, under a chair, under a bed, and once even tried to crawl underneath a refrigerator. I reached a conclusion: Sleepy did not like girls.

I had some friends who practiced veterinary medicine at a large clinic in Manhattan. One of them specialized in the study of artificial insemination. When I explained my problem, or rather Sleepy's problem, he said, "No problem, just bring Sleepy and little Effie into my clinic and we'll get them together."

I was excited, Sleepy was going to be a dad whether he wanted to or not. I asked if I could watch the procedure and Doctor G. said, "No problem." Into the operating room I went. One doctor put a mask on me. Two more doctors came into this rather large operating room, each carrying one of the two dogs on pillows. The dogs seemed quite relaxed. Doctor G. told me that they had been given a sedative. I asked for one myself because I was a nervous wreck. My request was ignored.

Effie and Sleepy were put on an operating table. One doctor was holding Effie and another held Sleepy. I still couldn't figure out how they were going to accomplish this artificial affair.

All of a sudden, there it was. The answer. Doctor G. pulled off one of his gloves, took Sleepy's lipstick in his hand, and pushed and pulled back and forth, back and forth, back and forth, but nothing seemed to be happening. This went on for what seemed like hours to me, but actually it was only three or four minutes.

The doctor was getting tired. He stopped, turned around to one of his associates, and said, "I guess this isn't working." I was trying to keep from laughing, but the veins in my neck were about to bust if I didn't. Well, I couldn't hold back any longer. Laughingly, I suggested that maybe if Doctor Susan tried it, we might get lucky. I thought any father would say the same thing. Doctor Susan laughed, but Doctor G. didn't think it was so funny. I was thrown out of the operating room.

Sixty-two days later, Romeo Sleepy became a father and his Juliet, Effie, had four, healthy, happy, Maltese babies. To be or not to be, it be.

The Bryn Mawr Mascots

My daughter was attending Bryn Mawr College in Pennsylvania. She wanted a dog, but I got her a beautiful pair of South American long-haired guinea pigs instead. I told her that this way she wouldn't have to walk a dog four times a day. She thought that was a good idea.

The pigs became welcomed mascots. To control the prolific breeding habits that this species is known for, one of the two little piggies had to be kept from either getting pregnant or making the other one pregnant. A decision had to be made. Bryn Mawr, an all-women college, a democratic institution, decided to have a vote. The vote was unanimous . . . castration. It was fair. It *was* fair, I think.

Sometimes dog owners bring up the sensitive subject of castration or hysterectomies for their dogs. The questions they most ask are: Should they do it? If so, when should they do it? Or why should this procedure be done at all? Will it change the personality of their dogs? Will their dogs get fat? Will this procedure calm down my dog's aggressive nature? My dog is biting people, will this operation stop his biting?

First of all, call it what is really is. It's an ovario hysterectomy for the girl dog. And it's castration for the boy dog. Not all of those other terms that mask reality, like spaying, fixing, neutering, altering. These polite terms might make a person feel better, but we think that it also masks true feelings and understanding of what your dog is going to go through. When a human being goes for an operation of this sort, even though the doctor makes the conversation as pleasant as possible, he still uses the most direct terms. It's fair. And it's only fair that you know about what your dog is going to go through.

If a man goes for a vasectomy, or he's going to have his

prostate removed, or if he has a cancerous growth on his testicles and they have to be removed, the doctor doesn't say, "You're going to be fixed, or neutered, or altered." You are told exactly what it is that's going to happen.

If a woman goes for a hysterectomy, or to have her tubes tied, she's not being spayed or altered. She's told exactly what it is that's going to happen.

To use these terms on a human being would be dehumanizing. So, to use these terms on a dog, we can't call it dehumanizing the dog, because dogs aren't human, but it still is de-dog-iz-ing, for lack of a better word.

For Health Reasons

Girl dogs should have an ovario hysterectomy for health reasons. It will almost totally prevent mammary gland tumors. It will also guarantee the prevention of unwanted pregnancies, so as not to add to the already overpopulated world of unwanted dogs.

It will not change their personality, nor will it make them fat. Too much food does that. They will not be traumatized from the operation. They will accept what has happened better than any human being. Many people who have had major surgery come through their operation successfully but then worry themselves to death. Dogs won't worry about it; they come through their surgery, they accept it and they forget about it. If their owners take good care of them, then they will live a full, healthy, and happy life.

What this procedure won't do is fully prevent a dog from being aggressive or from biting. That's a behavioral problem that's up to you to stop, not your veterinarian.

When should you have this done? There are two schools of thought. The school we follow says that this procedure should be done after your dog finishes with her first heat. That way we know for certain that the dog has fully matured and everything is in working order. Other experts believe that this procedure should be done before the dog's first heat. But all know not to have it done during her heat period.

For the boy, castration should be done when he's about nine months to a year old. It helps prevent the dog from having prostate problems later on in life. What it will not do is completely change or control aggressiveness. Maybe if you could find a way to threaten your dog with castration, he might behave, but how are you going to find a way? We can't help you threaten him. We don't know how.

A dog named Mercury was castrated because he was very aggressive. He bit everybody he came into contact with—dogs, people, he didn't care. After he was castrated, he still bit, just as hard and just as much. As a matter of fact, maybe a little harder and a little more. Because as he got older he got smarter and knew just where to bite and when. He would even wag his tail to get you closer to him and give you a false sense of security, pick the spot he wanted to bite you, and do it. Very smart, very enterprising. He didn't realize that his owners were thinking about having him put away for good. We're sure if he had known this, he wouldn't have bitten anymore.

There are two prime drives in the animal world. And that includes the human animal world. A sexual drive and a territorial drive. Medical procedures will stop the dog's sexual drive and prevent reproduction. But if your dog owns a car or a house or an apartment, he's not going to give up an inch of that.

I Can't Do It! It Isn't Fair to the Dog

Some dog owners can't bring themselves to have their boy dogs castrated or an ovario hysterectomy for their girl dogs. We sympathize with their reluctance and their feelings not to do this, but the long-term benefits, the health and well-being of your dog, should outweigh any of your fears and hesitation.

If you are thinking of breeding your dog because you feel that it's a natural and wonderful experience and your dog should feel the experience of love and the joys of motherhood, think about this: think about the puppies' traumatic experience when you take them away from their mother, and their mother's emotional trauma when you take her babies away from her. If you are still not convinced and you don't believe any of this, then there is your responsibility of placing the six or eight puppies you might not want to keep. What happens to them? You must know that animals do have feelings and form strong emotional attachments.

They Are Not Puzzles and Mysteries, They Are Just Collars, Medicines, and Hidden Danger

In the forty years that I've been practicing, my clients have numbered in the thousands. I have worked with their dogs, cats, horses, birds, all their different pets. Many of these clients have stayed with me all this time. As they acquired their new pets, they would be in touch with me. Sometimes I would go to California, Florida, and even out of the country to work with their pets. Wherever they were. To me, that's the greatest compliment of all. To have these people trust me with the health and well-being of their animals throughout these four decades.

Once we've worked with our clients' dogs, we consider them all part of our extended family. There's no way that we can spend time interacting with these lovable characters—we mean the dogs—and not become attached to them. So we continue to make available to our clients information that will help them with the practical everyday problems, puzzles, and mysteries that happen throughout the dog's life.

Because everything that's going to happen in your dog's life doesn't happen in the first hours that we are there. Although he will be taught in approximately three hours to be successful in his life with you, remember, no matter how perfect the dog, we are still living in an imperfect world. There are many restrictions on dogs, many signs that read NO DOGS ALLOWED, even if they are man's best friend.

How do you and your dog fit into or get around this scheme of things? Where all gimmicks and gadgets are made only for your convenience, not your dog's. You use your common sense. Think things through. Read. Ask questions. Get second opinions.

You go into pet shops and are sold a bill of goods. If you question them and are told not to worry about it, you should ask, "Why shouldn't I worry?" When you take your dog on an airplane and they are going to put him in cargo, ask the questions about pressure and temperature. Don't accept "Don't worry." The more questions you ask the more answers you will get. The more information, the better your decision will be.

There are accidents just waiting to happen, things that you might not be aware of. We want to make you aware of them and help you prevent as many of them as possible with good information.

That's why whatever relevant or practical advice that we can give our clients and their dogs, we're offering to you.

A Dangerous Cover-up

Your dog lives in a world where his incredible senses are neutralized. The senses that he depends on to survive are tricked or altered. This means that the natural survival abilities the dog would have in the wild are rendered practically useless.

A quick and dangerous example is candy-coated aspirin. This can badly hurt or even kill your dog. Why? Because his sense of smell would fully alert him if the aspirin weren't coated. It would tell him that the aspirin is not for him, and he wouldn't normally touch it. But when the aspirin is candy-coated, successfully disguised to make it palatable for you, it will also be palatable to your dog and he will be fooled into thinking that he has found a candy treasure and eat the whole bottle. Your dog will pay a terrible price.

This incident happened with one of our clients' dogs. A friend of theirs came into New York City to run the marathon, and stayed at their apartment. This person discovered that a couple of candy-coated aspirin taken just before her run would help her get through the marathon relatively pain free. And the candy-coated ones didn't bother her stomach. This is what she told us. After taking what she needed, she left the rest of the bottle on her bed instead of locking it up somewhere when she went out to run.

The dog found the remaining tablets and ate them, all of them, thinking they were candy. It was nothing for him to break that plastic bottle open. No problem at all. The runner said there must have been about twenty or so tablets left in the bottle. The dog became very sick. He was rushed to the hospital, his stomach was pumped, and they were able to get out some, but not all of the pills, which ulcerated his stomach. He almost died.

Just as you keep all medications and all cleaning supplies away from your children, keep them away from your dog. Even though dogs have a good built-in warning system, it's useless in our world with everything being disguised as something else. Unless your dog can read those warning labels, the ones that manufacturers put on their products, and you know he can't, and even if he could, he would still need a magnifying glass. Be aware of hidden dangers.

They Are in Your Medicine Cabinet

Sometimes we do recommend aspirin for our dogs. Usually for an older dog with arthritis or rheumatism. We're not saying your dog should or would run a marathon on an aspirin, but it will help his aches and pains. Being an old dog myself, I have found Anacin works the best for me and my dogs.

This is the way we would do it for our dogs. One tablet for every fifty pounds of dog, or half a tablet for twenty-five pounds of dog. And no more than twice a day, tops. Once in the morning when he gets up, and once at night before he goes to bed. If you are not sure of the proper amount, consult your veterinarian. Or maybe even your family doctor.

A useful remedy for your dog if has an upset stomach is Pepto-Bismol. You can give your dog the appropriate amount for his weight. Follow the directions on the bottle. A human being gets two tablespoons, so a fifty-pound dog should get one-third of the human dosage. And a five-pound dog should get one-tenth of what the fifty-pound dog gets. Whether your dog is a puppy or an adult dog, follow these rules.

People always seem surprised when we suggest an Anacin or a spoonful of Pepto for common problems. Remember, these products were tested on animals before they were approved for you. Oh, yes, before we forget, if your dog is on any antibiotics, antibiotics will kill bacteria, both good and bad bacteria. So you can go to your neighborhood health-food store and get some cultured yogurt that contains acidophilus, which will help replace the friendly bacteria. Your dogs will love it, so don't give them too much.

This One Is in Your Kitchen

Chicken soup, or any warm broth on a cold day, is good for you as well as your dog. It will help warm him up after he comes back from a nice romp in the snow. Don't make the soup too hot because he can't blow on it to cool it off. He's not built that way.

Collars and Powders for Fleas and Ticks

You are told that your dog needs a flea and tick collar, and that he also needs all those powders and sprays and baths for getting rid of those fleas and ticks. If you read the labels on these products carefully and with powerful glasses, they say, "Keep out of the reach of children." Well now, children and dogs have been synonymous since time immemorial. So it would seem that if it is to be kept out of the reach of children, shouldn't it be kept out of the reach of dogs?

If a dog is wearing one of these collars, does it mean a child can't play with his dog? How does a child play with a dog when he is wearing one of these collars? Or what about a dog that has just been sprayed or bathed with a product that says, "Keep out of the reach of children." If he has this stuff all over him, should a child be kept away?

Maybe that also means an adult with sensitive skin should be kept away from a dog treated with all of this stuff, whatever it is. How will these products, which could be harmful to children—and they are, otherwise the labels wouldn't have to warn you—how are these chemicals going to affect the health of your dog?

If your dog could talk he might say, "I wish they would spray themselves with that damn flea and tick stuff, it burns like hell and the smell makes me sick." Remember a dog's sense of smell is so much more sensitive than ours, and what seems harmless to you is not necessarily harmless to him. And anyway, a flea and tick collar only keeps fleas and ticks away a couple of inches on either side of the collar. What about those fleas that are having a circus on the tail end of the dog or on his head or on his ears?

We've seen dogs play with other dogs and then get sick after chewing on each other's collars. You know, dogs play by grabbing the other dog by his neck. That's where the collar is. We've seen dogs and cats that have always played together just refuse to play with each other once any of these collars, shampoos, or sprays were used. As Shakespeare might have said, "A poison is a poison is a poison, even by another name, it's still a poison."

Ellen's cat and dog stopped playing with each other when flea and tick collars were put on them. These two animals have been friends for nine years. Paula and Mickey's dogs were wearing new flea collars and they played with each other as they always did. Zoie, after playfully biting Matisse's neck, as she always did, keeping him in line as a good matriarch should do, became quite ill and had to be brought to the veterinarian's office.

Paula's instincts were right. Zoie became sick because of the new flea and tick collars. When she removed them, the problem was solved. In Mickey and Paula's case, good food, a nice refreshing swim in their chlorinated swimming pool, plus a little social grooming took care of the flea and tick problem.

Dogs will have a couple of fleas or ticks stay with them from time to time, but that's normal. They have had a scratch-bite relationship forever. Instead of using these collars and chemicals, the simpler way to prevent the flea and tick problem and to keep most of them off your dog is a proper diet, which allows the coat and skin to be naturally oily and that means no friendly landing zones for the pesty intruders. Remember, dry food is user-friendly for fleas and ticks.

Once in a while a flea bath is okay, but that's only if your dog is infested with fleas or ticks. Otherwise, just pick them off with your fingers, not a tweezer. You have much more control with your fingers.

By the way, don't worry about the tick's head staying on your dog. I have never seen a tick that has lost his head when being removed. Heads will generally stay on the bodies they were born on. Mother Nature made it that way. Once you've pulled the tick off the dog, flush it and send it out to sea.

When you walk your dog outside, be aware that there might be some antifreeze from a leaky automobile radiator, or salt or a salt-type product put down to melt snow. Or anything that might have been dropped or spilled. These products are harmful to your dog.

Normally, your dog would smell this and walk around it or stay away from it. His sense of smell would help him the same way it helps him avoid stepping in dog poop. Have you ever noticed that he never steps in it? But sometimes he is walked through these hidden dangers through no fault of his own and will get it on his paws. He will bring it home, lie around, and start cleaning himself. He could inadvertently lick this poison and become ill. Be aware of it. You might want to wash his paws when you bring him home from one of these potential mine fields.

In the Bag: Taking a Small Friend Along

Your dog isn't just a piece of furniture, he's your pal. You can and should take him with you when you go somewhere, if you so choose. He will, however, have to learn some table manners if he is going to a restaurant with you or to a friend's house for dinner.

Once he understands what is expected of him, then you will have a splendid and loyal companion to accompany you. He won't argue or complain about anything you do or say. He will like your choice of restaurants, he will like what you order, he will like your choice of lodgings, he will like your favorite topics of conversation, he will laugh at your jokes, and treat your philosophical depth with wise and deep looks. Most of all, he will love you very much for not leaving him home alone. That is, unless he has made other plans.

If you can teach your dog to stay in your bag quietly, then you can take him on a plane, right into the cabin with you. He just needs to be able to fit under your seat. After takeoff, you can bring him up on your lap.

Remember, like everywhere else in the world, there are people who like dogs and people who don't like dogs. Flight attendants are no different. Some will allow your dog the luxury of sitting on your lap and fill him with treats on his trip, all first-class stuff. Others will tell you that all baggage and pets should be under the seat.

You might want to tell the flight attendants who think that all dogs are baggage that your dog is an actor on television or in the movies. Many people are inclined to give special treatment to stars, whether they deserve it or not.

Should you give your dog a tranquilizer before traveling? If you teach your dog that it's fun to go into his traveling bag, and that it is fun to travel, then he won't be nervous and he won't need a tranquilizer.

Your dog relies on his extraordinary senses. When you give him a tranquilizer you are neutralizing his ability to adjust and cope with the world around him. Outwardly he will look relaxed, but inwardly he will fight the medication.

Think about this. When you take a tranquilizer or a drink before a flight it might relax you, or it might not. The reason you are taking a tranquilizer might be because you're frightened of flying. Frightened of the thought of what might happen to you when flying. You are also able to understand what effects the tranquilizer might have on you. So you are prepared. Your dog can't read the label, so he isn't prepared for the effects of the drug and it could easily frighten him. As for the natural fear of flying, your dog doesn't worry about it. And he doesn't have to worry. He doesn't know what flying is. All he cares about is being in the cabin with you. He will react and key off of you. If you are frightened or nervous he will pick that up and could become nervous or anxious. So perhaps you might want to take his ration of tranquilizers. Only, we do hope you don't fall out of your seat while trying to scratch behind your ears.

How to Have Your Dog Stay Happily in the Bag

The best way to accomplish this is by putting him in a bag and getting him used to it from the very beginning, from the time you first bring him home. Start by making a game out of him being in the bag. Put some tasty surprise in the bag and let him find it. Once your puppy or small dog goes into this bag looking for something good to eat, then start picking him up and carrying him around."

Now comes the important part. Up until now he went into his bag, but only because it was food time for him in there. This time, don't put anything in the bag but your dog. When he finds there is no food he might try to get out. Don't let him. Make him stay there, the way we taught you how to make your dog stay anywhere. Praise him if he stays there. If he doesn't, then slap the side of the bag and make him understand that he has to stay where he is. At times you must even let him know that he has to lie down in his bag. You must insist that he does.

When he does what you want, then praise him and give him a tasty treat. He will learn very fast when you let him know his choices are limited. Once your dog learns that the bag is his home away from home, you and your dog can become traveling companions and you can take him anywhere, even if the signs all around you say NO DOGS ALLOWED! You must remember to make sure your dog is safe hiding in his bag.

If you don't want to always travel with your dog or bring your dog to work with you, but you feel guilty about leaving him home alone, you might be thinking about a playmate for him. If you think that by getting a second dog your first dog will have good company, you had better make sure that the first one is completely shaped and taught to your satisfaction, or you might be asking for twice as much in the way of problems. You might be able to double your pleasure and double your fun, but it can also be double, bubble, toil, and trouble with a second dog if you haven't brought up the first one properly.

Remember: There are many, many things in our world that could be a problem for your dog. We covered some of them, but more than that we hope that you have been made aware of what is out there. Just use this rule of thumb. If something could be harmful to you, then it could be much more harmful to your dog.

Read the labels on all the products you buy for your dog. And use your common sense. Your dog will thank you for it with a long, happy, healthy, life. And again, we can't emphasize enough for you to use your common sense and your instincts, ask questions, and get second opinions. No one person knows all. Remember, in this world almost every product you buy, or any service you use for you or for your dog, turns a profit.

CHAPTER 9

How Smart Are They?

They are all pieces of the smarts puzzle. Education and learning. Background. Born on the wrong side of the tracks? Who's the teacher? How old? Girls and boys. Super senses. Imprinting. Behavior as opposed to genes. Where does one stop and the other begin? Or are good looks and a great personality enough?

Three Success Stories

Big Jake Taylor belonged to my friend Susan, a premier breeder of golden retrievers. Jake won best of breed for goldens at the Westminster Kennel show three years in a row. He was seven and a half years old when he came out of retirement to accomplish this triple play. He also won the nationals three times. Big Jake was a real champion.

Good-looking Jake was sporting a gray beard at the time he was written up in the *New York Times*. They compared him to that great gray-haired Yankee pitcher, Catfish Hunter. Not Jake's pitching abilities, just his gray beard.

I had a talk with Jake one day while we were shooting a commercial. He let us use his tail to knock some dishes off a table. The trooper that he was, he said he liked the senior look; there were certain benefits that went along with age. "I am a lot smarter now," he said as all the dishes flew off the table. He must be a lot smarter, for he did it in one take. And for pay, he wouldn't settle for a dog biscuit, not Jake. He would take only the director's filet mignon. He knew that by following direction and by being the best, he could get anything he wanted.

Crying Mike was a textile salesman in New York City's garment center. He had a successful selling technique. He would cry and cry until a manufacturer would give him an order just to stop his crying and get rid of him. When Mike left with an order in his hand, he would laugh all the way back to his office. Mike eventually went into business for himself, and tearfully succeeded.

When I met them, Mindy's daughter Colette was six months old. Frankie, their four-pound Yorkie terrier, was also six months old. Mindy, who was a gourmet chef, spent lots of time in the kitchen. Frankie and Colette kept her company. Frankie had the freedom of the kitchen because she could be trusted not to get under Mindy's feet, not to make a mess on the floor, and not to be destructive. Colette could not be trusted and she was kept in her walker for her own safety as well as everybody's else's.

Frankie learned very quickly what a great food source Colette was. She would devise ways to get Colette to drop or throw her food on the floor. Frankie loved this wonderful food dispenser. Colette also had many toys; Frankie would inherit them as well, in the same way. Colette threw them on the floor, and Frankie would collect them and put them in her personal corner of the kitchen.

Colette loved Frankie and would watch her for hours. Colette would talk to her, scream at her; she would do anything to get Frankie to pay attention to her. Frankie would tease Colette, jump up on her, and kiss her. They were pals.

Frankie learned that if her water dish was empty, by picking it up and bringing it over to Mindy, Mindy would fill it up. The same went for her food dish, and not only at feeding times but whenever Frankie wanted to eat or just to have a little snack.

The first time Mindy took Colette out of her walker and put her on the floor, she crawled straight over to Frankie's water dish, picked it up in her mouth, and crawled around with it, spilling water all over herself and the kitchen floor. I guess Frankie wasn't too good a teacher; Colette didn't understand the concept of full or empty.

Mindy could be in another part of the house having lunch or dinner with friends. Frankie would never beg for food, not Frankie, she was too dignified for that. Frankie would go into the kitchen, get her food dish, and bring it over to Mindy. "Let's eat," she would bark.

Frankie learned how to get what she wanted, when she wanted it. She knew the score. She even knew how to get a good rub or a scratch once in a while. She was able to accomplish all of this at six months of age. It would take Colette a little bit longer, but with Frankie's help, not too much longer.

In the human world, the arguments and the searches for what constitutes intelligence and what are the best means to measure it are highly charged, emotional subjects. In the dog world, the arguments on intelligence are now becoming just as highly charged and emotional. Some believe intelligence is genetically inherited. Some believe intelligence is a learned behavior.

Where does genetic imprinting stop and behavioral im-

222

printing begin? Good question. We don't know all the answers in our complex human society, but we do have a good idea when it comes to our four-footed furry friends, the dogs.

In this arena, no less complex than the human one, certain simple and obvious criteria should be considered before passing judgment on your dog's smarts. There are different advantages and disadvantages existing in the dog's world.

Different breeds have different specialties that they use in their learning process, especially when it comes to fitting into our world and learning our ways. Is your dog a sight hound, scent hound, working dog, or a toy? Then, is your dog a boy or a girl? Is he a puppy or an adult? Does he live in the country, the city, in a house, or in an apartment? Is he going to be a professional dog—a racer, a herding dog, a tracker, seeing eye, companion aide—or a pet? When can he start learning, how much can he learn, can you teach an old dog new tricks? And, finally, most important, who is his teacher and what is the test? Knowledge is a terrible thing to waste, and getting it wrong is just as bad.

All these pieces of the puzzle have to be factored in before you can make any judgments as to how smart your dog is. Your dog is a much more complex being than you might think. It takes more understanding, education, and intelligence on your part to bring out the best in him. Sweeping judgments of intelligence by broad classifications of dogs should be kept for sweeping floors.

What You See Is What You Get

If your dog is a specific breed, bred for a specific, physical purpose—for example, a greyhound to race, a bloodhound for his incredible sense of smell, or a toy dog for the purpose of fitting into your bag or even your pocket for convenience and traveling—then in these cases he has a specific physical purpose and no other dog can accomplish these needs any better. Then his genetic imprinting is important.

His genetic imprinting is also important if you are getting a dog for a specific look. Then you might be influenced by what look is in fashion at the time. There are contests and major dog shows that set standards for what a specific breed should look like.

In these areas there is no argument because nothing is faster than the greyhound, no dog has a better sense of smell than the bloodhound, and nothing is smaller than the smallest toy dog. And finally, nothing will have more of an influence on you than the dog whose looks and personality you fall in love with. All of this is purely academic.

In these categories if you think you have, or can get, another breed that's better equipped to do these above jobs, we say, "You're dreaming." Even though there are exceptions to every rule, we still say it's wishful thinking.

Some dogs can't physically do what other dogs can do. A small Maltese spaniel, for example, which we consider a nose dog, might have a tough time tracking. Because of his size, whatever he's tracking might be too fast for him or could even turn around and eat him. If he has people following him while he's tracking, he could be stepped on. He's too small for the job.

Whether your dog or puppy is a purebred or just a charming, irresistible mixture, it will make no difference what he is as far as his capacities and abilities to learn. Those smarts are all there in all of them.

When you bring a dog home to be your pet, what is important for you to understand is that the basic physical genetic abilities, the purpose that your dog was originally bred for, is only one of the many tools that you will be using to your advantage in his education.

All dogs should easily learn their main behaviors in the first thirteen weeks of their life. After thirteen weeks, you can still teach them, but you will have to break old habits and teach new ones. Still, all dogs can be taught very quickly, if taught in the right way.

Remember, in these first thirteen weeks, if your dog is a sight hound, you had better start teaching him his main behaviors as early in the game as you can. And "sit" is not one of them. With a scent hound you have a little more time, but still the earlier the better. And with the working breed, you have even more time than with the other two, but the earlier you teach him the better.

By Sight

An Afghan hound, or a greyhound, or a whippet, or a Russian wolfhound, or an Italian greyhound, or a saluki, or an Egypt hound—these dogs are all sight hounds, bred specifically for their sight and speed. They have a more highly developed sense of sight, and their sight develops much earlier than the other breeds.

The sight hound will respond to movement faster than all other breeds of dogs, and the only other animal that we can compare with the sight hound is the cheetah in the cat family, who also depends mainly on sight and speed.

Because of his early sight development, this dog should be taught as early as possible. When you are teaching a sight hound, hand signals and body language are most important. You must use hand signals first, and then once he's responding to your hands and body language, you can start teaching him with your voice.

That doesn't mean you have to teach him all of his behaviors by hand, and then by voice. It means at the start of each behavior you are teaching him, you first use your hand signals. When he starts to respond to your hands, and that could be in a matter of minutes, then you add your voice to it. This seems quite simple, and it is, but if you watch him key into movement, you'll understand the importance of it.

By Scent

Beagles, retrievers, bassets, bloodhounds, spaniels, labradors, weimaraners—any sporting or hunting dog, including the dachshund—these are all scent hounds, or nose dogs. You use a combination of hand signals, body language, and voice together when teaching these dogs.

Their sense of smell is more highly developed and develops faster than all other breeds. These dogs also should be taught as early as possible. You have a little more time than with a sight hound, but not too much time.

Because a scent hound's sense of small does not directly help us to teach these dogs their main and basic behaviors, and his hearing and sight aren't as good as the work dog or the sight hound, then the combination of voice and hand is very important. Unless, of course, you are teaching your nose dog certain scent discrimination behaviors. Then, in this area, he wins hands down, or nose down.

Working Breed

German shepherds, huskies, malamutes, all types of collies, Saint Bernards, poodles, Newfoundlands, Kerry blues, Airedales, all terriers—these are working breeds. These dogs have a more highly developed sense of hearing than the sight or scent hounds. Therefore, they can be taught with both voice and hand signals, but voice should be taught first. Then add your hand signals and body language.

The working breed has all the super senses that the other two classes have, it's just that the sight hound has the best sight, the scent hound has the best nose, and the working dogs have the best hearing. To you, these slight differences might seem insignificant, but to your dog, there's a world of difference.

Human beings communicate mainly by voice. Work dogs, with their highly developed sense of hearing, can seem smarter to us because of this, but it ain't necessarily so. Once you understand how and when these super senses develop in these different breeds of dogs, then the playing field of learning becomes level, at least in this area.

And Don't Forget Small Dogs and Toys

Small poodles, toy poodles, Westy terriers, Maltese spaniels, Yorkie terriers, the mighty little dachshund, etc. etc. etc. If you think all small dogs are just for fun, you're wrong. These dogs were all bred from the three classes of work, sight, and scent, and they all had a real purpose. If you look up their family trees, you will find out that they were originally nose dogs, ear dogs, or eye dogs. And you should teach them in the same way you would teach their bigger cousins.

Who's Smarter, He or She?

William, the conquering Westy, went out through a hole he dug under the fence. Jaime, his sister Westy, watching him go, was not amused. In no uncertain terms, she ordered him back. But William, pretending not to hear her, and looking for greener grass, was already gone.

Up to the house Jaime went, and barkingly reported on the situation to her owner, Catherine. Jaime marched with Catherine around the perimeter of the fence, and each time Catherine stopped and searched in the wrong place, Jaime brought her back on track. "There it is," Jaime pointed, clearly indicating the escape hatch.

Catherine immediately got her car and went after her best

boy, William, who wasn't far away. He was just down the road, peeing contentedly on a tree. Seeing Catherine and the car, William, tail wagging and excited, happily jumped in to go home. I guess William figured that that was going to be that. He didn't figure on an irate Jaime, the boss.

She chased him round the yard. He had to run and hide in the bushes. From there, he ran into the house and under the bed, and then into a closet, but there was no safe place to hide from Jaime. "Jaime, I swear, I'll never do it again," William gasped. "Don't swear, it's not polite," Jaime warned, rolling him over, growling. "You caused a lot of trouble around here, and a lot of trouble for me." But after all, it was dinner time, there were now more important things to do than chase William. After beating up on William to her satisfaction, Jaime decided to move on and into the kitchen for her dinner. Leisurely, she ate her chicken, broccoli, and rice mix. William watched from a safe distance. He didn't dare go in for his dinner until Jaime was through with hers. When she finally sauntered off and lay down on the couch for a nap after all her trouble and hard work. William came in to eat. "That was a close call," he thought.

"She's so smart," Catherine said. "She's so smart." She couldn't find exactly the right words to convey her admiration of Jaime, so she could only repeat in amazement, "She's so smart." What a dog. Catherine told us that Jaime reminds her of her grandmother. Catherine's grandmother would walk up to her husband and smack him. When he would ask her, "Why did you do that?" she would say, "Because you're probably going to do something wrong today, and this is what you get in advance."

This is not an isolated or even rare occurrence. We've heard this same story from many of our clients who have both boy and girl dogs. The boy wandered, and the girl went for help to go find him. And took it upon herself to chastise the wanderer when he got home. Tibby has located her Willy several times. He goes out through a hole in the fence, Tibby gets help, and when Willy gets home from his adventure, she punishes him.

Girl dogs mature earlier than the boys. They have their first heat anywhere from six months of age on. At that point, they are able to reproduce. Boy dogs learn about the birds and the bees at about a year old. That's why we say the first year of a dog's life is equivalent to fifteen or sixteen years of a human being. The second year is equivalent to nine or ten years. After that, you can figure five years to one.

The reason we calculate it this way is that a fifteen- or sixteen-year-old human being can reproduce. We don't know of any human being seven years old that can reproduce. Seven years to one used to be the accepted wisdom of comparison between human and dog years.

Girl dogs also mature intellectually faster than boy dogs. They have to. They have to learn motherly survival skills early. The young girl puppy will get an idea how to bring up her own young, how to nurse and how to care for them, by watching and learning from her mother. Getting born might be genetic, but taking care, bringing up, and protecting are learned behaviors. Chances are a girl puppy that has been taken away from her mother right after birth would have a problem raising her own puppies later on in life. She wouldn't know how and would have to learn by trial and error. And many times the trial and error could be fatal for her newborn puppies.

Because girl dogs mature faster than boy dogs, we find that it's easier to teach the girls and they obviously will learn faster than the boys. However, at six months of age, the boys start to catch up.

A potential problem here is that by the age of six months all of the basic behaviors should have been taught. Keeping this in mind, you would have to say the girl is smarter, because she was able to learn faster at an earlier age. That doesn't mean the boy dogs can't learn, it just means it can take a little more patience and a little more work. Knowing this, we've leveled the intelligence playing field a little more.

Another factor to consider is your dog's priorities. As dogs get older, girls usually show more interest in their immediate human family and its workings. They want to be part of it. As for the boys, they feel your family is their family also, but their interests are now being strongly pulled in other directions. Wandering, checking out the neighborhood, its trees, its pumps, and the other dogs. The boys are interested in the competition and want to establish territorial boundaries. Girls will also establish boundaries but not as aggressively as boys. And they won't wander as far, although there are exceptions to every rule.

Both boy dogs and girl dogs are loyal and smart, but the boy's loyalties, and smarts, at times seem to sway and stray from home. Sometimes far from home. The outside influences are very strong on boy dogs. So, you will have to remind the boys and refresh their memories from time to time, sometimes very strongly, and guaranteed much more often and much more strongly than you would a girl dog. We guess, that being the case, girl dogs are smarter, because they seem to know better.

The Puppy, His Background, Dog-Smart Dogs

The first thirteen weeks of a puppy's life are very important. If he spends this time with other dogs and has minimal contact with humans, he will be imprinted to other dogs and get his education from dogs. He will become dog smart. This will make it very difficult to teach this puppy to fit into and learn in a human environment.

You can teach an older puppy that has not been socialized with humans, but it will be difficult, and you will have to make many compromises. If the puppy was brought up in a human environment, even one without any training, it won't matter, this puppy will be fine and can be taught people ways. Even very successfully. If the dog is an adult, however, and has never been socialized with humans, he will be virtually impossible to teach.

Then there's the country dog, the one who sleeps outside, the one who has free roam, the one who finds his own way. He can either hunt his dinner or come home to get it. We call this dog the halfway dog.

The halfway dog and the dog that has no human contact, both of these dogs are still smart; they're street-dog smart. These street-dog smart dogs live successfully in the country, on farms or ranches, or even on the city streets. They are primarily on their own and have street-smart survival skills.

The Puppy, His Background, People-Smart Dogs

Many experts and many books will tell you that a puppy hasn't the ability to learn anything substantial until he's about six months old. So you shouldn't start teaching him until then. They go on to say that a puppy cannot retain too much information at one time. It's nonsense. If you want testimony from a real expert, just watch the dog's real mother. She starts his education at birth and she is 100 percent successful.

In the first thirteen weeks of a dog's life, he will learn no matter what the circumstances are. Good habits, if you teach them to him, or generally bad habits if you leave him to his own devices. But in those first thirteen weeks you should teach him everything that he needs to know to live in your world. Because he is going to be part of your life, one way or the other, he will bond to you, and what imprints he learns will be permanent.

When a puppy comes into your life, he is probably six to eight weeks old and the only things he knows are what he learned in the few weeks that he spent with his mother, his brothers and sisters, and his breeder. He knows nothing about you. What he has learned in those first few weeks of his life probably won't be of any help to him, or to you, when he comes into your life.

When you get your new puppy, you're taking him from one world and putting him into an entirely new world, yours. You must start teaching him from scratch who and what you are. What and when to eat, where to sleep, his toilet training, where and when, how to walk with you, how to come to you, how to stay with you, everything on the move and everything stationary. The earlier you get him, the faster you can teach him all of this.

Puppies that are allowed to socialize with other dogs before they are totally bonded and socialized to you could become halfway dogs. They can never really be taught to be the dog that you always wanted. Instead, they might become the dog that the other dogs always wanted. While you stand there and smile and say what a great time your dog is having playing with other dogs, they will be bringing him up their way. They won't make any mistakes, and they won't worry about public opinion if they get rough and tough with your dog.

An adult dog usually comes with built-in smarts that he has acquired through his years. They might not necessarily be the smarts that you are looking for. You definitely will have to break his old imprints and restructure them with ones that you can feel comfortable with. Or, you can make excuses and rationalize and blame the dog and his past life, but you will still have to accept what you've got.

The Teacher

Once you have taken into consideration your dog's specialty, whether he is a nose, eye, or ear dog, then bring in his gender; and to this mix add his background, where he came from; then his age and his social conditioning. You're now ready to fit in the next piece of the puzzle. And that is a big one. Your dog's education. His teacher and his teacher's abilities. Who is the teacher? You, or does he have a personal trainer?

If a dog owner feels he needs help teaching his dog, he can hire a dog trainer. If he doesn't like a certain trainer, he doesn't have to hire him. He can find another one and another one. He has many choices.

But what about the dog? Some dogs might not like their teacher. And the reasons can be as simple as the teacher is annoying or irritating and getting on his nerves. Just as people can be irritated or annoyed by certain sounds or voices, by certain looks and smells, in the dog's case, because they are more sensitive to sound, sight, and smell than we are, these annoyances can become magnified.

Your dog has a variety of creative ways to deal with these irritating people. He can make believe that he didn't learn anything—you know, act stupid. That way the trainer gets fired as an incompetent. Or the dog can just growl at, or even bite, the hand that trains him. He can also choose to leave the room, pretending to be too tired, very bored, or that he has a terrible, terrible headache. Or finally, he can scream his head off as if the world were coming to an end and the trainer was responsible.

Your dog might have had some past life experience. We don't mean that he thinks he might have been a pharaoh in ancient Egypt in a past life; we mean he might have had a negative experience before you got him, and because of this he can have personal likes and dislikes. Just like human beings.

Maybe he was stepped on, or picked up and dropped by accident, maybe he was fed the wrong food, maybe a child bit him, or he was attacked by another dog, or a million other things. Who knows what goes on behind closed doors? But whatever it is, he is not going to just forget his past experiences. He's like anybody else who has good or bad experiences. A dog doesn't forget anymore than a person does. We all remember certain experiences, and consciously or subconsciously we are affected by them.

A good teacher will be able to work around these hurdles, or make them disappear. Your dog will know if you are a good teacher. He will show this by being an excellent student. If he is being trained by a dog trainer, he will know if the trainer is any good, not because he will listen to the trainer, but he will learn from his trainer to listen to you.

We also know dogs that have had three and four trainers, or who have been away to school just as many times. These dogs have grown older with their problems still intact, and the owners are now armed with the most incredible and sophisticated reasons and excuses as to why their dogs aren't trained or why their dogs can't be taught.

These excuses range anywhere from brain damage, to lack of intelligence, to minor therapeutic mental problems, to major psychological problems that only Sigmund Freud or Carl Jung might be able to help with, but since these two doctors are not available, there is just no help to be found for these lost causes that truly aren't lost. The real deal here is that there has just been a lack of communication, a breakdown.

If you put your dog in a crate and teach him a single-word language, if he is bored to death with constant practice on lessons he has already learned, if he is kept separated from you and doesn't bond with you, how is he supposed to learn anything?

If you keep your dog with you, bond him to you, teach him your language, he will become part of your life. Give him time to think, and he will think. He will learn very fast because you will be setting up a communication line that your dog will truly understand.

Body language affects the way he learns from you. If you say one thing to your dog and your body language says something else, he could very well become confused. He won't know what you want. If you give him hand signals and then the wrong voice signal, or you are not consistent in your communication with him, he will become confused.

If you scream at him and get angry, your body will be giving off bad vibrations that he will pick up with all of his super senses. This will show up to him as if you were a thousand-watt lightbulb, glowing in a tiny, dark, closet. He will not know what you want and become confused. He will probably only learn how to be confused.

Teach him the right way, make your communication direct and simple, and let him know how appreciative you are with his learning, and he is going to learn. Without a doubt you will bring out all his potential. An enriched environment as opposed to a deprived one always brings out the best potential. Even human beings thrive and excel or fail depending on their positive educational support.

If you want to compare people to people, or people to animals, or animals to animals, then you better take into consideration their teachers, their parents, their environment— everything they have come in contact with, including the weather. With dogs, a good teacher will always have the smartest dogs.

Masters of Manipulation: The Cunning Canine

In his new environment, which is your world, your dog will learn many different ways of succeeding. Unless he has other dogs around to teach him the ropes, he is going to discover on his own, by trial and error, the best ways to get around you or to manipulate you if you let him.

If he feels he doesn't have to listen to you, then his manipulation will be very basic. This simple type of manipulation can run the gamut from direct aggressiveness to silly buffoonery, and these games won't necessarily be pleasant or to your liking.

If your dog feels that you are a strong and a good teacher, he might still try to manipulate you, but the manipulation will become more complex and more subtle and a pleasure to behold. Your dog's unique techniques and abilities to get the best out of his life should be quite enjoyable to you. Especially the complex and subtle kind of manipulation, where your dog takes the time to figure out, plot out, and think through how he's going to succeed in getting his way. In this area, passive aggressiveness, cunning, basic reasoning, and an incredibly intelligent clowning around become his calling card.

A Range of Emotions

Simba and Pebbles were both adopted from shelters. Simba was four years old, and this was her third time being adopted. Pebbles, only six months old, was adopted for the first time after being given away to a shelter. They were adopted by different families and came from different shelters, but both had similar experiences later on.

When they were taken for checkups to the shelters where they were adopted from, they were nervous. Maybe they thought they were going to be returned. That's a fair guess, but only a guess. When they went home with their adopted parents, the dogs were depressed for the next few days. They wouldn't eat, they moped around, and they stayed very close to their owners. Especially Simba, who was working on her third family, having passed two repeated sentences at her shelter.

The experience of going back to the shelters, even temporarily, had a profound negative effect on these two dogs. The emotional stress must have been terrible to have lasted that many days after they got home. These two dogs had similar feelings and showed a similar range of emotions.

In the four decades that I've worked with animals, including more than twenty-five thousand dogs, I have no doubt that they can think, they can reason, and that they have the full range of emotions and feelings, including empathy.

They can't communicate verbally the way we do because they haven't the physical ability to speak. But they can listen to what we have to say and act on that information and they can use their body language and simple sounds to communicate with us. These are their words.

Dogs do express emotion: happiness, sadness, fear, anger. They do get frustrated and depressed, and they definitely do feel pain. Dogs are totally forgiving, totally loyal, and honest in their feelings. What they have hands and nose down over us is their unconditional love, trust, and acceptance of you with all your excess baggage. They don't know from revenge. That trait is strictly reserved for us humans.

They might not always show their feelings in the exact same way that human beings do, although sometimes they show their feelings exactly the same way. Remember, they are built differently than we are, so the body language can look different on the surface, but they do have the full range and intensity of emotions and feelings.

Emotions do relate to learning. If a dog sees that you are pleased with something he is doing, then he will happily do it again and again for you, and he will even try to improve on it. That's learning. If a dog sees that you are not pleased with something he is doing, he will stop, or try to find another way.

If a dog sees that you are angry and out of control, he will either become like you, angry and out of control, or try to get away from you and hide somewhere because he's frightened.

If a dog is angry you can't teach him anything. If a dog is happy you can teach him. If a dog is sad, you have to make him happy before you can teach him. Emotions do relate to learning. The dog and the teacher have to be in harmony. The teacher has to feel that he can teach and that he wants to teach. The dog has to feel that he wants to please, learn from, and do for his owner. Emotions most certainly do relate to learning, and learning relates to smarts.

Harmony between owner and dog allows for a strong identification. If you ask most dog owners they will tell you that when they are feeling sad, angry, or happy their dog will respond to their feelings with feelings of their own. Dogs can identify so completely with their owners that they know their owners as well as, or maybe even better than, their owners know themselves. Without this harmony an owner wouldn't recognize a true emotion from his dog if it was staring him in the face or unless it bit him.

In trying to figure out how smart a dog is, where do you fit in emotional learning? This is another piece of the puzzle.

Complex Design

A dog can sense an impending disaster such as an earthquake. It is said that a dog's sense of smell is anywhere from hundreds, to thousands, to hundreds of thousands of times more sensitive than ours, depending on which expert you talk to; a dog can see so much better than we can; a dog can hear things that we can't hear. A dog can respond to complex behaviors as long as you give him time to think things through, so that he can take in information, process it, and then act on it.

Different breeds of dogs have different sense specialties that should be taken into consideration when teaching them. The different sexes, boy or girl, should be taken into consideration when teaching them. So should the background of the dog, his teacher, his age, and any individual idiosyncrasies, like the cunning games and the manipulative bag of tricks he's learned to make his way in your world.

Once all of this is taken into consideration, how can you possibly attribute intelligence, or a lack of it, to classes of dogs? You can't do it. Judgments on intelligence should always be measured individually.

If you feel you must make judgments, then also judge the judge. Who is giving the test? What is his cultural background? What is the test? Who tested the tester? What is being tested? What language is the test going to be given in? How much time is there to prepare for the test? At the end of all of this, the question still remains, what constitutes intelligence? How can you test for something if no one is certain what it is?

What About Prejudice and the Bad Rap?

Is there any? Some people don't like certain breeds of dogs. Some dogs are blamed for things that they have no control over. A Staffordshire terrier, commonly known as a pit bull, has achieved such a bad and unwarranted reputation that this poor guy is born with a bad rap before he even starts out in life. He was not born vicious, he was only born, but burdened with a bad reputation. And the same goes for the Doberman, the German shepherd and the rottweiler. They are all nice dogs, and deserve better public relations, not nonsensical bad raps.

Harley Conetta is one of these Staffordshire terriers. This guy is big, about seventy-five pounds, has a great personality, and he wouldn't hurt a fly. He loves children and he knows that everybody's hands are always for scratching his back, or his behind, or for giving him treats. Actually, Harley has the perfect personality for a run in politics, kissing babies and getting his way with a smile.

Then there are the breeds of dogs that some say are not too bright, even before they are given a chance to prove their smarts. What about them? Hearsay evidence. For example, we've sometimes heard words to the effect that certain breeds of dogs are "stupid." Where did this information come from? Well, "people" say. Who are these people? Someone knew someone who had a couple of dogs of a particular breed whose owner figured they had to be "stupid" because they couldn't be taught, because they apparently couldn't learn anything. Now someone will theorize about that entire genre of dog being stupid, and the misinformation goes on and on and on. When what should have been said at the beginning was not that the dog was "stupid" but that the owner wasn't smart enough to train him.

No matter how many dogs we've taught, at the end of every session there is the standard remark all the dogs owners will say as if it were scripted: "My dog learned so fast, and it was so easy for him, he's so, so, so, very smart, I just knew it!" Hey, how about us, shouldn't we, his teachers, get a little of the credit?

As to the question "Who's the smartest dog of all?" We have the answer and the only viable test. The magic mirror test. You look in the mirror and you ask, "Mirror, mirror on the wall, who is the smartest dog of all?" Of course, it's your dog, your dog, your dog, who is the smartest dog of all, and the most beautiful, the nicest, with the best personality—he's just the most wonderful dog in the world.

"Becky is the most intelligent dog I've ever known!" Carol said.

Becky, who belongs to Karen, is a little Yorkshire terrier, brought up with the techniques in this book. She was taught sentences instead of a single-word language. Carol, a friend of Karen's, related this story to us:

Carol and Lori were sitting on a stoop next to a parking lot, smoking. Becky was sitting on Carol's lap. Lori, feeling left out, said, "I wonder why Becky is ignoring me?" Carol explained, "Well, she's stayed with me several times, she's never been to your house." No sooner had Carol finished explaining than Becky jumped off her lap, went out to Lori's car, turned around, and looked at Lori as if to say, "Well, I'm ready to go to your house if you want."

Lori and Carol could only look at each other in amazement. Carol said to me, "It was unbelievable, spooky even. She knows things she's not supposed to know." Carol has also told me that since Becky understands sentences and words, she has started having to spell words like, c-o-o-k-i-e, but now Becky has even figured out the spelling of words. She goes to the refrigerator when she's asked if she wants chicken, or to the cookie jar if c-o-o-k-i-e-s are offered.

Carol has concluded, "I've been around animals all of my life, but Becky is the smartest dog I've ever known. And she reads minds. I think?"

Sixth Sense

Whether or not you believe in psychic phenomenon, extrasensory perception, supernatural energies, out-of-body experiences, life after death, or religious or spiritual interventions in our lives is all a matter of personal belief, opinion, or conjecture. Spiritual concerns can also be with consciousness, how to raise it, change it, enlighten it, and transform it.

But much information seems to indicate some or all of the

above are around. Including our heroine, Mother Nature. Mess with her and you call down all the elements. As far as we are concerned what exists for humans exists for other animals, especially since their senses, their super senses, are so much more highly charged than our own.

Dogs have the experience of listening to their senses much more than we do. We're too busy listening to the radio, watching television, reading newspapers, and listening to experts and experts in all forms of media, giving us so many different arguments and views on the same subject that it gets rather confusing.

Human animals have to find many ways to commune with nature or the powers that be. Retreats, gurus, Transcendental Meditation, chanting, whatever. A dog, on the other hand, reads the wind. Watch him sometime as he looks off into the distance and possibly the distant future. Your dog is already there, all the time; he doesn't have to go away to a retreat or get help from a guru on ways to commune with nature or whatever powers that be.

Over the years of working with thousands of clients, the subject of "mind readers" comes up quite frequently. Many dog owners simply believe and report that their dogs can read their mind. They say that their dog will react or respond to a thought. If they were thinking of asking their dog to do something, go somewhere, leave them alone, or come to them, and they hadn't yet asked the dog, the dog will respond as if they had.

Whether they read changes in your body chemistry or body language, or whether it's because they know you so well, dogs can predict your behavior and actions.

Then, there are some dog owners who feel that they can read their dog's mind. Of the two readers, if mind reading does exist, we would have to come down on the side of the dog. The dog owner has too many different theories to weed through, and too many different experts to listen to, and one lifetime is not enough time for him to get enough information to accurately read a mind or a body.

Now, as far as the dog goes, it's pure, with no interference from the outside world of experts. Either he knows, or he doesn't know. And since there are no color receptors on a dog's retina, to him everything is just black or white, he must know.

Misty: Did She Put Herself into a Trance?

Misty and Magic are the two giant black schnauzers, the swimmers that you met earlier. They live in Westhampton, Long Island, in the summer and winter in Palm Beach, Florida. Susan and Dan, their owners and best friends, asked us if dogs can meditate? We asked them, "Why?" They said, "Misty likes to meditate under a palm tree in the corner of our living room, and she does this whenever she feels like it, but generally, after her meals."

We saw what they meant. Sure enough, around noontime, after a light snack, Misty walked over to the palm tree and started walking slowly under and around it. As she moved slowly under the small tree, the fronds lightly fingered her back. Misty shut her eyes and went into her own world, a reverie of her own. And the movement became the slowest slow motion we've ever seen. She forgot about her pal Magic, her house, her owners, and everything around her, walking in a slow, meditative trance, around this tree. She kept this up for about fifteen minutes, and then slowly came out of it.

The palm fronds are not stiff enough to be used as a back scratcher, so it couldn't be a scratching behavior. For just scratching her back she uses another plant altogether, a bougainvillea. Susan showed us that Misty reacts completely different when her back is being scratched. Magic doesn't do this, and he loves to get his back scratched. As a matter of fact, he follows with interest most of the things Misty does.

We just heard that now Magic is meditating as well, but it took him a year longer to reach his enlightenment.

We thought we'd seen everything, but this stopped us in our tracks. This was amazing. All we could do was put this whole sequence on video.

We do believe that because dogs have such highly developed and incredible senses, they can feel, see, hear, and smell things that we aren't even aware exist. But self-hypnosis? Meditation? This was new to us.

Dreams

Every owner knows that his dog dreams. Most speculate that what he's dreaming about is something very dog-ordinary, like chasing a stick or a rabbit if he's ever seen one.

Humans are credited with having dreams that are very complex and that are analyzed from top to bottom, stem to stern, port to starboard, and any and every other which way. That the dreams hold hidden deep meanings for the dreamer. Your dog dreams. His dreams affect him the same way your dreams affect you. Holding messages or special communications for the dreamer. And that goes beyond the chasing of imaginary rabbits or thrown doggy bones. The only difference we can see is the number of experts that humans have to analyze their dreams.

We all—humans and animals—interact with our environment every day. We have dreams of the future and the past, dreams of far-out fantasies, and dreams that work out problems so that our present life can be more enriched and rewarding, working"stuff" out. We believe that dogs do, too.

A traumatic experience for a dog, or for a person, is still a traumatic experience. Fire, an earthquake, being hurt, being abandoned, death, divorce, even moving to a new home where you and your dog are uprooted from your basic security. All of these experiences could present themselves in dreams or nightmares. A happy experience, good times, good food, and love could generate positive dreams for the dreamer. And they do.

Healing As Opposed to Heeling

A friend of ours was told that if he had a dog he would live longer and stay healthier. So he bought two dogs, hoping to live forever. In all the years of bringing my animals into New York City hospitals, foundling homes, and schools, I saw people from the sick and elderly to young children brighten up as if by magic. Animals do help people get through emotional problems. To us this is healing.

There are spiritual beliefs that have always reserved an important place for animals. Believing animals to be reincarnated ancestors, or raising animals to the level of gods and appreciating their incredible abilities. Two that come to mind, and there are many more, are the eagle and the killer whale, both respected for their power and grace. Animals have influenced human experience and knowledge forever. But the dog, helping man wherever he can, is intricately tied to us because he lives with us, sharing our emotions and our lives. He contributes more to us on a personal level than any other animal.

Your dog will accept you with all of your shortcomings. It's called unconditional love. Your dog is a physical, emotional, and spiritual animal just like you. And he does have a soul, contrary to certain beliefs.

To the question, "How smart are they?" With all of our pieces of the puzzle put together, even posing the question implies limitations and judgments. The question maybe should be, "How smart are we?" To respect an animal is to respect his intelligence, in all of the various ways that it is manifested.

EPILOGUE
The Tale's End

There is a popular belief out there that when you want your dog to do something for you, you must give him a command and command him to do it. You can give a command to a computer and it will perform a function for you. Commands might be given in the military; that's understandable too. But you don't have to command your dog. He's not in the army and he certainly isn't a computer. It isn't necessary to talk to your dog in that way. The single-word command language, "sit," "no," "stay," "come," "heel," if you want him to do something or not to do something, to move or not to move, is truly an insult to his intelligence and to yours. Your dog is capable of understanding far more than that and you are capable of setting up and delivering a more complex form of communication. It's called your language.

When you command your dog he becomes a workable possession and not a friend. This command mentality shifts him in your mind subtly, separating him from your world. How can the two of you communicate, how can your dog get to know you, if he is taught a different language than yours, if he eats a different food than you do, and if he lives away from you in a cage or a crate?

Your dog is coming to live with you, in your world. Teach him your way, who you are, and what you want of him. He will listen, he will learn, and he will happily do everything willingly. He might even improve on what you're asking of him. More importantly you will appreciate his individual style, character, and unique abilities to integrate his life with yours. When you develop a true awareness of your dog, you will be able to see this. Otherwise you could miss out on truly appreciating him altogether. Because you won't know him.

Let's not have our dog, our best and loyal friend, merely exist and get by on minimum daily requirements, but get the most and the maximum benefits out of his surroundings, without making life uncomfortable for either of you. He should add to your life and you should add to his. The happier you are with each other, the more you will give to each other.

You now can have the dog that you have always wanted and your dog will finally have the well-informed owner that is sensitive to all of his needs and who will be able to take care of him in the style that he should be taken care of and that he deserves.

No more "I wonder what he's trying to tell me," or "I wonder if he understands what I'm trying to teach him." And if you think we're just talking about you, the owner, you're wrong. Now you both can understand each other and break down the silent wall between you, because that wall was always and only an illusion. It was a lack of communication.

No matter who or what you believe in—God, Christ, Allah,

Buddha, or Mother Nature—it seems the dogs heard the voices and listened to the messages: unconditional love, complete acceptance, great compassion, and total and unquestioned loyalty—no room for intolerance, hate, exclusion, or greed.